The Three Faces of Mind

The Three Faces of Mind

of Mind

DEVELOPING YOUR
MENTAL, EMOTIONAL, AND
BEHAVIORAL INTELLIGENCES

Elaine de Beauport

with Aura Sofia Diaz

A publication supported by
THE KERN FOUNDATION

Quest Books
Theosophical Publishing House

Wheaton, Illinois ♦ Madras, India

The Theosophical Publishing House
P.O. Box 270
Wheaton, IL 60189-0270

A publication of the Theosophical Publishing House,
a department of the Theosophical Society in America

Library of Congress Cataloging-in-Publication Data

De Beauport, Elaine.
    The three faces of mind : developing your mental, emotional, and behavioral intelligences / Elaine de Beauport with Aura Sofia Diaz. — 1st Quest ed.
        p.   cm.
    Includes bibliographical references and index.
    ISBN 0-8356-0748-8
    1. Emotions and cognition.   2. Intellect.   3. Brain—Localization of functions.   4. Brain.   I. Diaz, Aura Sofia.   II. Title.
    BF311.D37   1996
    153.9—dc20   96-22709
                                                                                CIP

        8   7   6   5   4   3   2   1   *   96   97   98   99   00   01   02

Excerpts from *Healing and the Mind* by Bill Moyers. Copyright © 1993 by Public Affairs Televison and David Grubin Productions, Inc. Used by permission of Doubleday, a division of Bantam Doubleday Dell Publishing Group, Inc. Permission from Paul D. MacLean to quote from his book *The Triune Brain in Evolution*. New York, Plenum Press, 1990. Illustrations on p. 211 reprinted by permission from *The Human Body: The Brain: Mystery of Matter and Mind*. Copyright, 1981, U.S. News & World Report. Sylviane Sans for illustration on p. 78. Luis Camejo for illustrations on pp. 6, 83, 243.

Book and Cover Design by Beth Hansen

This book was set in Bembo, Janson, and Ultra Condensed Serif.
Printed in the United States of America.

THIS BOOK IS DEDICATED TO:

The Presence of Energy in All Life

With the hope that energy may become the common language that
unites us and enables each of us to appreciate and orchestrate our
diverse intelligences on behalf of life.

Contents

List of Illustrations

Acknowledgments

Above all I am grateful for the continuous company of my sons Patrick and Pierre de Beauport. Without them I would not have been inspired to search out the many pathways of human development described in this book. I owe them for their patience and sense of humor during this long exploration. I thank them for enriching my life with their presence and, together with Carolyn and Christian de Beauport, I look forward to further adventures.

I am especially indebted to Paul MacLean for his long years of scientific investigation which made it possible to understand the different human processes in relation to his research elaborating a triune structure of the brain.

It was Mary Schmidt who brought my attention to MacLean's research and who then spent endless hours answering my questions. It was her love for life as well as her knowledge of neuroscience that inspired my interest in the study of the brain.

Other great teachers enabled me to experience the different human capacities involved in this model of multiple intelligences:

Jacinto Vallelado, Spanish philosopher, who helped me believe in the power of my mind.

Ross Hainline, Jungian therapist, who offered me careful guidance for my life and opened me to the world of dreams.

John Lilly, great explorer of states of consciousness, who helped me to open the smaller world of myself.

Jean Houston, philosopher and midwife to the many dimensions of spirit, offered me experiences that were key in the development of my life and in the understanding of human life as energy.

Michaleen Kimmey, whose dedication to emotional ranges opened me to finding the road of feeling my way carefully on this earth as well as distinguishing between the vibrations of thinking and feeling.

Sue Bender, Gestalt and Transactional Analysis therapist, who helped me to understand some of the energy transactions involved in my own behavior.

Dorothy Smith and Carmen de Barraza, who by their presence gave witness to the intuitive and psychic dimensions.

I also wish to express my appreciation to those who participated in the creation of the Mead School for Human Development, an experience which permitted me to observe very closely the diverse capacities of children that in turn motivated me in the search for a more complete explanation of human development.

I want to thank those who support the existence of Smith College, a place of learning that was so important in my life, as well as those who helped me personally, especially Allen Burr Overstreet, Gwendolyn Carter, Mary Mensel, Allison Cook, and Helen Kirkpatrick Millbank.

I wish to thank Catherine Ogilvy for her support of my doctoral studies in which I began the research for this book.

Many were especially helpful in the development of courses based on the information presented in this book:

Jane Prettyman offered her extraordinary writing and artistic abilities as well as her initiative and her perspective of the human condition.

Sylviane Sans provided sensitive and continuous assistance in the first workshops on Multiple Intelligences and Self Care as well as her artistic capacity in the creation of the banners illustrating the three brain systems.

Gail Weissman and Carol Nicols for their vision and support for three years in the Mount Sinai Medical Center of New York which made possible the development of many of the exercises and concepts in this book. I also appreciate Annette Vallano's insistence in the creation of the first Self Care Course and her assistance in the teaching of the courses at the Mount Sinai Medical Center.

Althea Whyte for her many years of dedication to doing anything that was necessary, from redordings to typing to a sophisticated selection of music for the workshops.

Beatriz and Manuel Kohn for their unlimited kindness and support.

And the last who are also the first: all those who have been with me in the study and exploration of energy and our three brain systems. It has been the presence and love of you who have for so many years been close and enthusiastic about this work, that have continually encouraged me. Please know that I am extremely grateful to each of you.

In the direct participation of this book I want to express my appreciation to the following people:

Maria Eugenia Yanes de Gonzalez for her constant assistance in the correction and translation of numerous first drafts.

Bibs MacIntyre for her initial editorial assistance.

Luis Camejo for enormous patience as well as his creativity and artistic talent in the creation of the illustrations.

Kitty La Perriere for her support and careful reading of the text.

Roz Targ, our dauntless agent, who believed in us and offered her optimistic spirit and many years of experience.

Brenda Rosen, Executive Editor of Quest Books, for her recognition of the potential importance of this work. We especially appreciated her comprehension of the material and invaluable suggestions of areas to be further developed. We felt accompanied by a professional and a caring human being at every stage. We also want to thank others at Quest who assisted in this process.

Words do not adequately define the participation of Aura Sofia Diaz de Melasecca in the realization of this book. She was the motor that made it happen. Her perspective and ideas, based on her feelings and experience working with human beings as well as her many years studying individual and family therapy with Virginia Satir, made her contributions invaluable. She helped to clarify and elaborate many concepts that otherwise might have remained obscure. It is thanks to her capacity in grasping the overall vision as well as the details, thanks to her sensitivity during my sporadic rebellions, and also thanks to her love of humanity, that the book exists. I am eternally grateful for her presence and collaboration.

Foreword

JOSEPH CHILTON PEARCE

his book, one of half a dozen really important ones I have read in my short seventy years, could be a major vanguard in our species' growing attempt to become more aware of itself. With remarkable simplicity and clarity, de Beauport offers a treasure chest of insights into the workings of the mind, as revealed through current brain-mind research, and equally simple exercises for making that information one's own transformative knowledge. Through works of this nature (and stature), I see the possibility of our rising out of the shadowy mythical-religious projection-stage of our evolution, with all its wars and terrors, and breaking into the light of full self-consciousness and empowerment, a true childhood's end and coming into maturity.

Much of the credit for this shift, were it successful, would lie with science, if only by default, as interpreted by authors such as de Beauport and Diaz. For, even as science as an activity has provided us with ample means for self and global destruction (means we seem eager to employ to their full), it has also provided us with a knowledge of ourselves never before available, certainly not on a general level as translated by this book (of which we *must* learn and employ to survive).

Many scientific discoveries remain outside the common domain because of their complexity and the general hesitancy of scientists to make philosophical or "meta-physical" statements or observations about their own work. De Beauport fills this communication gap with a cascade of brilliant observations, syntheses, and functional guidelines for personal application. She presents these findings in so clear and logical a fashion as to please any academic critique, while at the same time embracing and enlightening us on such unscientific issues as the human spirit.

Among research contributing to this evolutionary shift is that into the brain-mind; the heart-brain dynamic (the heart emerging as a major intelligence in our experience); child development; quantum physics' "non-local" energy, and its corollary, discovery of non-localized "fields of intelligence" on which our brain draws to form our lived experience. De Beauport is familiar with these disciplines, with the exception of the extremely new, largely unknown, and most extraordinary of all research discoveries to date, the heart-brain dynamic (as brought to full synthesis through The Institute of HeartMath*). What is intriguing to me, however, is that the author is actually familiar with heart-intelligence itself, through her own intuitive understanding and experience, though she doesn't label or describe it in as direct and formal language as that given us by The Institute of HeartMath.

So *The Three Faces of Mind* draws and elaborates on those areas of brain research that open new vistas to human understanding and potential. Among the most important areas of this research, I would list Karl Pribram's theory that the brain functions by translating from a "frequency realm that is not in time-space," a realm from which our experience *of* a time-space world is translated. De Beauport skillfully incorporates this "frequency aspect" of brain function into her own creative presentation, as well as its relative, the non-local energies of quantum physics. Equally important is the "neural field" theory of Gerald Eddleman, how the "sensory maps" of the brain develop for this translation work itself (which is critical to our understanding of child development). And last but not least, the "triune nature" of brain and behavior as presented in the life-work of neuroscientist Paul MacLean, which throws as much light on child development and human nature in general as any contemporary work. In light of its profound importance, MacLean's work seems to me to have been woefully ignored, so we are doubly fortunate that here, in *The Three Faces of Mind*, de Beauport brilliantly weaves MacLean's wealth of research into a breathtaking psychological, philosophical, and spiritual tapestry that offers us not only a simple and powerful avenue for self-transformation, but an opportunity for creating an educational system that would truly lead a child "forth into knowledge," a knowledge that would transform society.

Baldly stated, those creative forces that we have always projected outside ourselves onto cloud-nines, gods-goddesses, demons-angels, fates-destinies, historically considered beyond our control other than supplication, sacrifice, or worship, are now being revealed as part and parcel of our genetic brain-mind-body system itself, generated from within-and-through the awesome complexities of our mind-brain-heart-body complex. The indications are clear that these formerly projected creative powers are "interior" rather than exterior, making us ultimately responsible to and for them.

This doesn't imply that in discovering such forces "within" (non-localized would be a more accurate term), we thus explain them away or gain control over them as technology. Far from it. To be responsible *for* doesn't mean to "own" or be the creator of. For the more we discover about the brain-mind complex, the more awesome and mysterious it becomes, particularly when we encounter non-locality and its "frequency realms" on which our brain-mind draws and in which the heart plays the key role. Nor do I imply that we are gaining or even *should gain* "control" over these creative processes. But, as this book clearly demonstrates, we can, and for our survival *must*, learn about and develop far more *cooperative* responses to these "autonomic" processes than we have in our former, sleep-walking past, when we projected them as outward beings and powers.

That such understanding and employment can begin at any period of life and bring profound change to our awareness and behavior is one of the graces of this book. Our primitive projection-applications and/or efforts at "dominating" nature have equally failed us. Meanwhile, the means of gaining true "dominion over our world" (a proposal two millennia in gestation), are ready to be born into our personal lives.

The implications of brain research, particularly that centering on the emotions and heart, are radical, however, presenting a true quantum leap from our conventional images of self and world. A new image is forming, though glimpsed but dimly by scattered members of the scientific community, academia, or the public at large. Perhaps the extremity of the chasm between old and new paradigms explains the fundamentalist revival also taking place today, with its clear polarizations, inability to stand ambiguity, longing for ancient precepts, and rock-bound certitudes that relieve us of responsibility—a reversion to childhood, in effect. For we instinctively recoil against the uncertainties of the unknown trying to break forth. Even within the sciences, the split between old and new paradigms is a matter of passionate debate, while within most disciplines, there is *no* debate since there is little awareness as yet of what is implied or happening.

All of which point up the importance of the following work. In no way could I summarize or suggest the richness of de Beauport's ten intelligences, except to say a knowledgeable reader would do well not to think of her work as just an extension of Howard Gardner's "multiple intelligences" (which has proven so popular and been so distorted). De Beauport's intelligences arise from her understanding of the triune structure of our brain-mind and its multiple forms of interaction. If we are willing to look, she holds before us an uncannily accurate mirroring of ourselves. More positively, she shows, through her exercises, how we can bring to our awareness, and so learn to monitor, those hitherto automatic "knee-jerk" reactions leading to our chronic grief. As *The Book of Common Prayer* has lamented for centuries: ". . . having done those things which we ought not to have done and left undone those things which we ought to have done . . . there is no health (or wholeness) in us." Precisely because of the three-fold nature of our brain, we have been a house divided against itself. The following pages can bring our house to order.

The richness of this book has been, for me, an adventure of and challenge to, mind and spirit. The section on "associative intelligence" alone makes the book worthwhile, yet is but one of many equally rewarding insights. This is not a book to be read as entertaining hypotheses of "human potentials," nor just information, but one to be lived with, contemplated, worked with, even when, or particularly when, it encroaches on our self-image and generates uneasiness.

Surely this book has companions of like merit, though from different mind-sets and disciplines, each of which complement and strengthen the other. Those of greatest import to me and closest in spirit to de Beauport are *Journey of the Heart* by John Welwood, James P. Carse's *Finite and Infinite Games*, and the publications and training programs from The Institute of HeartMath. Chris Mercagliano's fascinating history of the Albany Free School, *Making It Up As We Go Along*, has a strong resonance as well. Intriguingly, all of these, so widely disparate in approach, content, and texture, point, as does *The Three Faces of Mind*, toward a single renaissance of mind and spirit generating at every hand. Thus we have, as readers longing to grow and expand in spirit and knowledge, a rich vein of gold readily available, and I urge you to plunge right in to the following wealth, respond with true intent to that offered, and reap rich rewards.

*Address for

The Institute of HeartMath
P.O. Box 1463
147000 West Park Avenue
Boulder Creek, CA 95006
(408) 338-8700

Introduction

It is that our normal waking consciousness, rational consciousness as we call it, is but one special type of consciousness, whilst all about it, parted from it by the filmiest of screens, there lie potential forms of consciousness entirely different . . . no account of the universe in its totality can be final which leaves these other forms of consciousness quite disregarded.

William James, *The Varieties of Religious Experience*

J*ames was right. We can no longer disregard forms of consciousness other than our normal waking consciousness. The label "unconscious" obscures our vision, limits our capacities, separates us from deep religious experience, and ignores the discovery that we are energy systems guided by artistic and spiritual processes as well as by rational processes and by two deeper brain systems, as yet little understood beyond the medical or scientific communities.*

In this book I have probed the veil of the unconscious and examined recent research in order to offer ten pathways of intelligence and consciousness, pathways I believe every human being needs in order to explore the immensity of our universe as well as the depth of our individual self and our daily living. These ten pathways are based on my own explorations, my thirty-three years of experience in teaching people of all ages, the new paradigm put forth by the new physics, and the brain research mainly of Roger Sperry and Paul MacLean.

Prior to 1981 human intelligence was considered to be primarily rational intelligence, and from the perspective of brain research, this intelligence occurred in the left hemisphere of the neocortex. Researcher Roger Sperry won the Nobel Prize in Medicine in 1981 for his discovery that the right hemisphere also contributes to human intelligence. Nevertheless, Sperry's findings referred only to the two hemispheres of the neocortex and left untouched the important brain structures lying just below the neocortex. To open pathways into what was labeled the "unconscious," the brain research of Paul D. MacLean was fundamental.

MacLean, now Senior Scientist at NIMH, in 1972 was Chief of the Laboratory of Brain Evolution and Behavior at the National Institute of Mental Health in Bethesda, Maryland. According to MacLean, the brain includes three different structures which fulfill three distinct functions: the neocortical system of thought and image, the limbic system located below the neocortex that enables us to desire and to feel, and under both of those, a third R-complex structure related to behavior. MacLean wrote:

> *Radically different in chemistry and structure and in an evolutionary sense countless generations apart, the three neural assemblies constitute a hierarchy of three-brains-in-one, a triune brain . . . Stated in popular terms, the three evolutionary formations might be imagined as three interconnected biological computers, with each having its own special intelligence, its own subjectivity, its own sense of time and space, and its own memory, motor, and other functions.*
>
> *Improved anatomical, chemical, and physiological techniques have afforded a clearer definition of the three basic formations than was previously possible. It has also proved that the three formations are capable of operating somewhat independently.*
>
> *Moreover . . . the triune relationship implies that "The 'whole' is greater than the sum of its parts, because the exchange of information among the three brain types means that each derives a greater amount of information than if it were operating alone."[1]*

I saw MacLean's presentation of a triune brain of three systems—physically and chemically so different yet interconnected into one totality—as the map that we needed to guide ourselves toward full human consciousness. If two brain systems were beneath the level of consciousness, then the human question became how to access and guide others into accessing these deeper brain systems. If each system contributed to the whole, then how could each system become educated or brought to human consciousness? I became interested in both the independent functioning of each system as well as the overall potential impact of three systems within a unified whole.

From my years of observing children, I knew there was an emotional as well as behavioral intelligence that it would be important to identify if we were ever to improve education. In the school I created I had seen children rewrite the twenty-minute attention span alleged to be the norm in most child development textbooks. When they were in love with what they were doing and no bells were ringing, they could be concentrating for thirty to forty minutes. Love and emotion certainly had something to do with learning. I saw children learn what to do with their anger and then be able to feel good as well as control their behavior. When we helped them with their behavior, rather than expecting it or talking about it, I saw them learn to act in helpful rather than harmful ways. I knew behavior had a lot to do with whether they would be able to go on learning and whether they would do anything meaningful with what they were learning. From ten years of close observation, I knew emotions and behavior were keys. MacLean's research enabled me to search out emotional and behavioral intelligence in relation to brain research, just as Sperry's research enabled me to broaden the scope of what was considered mental intelligence.

With this perspective, I began to develop and teach the ten intelligences presented in this book to over five thousand adults in the United States and Latin America. Adults found it extremely helpful to be able to separate their emotional and behavioral intelligence from the mental intelligence they were accustomed to. To know that there were diverse brain structures beneath what they had always considered "the brain" helped them to understand a lot of their own behavior and emotional difficulties as well as the difficulties of those they were living and working with.

Three nurses from Mount Sinai Medical Center reported that they had been able to improve their relationship with an extremely angry patient who had been unmanageable. After learning about the emotional brain and becoming more aware of their own emotional history, they were able to understand and not take his anger personally. They moved in and out of his room without being hooked and yet were able to treat him kindly. In another instance, a supervisor was able to make a list of all that she appreciated about the nurses working for her. She had not lost her critical rational intelligence; she simply had shifted to associative intelligence to associate with what would help her relate to those working with her.

The brain is like a crowded cocktail party where everybody is talking at once. You have an idea they are all saying something important, but you don't know exactly what it is. By treating each brain system independently rather than as an integrated whole, we are better able to hear the conversation from each. Exploring distinct intelligences teaches us how to focus on our emotions and behavior and when to shift away to use our reflective mental abilities. We can access the brain structures independently, depending on which intelligence we are focusing on. When I am with another person, I may focus on thinking rationally or shift to imagination; I may slow down and let myself be affected by the person, or act in cooperation with the other regardless of what I am thinking or feeling. Independent access to each brain system is important.

Meanwhile, we can remember that each system is not only independent, but also interactive and interdependent. One may be dominant, but the other two are always involved. My treatment of each brain structure independently is not meant to deny the obvious interconnections. What we think affects what we feel and do. What we feel affects what we are willing to think about or do, and certainly what we do affects how we feel and contributes to our thinking processes as reflective humans.

As excited as I was about brain research, there was still the thorny issue of how to deal with the prevalent mechanistic view of the brain that had been hindering a more complex understanding of human development and education. To transcend this limited view of the brain in order to engage us in a search for full human consciousness, I had to move beyond pure physiological description to research into new physics. According to the new physics all matter is energy and energy is not in a fixed state; it is rather in continuous movement. Brain matter, then, is energy and consequently also in continuous movement. Instead of inquiring ever more finely into details until discovering some fixed and specific features, such as an intelligence quotient, the new paradigm opens us to energy and allows us to work with the intelligences as different energy processes in continuous motion.

I also took seriously Einstein's famous formula, $E = MC^2$, as an invitation to see all matter as energy: a rock, a plant, a snake, an animal, and human beings. We divided the atom and liberated energy as destructive fire. The formula that threatens us with destruction may also be the formula that leads us to a greater vision of human learning. Energy now offers us a unitary perspective on all life, and from that singular perspective we can start to appreciate multiple and diverse realities. Einstein's formula, which applies to all matter, is therefore applicable to you and to me. I am equal to matter multiplied by the speed of light squared. Your energy equals your matter times the speed of light squared. You are energy in constant vibration.

All life is energy. I am energy and my brain is energy, and energy is vibration. What kinds of vibrations govern my brain structures? What kinds of vibrations will enable me to access them? It is obvious that my hand vibrates at a much slower speed than my eye, my heart at a different speed than my leg. Each of these physical structures is different and therefore vibrates at different speeds. Since the three brain structures are physically different, they also must vibrate at different speeds. The speed of the rational process of the left hemisphere of the neocortex would therefore not give me access to the two deeper structures of feelings and behavior lying just below the neocortex. The search then became how to discover the vibratory processes that would give me access to three different brain structures in order to become more conscious and better conduct the different realities of my life. More precisely, considering that the brain is not fixed matter but energy in continuous movement, I began to focus on the physical and chemical differences between each brain system in search of the processes that would give us access to more capacities within our brain.

The ten processes that have resulted from my search take into account both the major characteristics described in current brain research as well as human abilities, which I have been studying in myself and others for many years. Continuing brain and chemical research will undoubtedly throw new light on the functioning of the brain, either as a totality of many systems or in reference to each of the three systems. Certainly more research will show the interrelationship of each of these structures and, I hope, will enrich each intelligence. Independent of brain research, however, thinking, feeling, and acting human beings have always existed. The three faces of mind have been present throughout history and in all cultures. Brain research now gives us explanations, inviting us to be more conscious of these three elements of our being.

This book approaches the brain as an energy system instead of viewing it as a fixed-parts system. Perceived as an energy system, the brain opens us up to the proposal of different processes that vibrate from the thick waves of the finite to the finer waves of the infinite.

Recognizing the brain as an energy system comprised of billions of cells also enables us to quit pursuing a fixed intelligence quotient for each individual. In the first part of this century, our belief in a brain system of fixed characteristics rather than in a brain system of energy, supported the years of measurement that have harmed individuals and plagued school systems, only to be finally rejected by leading authorities as we close out this century.[2]

There are estimates that we actually use only ten percent of our brain power. We have, however, only one formalized process for accessing our brain and increasing our brain power: only rational intelligence has been trained and validated. Yet in different individuals we can easily observe the many different capacities of the human being: exquisite visual and musical capabilities, spiritual sensitivity, emotional profundity, the ability to take action, to move and survive—all indicating that there is much more than rational intelligence involved in our human capacities.

Many intelligences are available, latent within all brain structures, awaiting your interest and power of concentration. Each can be learned and practiced as you once learned and practiced the rational process. Each can open you to new horizons, increased intelligence, and greater consciousness.

Redefining Intelligence

THE MENTAL INTELLIGENCES OF THE NEOCORTEX

—*Rational Intelligence:* the process by which we perceive information through sequential connections, involving primarily the use of reason, logic, cause and effect

—*Associative Intelligence:* the process that allows us to perceive information through multiple connections, involving primarily the use of juxtaposition, association, and relationship

—*Spatial Intelligence:* the process of perceiving information at a deeper level, synthesized sometimes into images, sometimes into sounds, or other combinations received from the senses and deeper brain systems

—*Intuitive Intelligence:* direct knowledge without the use of reason; knowing from within

THE EMOTIONAL INTELLIGENCES OF THE LIMBIC BRAIN

—*Affectional Intelligence:* the process of being affected by something or someone; developing the ability of closeness with a person, place, object, idea, or situation

—*Mood Intelligence:* the ability to enter into, hold with, and shift from any mood, whether the experience feels painful or pleasurable

—*Motivational Intelligence:* being aware of our desires and knowing what excites us and moves us the most; the ability to guide our life in relation to what we love

THE BEHAVIORAL INTELLIGENCES OF THE BASIC BRAIN

—*Basic Intelligence:* the ability to move ourselves toward or away from; being able to imitate or inhibit anything or anyone on behalf of our own life or the lives of others

—*Pattern Intelligence:* the ability to know the patterns governing our behavior and being able to alter them when necessary

—*Parameter Intelligence:* the ability to recognize, extend, or transform the rhythms, routines, and rituals of our life

Aware of these many intelligences, the new thinker is like an orchestra conductor, focusing on music from one section, then another, then all together. Or the new thinker is a surfer, catching first one wave and riding it, then another, moving with waves in continuous motion.

You are the conductor of your brain. The results you get depend on where you concentrate, where your focus is or is not. Knowing that you have many intelligences to choose from, you can start guiding your life by focusing in an appropriate intelligence and shifting out of one you find inappropriate.

To focus and shift effectively, it is important to realize that each intelligence involves a different vibrational energy range. For example, the vibrational range of mood intelligence differs from the vibrational energy of spatial-visual intelligence. The mood of anger has a thick vibrational energy, whereas visualization has a faster, thinner dimension. The vibration involved in associative intelligence when we are looking at a sunset is different from the slow vibrations involved in affective intelligence, in which we stop to allow ourselves to be affected by the sunset. Even thinner vibrations are those related to psychic phenomena, or the extrasensory perception involved in intuitive intelligence. Each brain system is an energy system vibrating in ranges extending from thicker to thinner energy and from slower to higher speeds. Thicker ranges refer to physical existence, visible and sometimes tangible; thinner ranges refer to the invisible as described in spirituality and quantum physics. In between thicker material realities and spiritual or quantum realities lie all the variations of energy that we may discover as we learn to activate the billions of cells making up the human brain-mind-body system. Each intelligence charts a pathway through this tremendous energy potential of the human mind.

I do not intend to disparage the need for rational, logical, and critical thinking. On the contrary, I expect that through clarifying the other mental processes, rational thought will not be as contaminated as it now is in our culture. At present there are many other mental processes that are masquerading as rational, using a thinly veiled logic in order to communicate by means of reason—the only process intellectually and socially acceptable. Human beings and the rational process will both benefit when we become capable of clearly identifying the boundaries of different mental processes. We will also be able to focus deeply within one mental process, and at the same time remain aware that there are other mental processes we are ignoring.

Are these ten processes, ten pathways to consciousness, or ten intelligences? The answer is, all of the above. Each process enables us to access different vibrational ranges of the three brain structures. This deeper and diverse access lets us become more and more conscious of areas of our life that we heretofore considered or accepted as unconscious. The label "unconscious" served to mask our ignorance of the deeper processes within us. Hence, ten pathways to consciousness. Each pathway also enables us to gain more and more information about our life and all life around us. With this information we become not only mentally intelligent but also emotionally intelligent and behaviorally intelligent.

Each intelligence deals with a different kind of information. For instance, a woman who is intelligent in her thinking or visualizing process may be ignorant in her feeling process. That is, she may be unable to access information about her own feelings or unable to access emotional information about the lives around her. Or a man may be intelligent emotionally but incapable of acting; that is, incapable of integrating feedback about his own actions or those around him. Each of our brain systems offers us different information. Rational intelligence helps us access information through a certain process, but it excludes the other processes of becoming artistically intelligent, spiritually intelligent, emotionally intelligent, and behaviorally intelligent.

Perceiving ourselves as energy systems with multiple realities and various intelligences instead of perceiving ourselves as a single reality with a fixed intelligence involves a tremendous change in human consciousness. Our search has to be toward the discovery of as many mental processes as can electrify our brains and develop our capacities. Scientific research invites us into an exquisite complexity. Our responses need to be appropriate. We need to open our minds to a potential mental abundance and freedom.

Consider this book a beginning of the exploration of the billions of cells that make up your human brain-mind-body system. Please feel free either to read this book sequentially from cover to cover or to open it to any chapter that interests you. You might prefer to go deeply into one intelligence, reading and doing the exercises, before you proceed to the other intelligences. If you are interested in the relationship between brain physiology and intelligence, you will find an overview chapter at the beginning of each part of the book.

In Part 1 you will find an explanation of the characteristics of the neocortex, followed by the four mental intelligences.

Part 2 deals with the characteristics of the limbic brain, proposes a new approach to emotions, and then offers a map to guide you through the territory of emotions. Chapters on the three emotional intelligences are followed by a chapter describing emotional intelligence and the three openings (nose, mouth, and genitals) that affect the limbic brain.

Part 3 covers the characteristics and languages of the basic brain, also called the R-complex, reptile brain, or nervous system brain. Chapters on each of the three behavioral intelligences are followed by a description of the behavioral intelligence in relation to the openings of your body.

In the conclusion under the section entitled "Individual Action," I suggest that certain intelligences might be especially helpful for different life situations. Therefore you might wish to check the conclusion before deciding how to read the book. I also propose two theoretical changes as well as social actions in which these intelligences can be applied to make a difference in our personal and collective lives.

I hope you will enjoy this book and find it useful as a reference handbook, where you can look for the intelligences and exercises listed in an appendix as you need them. I also hope that groups will consider studying this book together.

PART I

MENTAL INTELLIGENCE:

THINKING, IMAGINING, INTUITING AND

THE NEOCORTICAL BRAIN

Network of Possibilities

THE NEOCORTEX

T wo years before Roger Sperry received the Nobel Prize in Medicine in 1981 for his research into a right-hemisphere intelligence, I met Mary Schmidt, a neurophysiologist who kept telling me about the split-brain research that in 1979 was being reported in professional journals. She took a great interest in the Mead School that I had founded in 1969. With the variety of imaginal and creative work going on in the Mead School, as well as the specific advances in math and science, she became excited that these results sprang from the richness of our structure, which was in some way stimulating both sides of the brain. The school was committed to the fuller development of the student's potential but without any serious interest in the brain. I was highly skeptical and had no particular interest in brain studies. Mary, however, was so convinced of the importance of the right hemisphere to intelligence that she persuaded the director of a lab in Boston to lend us an EEG machine for a month. Thus it was that on a rainy October afternoon I found myself driving with Mary to the lab, where with the aid of a handyman we loaded the large EEG machine on the back of a station wagon and returned with our prize to the school in Greenwich.

We asked twelve sixth graders if they would be interested in studying their own brains. Having first discussed the project, Mary and I decided that we would not be interested in a control group and therefore ours could not be formal research. Instead we would propose it to the students as another workshop, a brain workshop. Just as the students had cooking workshops and math workshops and printmaking workshops, this could be called a brain workshop. Volunteering her time, Mary one by one hooked electrodes on the left and right sides of each student's head. She then asked the students to do various tasks in language, math, and art as well as one in which they remained silent. They were fascinated with the whole procedure.

Mead School had centers for language, art, science, math, and music, so I had six years of reports that indicated when the child had learned to read and how well each was doing in math, science, or art. In other words, I had a full report on each student's learning process. When I looked at the results of Mary's simple EEG's studies and compared them with the students' learning records, I was astounded. Those students who had had difficulty learning to read but had done well in art were producing relaxed alpha waves in the right hemisphere when asked to do art and irregular sharp beta waves in the left hemisphere indicating difficulty when asked to read. Those who had learned to read at an early age registered beta waves in the left hemisphere just as we would have expected. What Mary had been telling me about the characteristics of right and left hemispheres seemed to hold true. The brain studies matched the academic reports that I had on the students for six years. I became an excited believer.

One of my best memories is of sitting down with the students and discussing the results. They were excited to understand why one had difficulty reading, why another read faster, why one could do better in art, another in individual sports, and another in math. They were able to talk about why some worked out math problems by writing the answers down, while others did it by going inside and seeing the answers. By this one experiment we had been able to remove six years of pressure, doubt, and confusion in the children's minds. I was deeply moved to see their openness in discussing the experiment with one another. They were curious and interested that they could develop a greater specialty in one area than in another.

I knew then that the right and left hemisphere studies would one day become famous. Indeed, two years later when I read in the newspaper that Roger Sperry received the Nobel Prize, I remember the tears coming to my eyes as I thought, "Now everybody will know and understand."

The neocortex is the brain system that distinguishes us as human beings as distinct from all other forms of life. It permits us to make distinctions and reflect upon our thoughts, feelings, and actions as human beings.

The neocortex has been called a "crown of jewels" and an "enchanted loom" by recent brain researchers. As an explorer in the field of education and human development, I have experienced many moments of exquisite subtlety and beauty created by this brain system in the realms of intellect, art, and spirituality. There are other moments when I am convinced that we are wearing our crown of jewels as a crown of thorns: we so often use it to distinguish what is wrong in ourselves or in others, to criticize and condemn instead of to clarify and appreciate. Rather than using the neocortex to improve life, we have been using this precious capacity of reflection to condemn ourselves or others for what we do not have or cannot do, often concluding that limitations and suffering are a fixed aspect of human nature rather than a matter of where and how we focus our mental attention.

It does not have to be that way. The capacity of the neocortex is tremendous. We now know that the neocortical system is composed of ten to one hundred billion neurons, capable of quadrillions of connections.[1] That is certainly enough connections to enable us to preserve our capacity for critical thinking, to develop a new capacity for appreciative thinking, and to coordinate both on behalf of human life.

The neocortex as an enchanted loom is a potent image, capable of guiding us into weaving thoughts for the improvement rather than the negation of life. With so many billions of cells still to be developed, we no longer need to get stuck in the limitations of the human condition, either individually or collectively. We can learn to use our neocortical loom to illuminate human life.

A Closer Look

The neocortex, largest of the three brain systems, consists of honey-combed convolutions containing billions of cells. Although usually pictured as gray and dead in our textbooks and magazines, when alive the neocortex is rivered with veins and arteries carrying oxygenated blood to the nerve cells throughout this vast network.

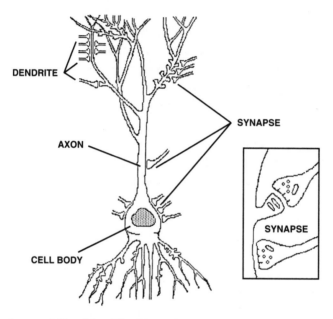

Fig. 1. Axon and Dendrite: The Physical Network of Mental Intelligences (Luis Camejo)

The axon sends impulses across an open area called the synaptic gap; those impulses are then received by the dendrites of other cells. This process, linking axons and dendrites, creates a vast network of vibrations or mental intelligence that expands from cell to cell. Recent chemical research focuses on the neurotransmitters that affect this process of connection between axon and dendrite.

What is intelligence? The impulses being sent by the axon and being received by the dendrite and the resulting synapse is the activity of the neocortex, which is commonly called intelligence or thought. Whatever label we use to describe the mental activity of the neocortex, by increasing the connections we increase our mental activity and therefore our intelligence.

What is significant for you and me as human beings in search of developing the vast potential of the neocortex is to know that the crossing of the synaptic gap consists in making connections between those ten to one hundred billion cells that make up our neocortex. Anything that can help to increase those connections will increase the power, mental ability, and intelligence in our neocortical system. We are born with this vast neocortical territory. It depends on us to make the connections between axon and dendrite. Without our conscious participation we would have billions of cellular bodies compacted together with life but without synapses, without connections. We make the connections. We create the impulses that cross the synaptic gaps, thereby increasing our intelligence. You and I without doubt have the necessary "gray matter" to become intelligent. The question is, how many connections will we be able to achieve during our lifetime? How intelligent are we going to be? Willing to be? What is important is to value all possible connections that occur and all sorts of activities that may stimulate those connections.

Territory of Intelligence Expands

Until 1981 we considered intelligence to consist of only the connections made in the left hemisphere that were associated with the rational process. Then Roger Sperry was awarded the Nobel Prize for the discovery that not only the left hemisphere but also the right hemisphere was actively engaged in important mental processes.[2] The neocortical network of axons and dendrites is divided into two hemispheres connected by the corpus callosum, a fibrous bridge serving to link both areas. In what was known as split-brain research, it became possible to isolate the characteristics of mental processing that occurred in the right hemisphere of the brain. Only when the left hemisphere was surgically isolated from the right did we become certain of the intelligence of the right hemisphere. Even when separated from the left hemisphere, the right was able to continue to process information, displaying characteristics that then became clearly associated with the intelligence of the right hemisphere.

J. E. Bogen, M.D., famous split-brain researcher and Clinical Professor of Neurosurgery at University of Southern California School of Medicine, later studied famous philosophers, authors, and scientists who, based on their own observations of the human experience, had already referred to two different types of mental processes. Both philosophers and scientific investigators therefore corroborate the presence of intelligent connections on both sides of the neocortex. The following list, compiled by Dr. Bogen, gathers together many terms used to make subtle distinctions between the mental processes of the left and right hemispheres.[3]

Source	Left	Right
Akhilinanda	buddhi	manas
Assagioli	intellect	intuition
Austin	convergent	divergent
Bateson & Jackson	digital	analogic
Blackburn	intellectual	sensuous
Bronowski	deductive	imaginative
Bruner	rational	metaphoric
Cohen	analytic	relational
de Bono	vertical	lateral
Deikman	active	receptive
Dieudonné	discrete	continuous
Freud	secondary	primary
Goldstein	abstract	concrete
Hilgard	realistic	impulsive
Hobbes (per Murphy)	directed	free
Humphrey & Zangwill	propositional	imaginative
W. James	differential	existential
A. Jensen	transformational	associative
Kagan & Moss	analytic	relational
D. Lee	lineal	nonlineal
Levi-Straus	positive	mythic
Levi & Sperry	analytic	gestalt
Lomax & Berkowitz	differentiation	integration
Maslow	rational	intuitive
McFie, Piercy (from Spearman)		
	relations	correlates

McKeller	relastic	autistic
Neisser	sequential	multiple
Oppenheimer	historical	timeless
Ornstein	analytic	holistic
Pavlov	second signaling	first signaling
C. S. Pierce	explicative	ampliative
Polanyi	explicit	tacit
Price	reductionist	compositionist
Radhakrishnan (per H. Smith)		
	rational	integral
Reusch	discursive	eidetic
Schopenhauer	objective	subjective
Sechenov (per Luria)	successive	simultaneous
C. S. Smith	atomistic	gross
Wells	hierarchical	heterarchical

In spite of the richness of this list, I decided to follow my own experience with students and selected the following five characteristics as basic and sufficient to illustrate the differences between the hemispheres.

Left	*Right*
Sequential	Simultaneous
Linear	Spatial
Logical	Associative
Parts-to-Whole	Whole-to-Parts
Time	Timeless

What interests me is not so much the physical location of the characteristics in one hemisphere or the other, as the existence of the different characteristics that permit us access to the whole neocortex without worrying about whether it be right or left. Before describing the four intelligences associated with this brain, I would like first to describe the characteristics of each hemisphere to show how they relate to the overall processes.

SEQUENTIAL . . . SIMULTANEOUS

Sequence is the most obvious characteristic of rational thinking associated with the left hemisphere. We speak in sequence, one word after the other. We also try to compute sequentially, first one number then the next. Sequence involves processing step by step. It is a succession where each operation precedes and follows another one. In rational thinking we process in a sequential continuity linked by reasons, causes, and effects. We try to conclude or close a process before beginning another: "Let me finish this before I start that."

In contrast, the ability to process simultaneously—to see things all at once or to catch glimpses—is associated with the right hemisphere. A person with a preference for the right hemisphere takes in glimpses of reality, perceives larger and larger fields of interests, has instant recognition, "a-ha!" moments of awareness, and all-at-once perception. Instead of a preference for exactness, there is a preference for generality, for softness and glimpsing, a preference for leaving a process open instead of coming to conclusions and setting limits.

LINEAR . . . SPATIAL

Someone who thinks sequentially sees reality as linear, while a person with a right hemisphere preference sees reality spatially. We usually write linearly, whereas the glimpses of painters, sculptors, poets, and artists are usually presented spatially. Images may be elaborated in external space through paints or texture, or in the many dimensions of space known as art. Images are also elaborated in the internal space of the human mind and become the inner arts of daydreaming, imaging, visualizing, or the receiving of intuitions or revelations, as in religious experience.

Sometimes we are more comfortable in the world of space, in endless glimpses, sometimes in the more confined sequences of line, exploring something with exactness and coming to closure or conclusion.

LOGICAL . . . ASSOCIATIVE

Logic, the exact linking of cause and effect into rational thinking, is the backbone of Western civilization. It is basic to all research, the foundation of science and universities. It is deeply ingrained in all our institutions. Logical thinking is basic to political freedom. It enables us to criticize and doubt the generalities of concepts and programs promised by our politicians as they struggle for power.

Most of us try to be logical, even when that is not our strength, because it is the dominant mental process of our social and intellectual training. We use logic to defend ourselves in difficult situations, be they professional, commercial, family, social, or political in nature.

Association is a characteristic of the right hemisphere. Associating is the ability to make connections, not of a sequential kind but of a random kind: free-flung, relating by whim, by taste, preference, shape, or nuance. Association is linking for the purpose of staying open: discovery by chance; stopping along the way; leaping over, around, and beyond anything that has even the appearance of being a fixed way or procedure. We easily identify this with a process of creativity, conjuring up the image of either artist or inventor. However, we might well ask if this process of creativity is held exclusively by the artist or whether it needs to be available to every thinking person.

PARTS-TO-WHOLE . . . WHOLE-TO-PARTS

The left hemisphere processes part by part and is confident of arriving at the "whole." The right hemisphere wants to grasp the "whole" before being willing to enter into the parts. Considering the vastness of the universe, it is questionable if anyone truly sees it as whole. Rather, we perceive or glimpse larger totalities than the smaller parts we have been accustomed to perceiving.

Some of us are content to listen to a lecture; some prefer an overview first, either visual or verbal. Some read a book chapter by chapter, confident of arriving at meaning and conclusion. Some open anywhere; some do both. Some of us are able patiently to speak sentences to conclusions; some of us burst and stutter, as we catch glimpses and paint pictures for the audience or for each other. Some of us see the forest, some the trees. Some see the background, some the foreground. Some of us walk into a room glancing from person to person; others in a single glimpse get a view of the entire room, which for them is sufficient.

A person with preferences for the left hemisphere sees parts first and builds into a whole, which is named conclusion, plan, or system. The left arrives at the whole by means of the parts, which are called reasons. A person with right hemisphere preferences sees wholes or glimpses first, calling them an image, overview, revelation, or system. The right arrives at the parts after framing the whole, penetrating or discovering parts in a random process of discovery and association.

Within the same family or the same office, some prefer wholes, some parts. Conflict often arises not over the content of the problem, but rather over how to start doing something about the situation. One person may prefer to begin by immediately focusing on a part of the problem; the other may need an overall view before beginning to act.

We can also create conflicts by defining which of the parts is more important before being able to begin. In this way a person with a left preference may get lost in definitions and postpone action. A right hemisphere also gets into difficulties: he has an overview and doesn't want the other to act until the other can see the situation as he sees it. "If you don't even see the problem as I do, then how can we begin to solve it? I see one part that needs immediate attention; you see other parts or you see a whole and don't want me to act until I see the situation as you do." Who is on first—the parts or the whole? Do we disagree, must we stay in endless conflict, or is it possible to appreciate the lens the other is using? Can we learn from what the other sees and develop both lenses? Meanwhile, can we appreciate and use each other's deepest development, whether it be a preference for parts or a preference for wholes?

TIME . . . TIMELESS

Some of us look at life chronologically, separating reality into parts we name past, present, and future. Others see everything as eternally present, refusing to make time distinctions. In the left hemisphere, measuring time is an aspect of sequence. We impose sequence on reality. We decide there was a yesterday, there is a today, there will be a tomorrow. While the right hemisphere perceives by glimpses and establishes its order through art or religious revelations, the left establishes order by means of time.

Even within the sequence of a day we number the hours. "At this moment it is precisely 4:20 P.M." "First this, then that." "Right now, it is six o'clock in the evening; then comes seven o'clock, and after that, eight o'clock." Within the week we need to know it is Thursday in order to meet someone, to feel secure, or to make our business contracts—"a week's work" or "three days' pay." Time is a social construct that helps us meet social conventions. It was, without doubt, invented by the left hemisphere. To a person with a left hemisphere preference, time is reality; to a person with a right hemisphere preference, eternity is reality.

Here again, preference for time or ignorance of time can tear apart an office or a family. "There is time for everything," says the wife's right hemisphere while she is putting on her makeup. Meanwhile the husband's left hemisphere knows that the show begins in ten minutes and they are going to arrive late. Some parents condemn children as stupid because they do not act "on time" or "know what time it is," when, indeed, children who live predominantly in the right hemisphere will see the parental demand for time as stupid—or, more likely, they will not even grasp the demand. Children and even some adults with a right hemisphere preference consider their daydreams intelligent because within their brain is a fullness and a richness of imagery that makes them feel intelligent. For them there is a place where the passing of time neither bothers nor intervenes in their mental processing.

We also involve ourselves in intense intellectual and religious struggles over whether to view the world through a sense of time or timelessness. Evolution versus creation—is this the left hemisphere looking at reality through the sequence of past, present, and future versus the right hemisphere seeing life as eternally present, life occurring all at once? Could it be that the existence of two such different hemispheric processes is the real cause of a mental war between science and religion? We now know that the same brain can perceive the cosmos through two different lenses. Could we make peace between religion and science by accepting both the totality of creation as proposed by the right hemisphere and the sequence of evolution as seen through the left hemisphere?

With all these characteristics as opposite as exactly two o'clock and eternity, parts or wholes, logic and randomness, line and space, sequence and simultaneity—how can we live with each other, let alone manage this dualism within ourselves? Until now the human community has existed more or less in perpetual war, with years of intermittent peace. What seems truth to one person or one culture is not truth to another. Only in rare circumstances has the individual succeeded in an integration reflecting the great potential of this neocortex.

The existence of two such different lenses through which we perceive the world helps explain our opposition to one another both individually and socially. Roger Sperry and his colleagues and predecessors in brain research now bring us to the possibility of a brain revolution in which we could expand the territory of intelligence by including and integrating the diverse characteristics of both hemispheres. It is for those of us in the fields of humanities and social change, of education and health, to accept this as the challenge of our century.

I propose that the diverse characteristics of the two hemispheres form the basis of four intelligences that we can learn and teach, just as we have learned and taught rational intelligence. The characteristics of sequence, line, logic, parts, and time are primary characteristics of rational intelligence. Simultaneity, space, associations, wholes, and timelessness are primary to three intelligences I have called associative intelligence, spatial intelligence, and intuitive intelligence.

The practice of each of these intelligences or processes will provide you with more of the connections you seek to develop within your own brain and will give you a way to begin to appreciate others who think primarily in a different way.

CHAPTER II

The Careful Process of Comprehension

RATIONAL INTELLIGENCE

Rational intelligence has been accepted not only as the very basis of Western civilization but also as synonymous with the word intelligence. *In recent years a great concern has developed over the lack of precise thinking in our culture and a potential decline in rational intelligence. Very often we fail to substantiate our thoughts with careful reasoning. I believe that this decline in rationality can be explained by our desire to be socially accepted, polite, or kind, which we often achieve by being vague, mixing images and feelings together with thoughts, or avoiding the precision of rational thinking.*

I believe that great problems confront the expansion of rational thinking in modern society. The answer is not to turn back to the past, where we valued only classical rational thinking. It is scientific rational thinking that has produced the new information about the brain available today in neuroscience. The discovery of the different mental characteristics involved in the right and left hemispheres of the neocortex can enable us to distinguish more accurately the essential characteristics of rational intelligence. As we identify and understand the traits involved in the other processes (associative, visual, and intuitive), we will be able to be more precise in our use of rational thinking.

The Process

The rational process invites us to make sequential, precise, and logical connections, in contrast to the associative process, which invites us to make more general, relational, and random connections.

Rational intelligence has different names: "rational thinking," because it persists in providing reasons; "logical thinking," because it is based on the links between cause and effect; and "critical thinking," because of its emphasis on discovering the critical difference by means of continuous questioning.

Rational intelligence is the capacity to be exact, to make detailed connections, ordering them in a sequential process in which reasons are given to substantiate every aspect of the discussion. We develop our thinking using reason, explaining step by step until we arrive at a conclusion. In rational thinking we observe the effect of any situation, analyzing the causes, each time searching more deeply and more specifically.

By linking cause to an immediate effect, rational thinkers make connections of a sequential kind until they come to closure by reaching conclusions. They verify this process by submitting the outcome to further tests of cause and effect. Carefully, sequentially, logically, they construct their thought processes until they reach understanding or comprehension. Every conclusion then becomes an invitation to open the process again by subjecting their conclusions to new doubt and questioning in a continuous and persistent search for truth. It is basic to rational thinking that any conclusion must be subject to doubt, in search of the critical difference that will provide the next logical step in order to continue the investigation. By means of questioning and doubt, rational thinking becomes a dynamic open process that leads to continuous discovery.

When something is missing, rational thinkers ask the famous questions who? what? when? where? how? and why? The answers provide them with an analysis of the situation and help them to a greater understanding of what they are facing. In this way rational thinkers understand the different aspects of the problem, which gives them the ability to begin to resolve the situation from various points of view.

Rational intelligence allows people to separate themselves from immediate action or an emotional reaction when facing a problem. They gain distance through the intellectual ritual of first analyzing all aspects of a situation. Analysis enables them to feel more at ease with the problem and satisfied that they are perceiving and taking into account the complexity of the situation.

Rational thinkers achieve satisfaction through analysis and comprehension. With analysis they put together all relevant data and make order in such a way that they reach a new understanding of the problem, a new comprehension.

In Search of the Cause

Rational thinking assumes that for every existing situation, there is one, several, or many causes. If you feel sad today, as a rational thinker you would begin to search for the cause of your unhappiness. Is it because you ate too much? Could it be because your friend did not call last night? Because you've stayed up late many nights? Because you have no exciting plans for tonight? Faced with the same situation, a person with a right-hemisphere preference would quickly answer, "Yes! All of the above!" or perhaps not even be aware of or interested in the causes. A more rational person would continue reviewing one cause after the other, in search of the principal cause.

A cause is "anything producing an effect or result,"[1] and in this way cause and effect are intertwined. If you observe the effect malaria is having on children's health, you would then proceed to study the causes of malaria. Every time we observe an effect, we begin to search for its cause. Cause and effect are logical twins, logic requiring that we explain both: "I am doing this because . . ."; "the effect of my doing this is . . ."; "this effect was caused by . . ."

A lengthy search for the more exact causes can lead us to isolate a factor that we consider will make the critical difference in resolving the problem. For example, the critical factor in malaria's spread may be whether or not mosquito-breeding waters are located near people's homes. Isolating the critical difference or critical factor is a crucial point for beginning to solve the problem.

Often in our personal lives, however, we use the rational process to analyze and criticize, and we forget the important phenomenon of action. We continue criticizing ourselves or our situation, breaking the problems into pieces, each time smaller and smaller pieces, until we fall into endless analysis.

What can you do after you have analyzed the behavior of your children, after you have taken apart your room or dismantled your clock and now you are staring at the parts? What will you do to improve your children's behavior or your own? Often we end up exhausted, throw out the clock, push the furniture back in place, or pray for our children. Sometimes we take a small step forward to help ourselves, or we return to the therapist hoping someone else can put the pieces together. It is sad that this rational process, which has given birth to great philosophies and great scientific discoveries, can also leave us, even those of us who are academically well educated, in such a mess. What are we doing wrong? Or not doing at all? What is missing?

The Full Rational Process

What is missing is the second phase: putting all the pieces back together to obtain a new result, a new solution. Scientists include the second phase in their scientific ritual of continuous exploration. They first observe the situation, breaking it down into all the parts. They minutely observe all the data, as shown in Figure 2, as the first phase. Then they develop a new solution or invention, as illustrated in the second phase.

FIRST PHASE   **SECOND PHASE**

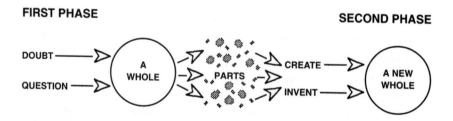

Fig. 2. The Two Phases of the Rational Thinking Process

Intellectuals and people not in the scientific field often content themselves with analysis and comprehension of the problem. To conclude is to understand. To be critical, to know what is missing, is to be aware, informed, and able to comment on what is needed. Very often, comprehension involves a lack of appreciation for action, either consciously or unconsciously. The intellectual usually believes that analysis in and of itself is enlightening, that understanding the problem is sufficient. However, to depict a situation and be able to verbalize what is missing can be a form of intellectual snobbery that leaves us talking about what is missing with little interest in developing alternative solutions or actions. We seem to be satisfied with only a part of the process. We are content with, even arrogant about, our analytic, critical capacity, using it on ourselves, our children, our government, our homes, our lives.

By contrast, a philosopher goes on to create a new theory, a new whole from the parts. A scientist goes on to invent. Businesses offer training courses in problem-solving—in how to find a solution—putting the pieces together again into a new whole, a new perspective. In everyday life, however, we often just live with the pieces. If we go on criticizing ourselves or our situations, our failures or our mistakes, we break our world into even smaller, sadder pieces. We entrap ourselves in a web of analysis that reaches no helpful conclusion.

Would the scientist have been successful or have achieved so much without that second phase of invention built into his training? The scientific process has given us many scientific and technological solutions. Compared to scientists, humanists seem helpless. Even those who develop social intervention programs consider them "less intellectual," and preference is given to investigation and analysis as representative of pure science. Research is favored over application. Do scientists know they are on a journey of discovery and intellectuals believe they are on a journey of analysis only? Solutions, inventions, and actions are as necessary to the humanist as to the scientist.

My criticism of rational thinking as practiced in the humanities is that frequently the second phase, the solution phase, is not included in academic training. From preschool we are trained in the first phase of rational intelligence, that of critical thinking. Remember the activity workbooks: What is missing in this drawing? What object does not belong to this category? Where is the mistake? We are consistently taught to observe, look at the parts, and see what is missing. For twelve to sixteen years, we write essays to analyze difficult situations, find what is missing, and conclude with sophisticated questions. I am not opposed to this half of the process: it is essential. I am opposed to having had no exposure through those sixteen years to the second half of the process: solution, invention, and construction of alternatives.

Critical thinking without construction of alternatives is destruction without creation. Critical thinking is necessary, but it is not enough. When we find the critical difference—what is missing—we need to go on to create alternatives, search out and test those alternatives in our human lives, and not tire until we reach solution or invention. If we are going to take apart, we need to put together again. If we are going to destroy what is, we need to create something new. The full rational process encompasses both stages. All the same characteristics are involved in both phases. We doubt systematically and sequentially, linking cause and effect as we break the problem into diverse aspects or smaller parts. We invent or construct a new solution by linking cause and effect and building sequentially toward a new outcome. Specificity, exactness, cause and effect, sequence, search, conclusion, doubt, and questions—all are elements continually in use in both the analytic and invention phases of the rational process.

How can the rational scientific process be used on our own behalf? Our doubts and criticisms can serve in the development of the new human being by making us aware of what we need in order to improve ourselves. At present we are skillful only at using rationality to destroy ourselves, complaining, doubting, and criticizing, leaving ourselves in a weakened condition, dependent on others. Just as we evolved from criticizing our outer physical condition to improving conditions through the scientific method, we now need this full mental processing for the development of ourselves. In your personal life, you can use rational intelligence for your development if you remember to use the entire process, creativity as well as criticism.

How can you expand rational intelligence so that you preserve its exactness without ending with criticism of yourself or others? First, continue the process instead of stopping in the middle. When you feel downhearted about having arrived at the critical point where you know what is missing, go on, as scientists do, to propose a hypothesis that can help. Continue on to the positive: identify several possibilities. If you are unhappy about your work, what alternatives are open to you? You can look for an office where you might be happier, a boss who might be more patient, or a course where you might learn to communicate more easily with your colleagues. You can return to school to learn a new career or change your career without additional education. Which seems the best alternative? Which hypothesis are you most interested in testing?

Proceed, then, to test your hypothesis, logically, precisely, step by step, until you verify it and find that it works in your real life. Great! If it does not work, start again with another hypothesis. Do not lose your excitement—search alternatives. The same who, what, how, when, where, and why you used in analysis serve you now in the search for a solution. Go on searching until you arrive at a solution that not only solves the problem but enables you to act.

To apply rational intelligence to yourself, do so very specifically. For example: "I don't know how to handle a computer. Sometimes the alarms sound; sometimes the keys don't make the right thing happen." If what is missing is training, if that is the critical factor, then, "I can call a technician and find out if he can come next Monday between 4 and 6 P.M. to teach me what I need to know." Look for what is missing, the person who can help you, and a time to be in contact with that person. Have as a final goal not only the understanding of your problem but also the solution and the action.

Doubts and criticisms when combined with solutions can be helpful in our social development as well as in our personal development. Just as we have evolved from criticizing the conditions of the environment in which we live to improving those conditions through science, we can now evolve to a more complete rational process for the development of action in our human society. What works on the outer physical environment, works on the inner physical environment, for we are all physical vibration. This mental processing, which we are all at least partially trained in, we can now convert to its fullest use on behalf of our own lives. The analysis, comprehension, and understanding achieved in the first phase of the rational process can be extended to the second phase of the process. We can guide ourselves consciously toward new solutions, inventions, and action in both our personal and social lives, as in the following example.

Martha was a successful manager of an important import-export office in Miami, her own boss, and able to travel frequently. She had an excellent salary and a sophisticated apartment. All this and she didn't feel happy. What was missing? She wanted to work more directly with people and less with office papers. Able to isolate this as a critical factor, she never lost sight of the many advantages that her work offered her, but rather went on to invent various possibilities for herself. What if she trained in psychology or therapy or went back to medical school? From many alternatives she chose to try out the possibility that being a massage therapist might make her happy. After a year of study she was convinced that she had the basis of a new career and could risk the action of leaving her job and her apartment. She spent two years learning and enjoying herself. Not only is she now a practicing massage therapist, but she also has found a second husband and is living in a beautiful new house. Hers is a wonderful story of carrying rational thinking from the analytical phase into the careful planning of an action.

Warning: Rational Thinking and Relationships

Is the logical, rational, sequential, questioning process an adequate mental process in all human situations? At present we try to use rational thinking for everything, everyone, and every situation. It is our ultimate answer, our sacred cow. Rationalism is an absolute we have decided to treat as sacred because it has been useful to us. It lets us know the parts of a whole, the specifics. It allows us to doubt, criticize, and question any whole to determine what is missing. However, we must ask whether or not rational thinking is an appropriate mental process to be used in interpersonal affairs. The human condition may require a different intelligence if we are to relate adequately to one another. If reality is energy appearing in multiple diverse forms, can one form of thought be adequate to serve us with diverse forms and in multiple realities? If reality is multifaceted, no single mental process can serve us absolutely, in all situations.

Each of us is billions of cells, capable of quadrillions of connections, and yet we look at each other and make judgments, always trying to identify the parts, pin down the cause and effect, come to conclusions about, and end up in criticism, doubt, and questioning. Yes, a rational thinker must conclude by doubting and questioning. Indeed, that is exactly what enables rational thinking to be a dynamic, open process.

However, try to understand that we have been taught to question and doubt since we were five years old, finding what was missing on those pages of our kindergarten workbooks. Understand that we practiced that criticism for at least twelve years and most probably sixteen years. Now realize that this training is like a filter we look through, essential for politics, science, and discovery but damaging for viewing human beings. When we meet a person or when we relate to human beings anywhere—in our family, office, stores, or on the streets—we look through that same highly-trained lens. We first discover important parts or characteristics, and then we come to a conclusion. Even if it is a favorable conclusion, even if we like the person, we will have an automatic predisposition to criticize and doubt. "Well, he couldn't really be that terrific." "Well, she is good in that, but I wonder if she knows how to do . . ." "He certainly did a great job, but don't you think he could also have considered . . ." This may well be the cause of much human suffering: our inability to believe in ourselves or others. Are we taking ourselves and one another apart as coldly and specifically as we would take apart an engine or a political concept?

If we end up questioning ourselves, will we end up in a million pieces, with no essential mental process able to relate those millions of pieces? Is our human condition a Humpty-Dumpty one of our own rational making with no mental process adequate to put Humpty-Dumpty together again? When applied to human beings, is our logic contributing to our deaths by entropy, a wearing-away process caused by the practice of doubt, eroding our self-esteem until we give up and prefer numbness or an impersonal world? Without knowing how to live well with persons, it may seem to us preferable to ignore them and control our lives through objects or problems.

Such was the case with Jim. He was comfortable with money but not with people and even less comfortable when harm hit the people in his own family. I watched him overcome financial disaster with careful and persistent logic. When the economy hit him hard, he was able to step back, analyze the causes, select the main issues, and develop a comprehensive picture of his situation. Even more important, he didn't give up. He was able to engage systematically in bold action and lead himself through the crisis to success. He knew how to relate to finances.

However, when adversity affected his own family, although Jim could apply his analytic capacities to the situation, he was unable to take personal action. He could deal with financial difficulties but not with his daughter being pregnant without being married. He stayed stuck in the analysis phase of rational thinking, unable to continue into the action phase because it dealt with action changes in his own behavior as well as that of his daughter and family. He became angry with his daughter, his wife, and sought rational explanations. He doubted everyone except himself. He was unable to accept that there was something missing in his family and to take action, such as seeing a family therapist. Instead, he took refuge in the pattern of family pride—it couldn't happen to me. Two months of inactivity robbed him and his family of tremendous energy as well as delayed effective emotional help for his daughter. Two years of family evasion passed before the daughter really got her father's attention by a severe car crash, which damaged public property and involved her with authorities. Public involvement broke down the walls of family pride, and Jim eventually was able to relate to his daughter and her new baby.

The rational process that served Jim so well when he was dealing with money failed him when he was dealing with his daughter. Although the story illustrates his inability to move into the action phase of rational thinking, it may just as well illustrate his inability to shift to any other mental process. I believe there is a difficulty in our persistent use of one mental process. The Western world fell in love with the rational process because it worked so well with the outer, physical environment. Is it safe, is it appropriate to rely solely on this process in the development of our inner human environment? There are other processes, other useful ways of making connections in the neocortex, as we shall see in the next chapter.

EXERCISE
FROM PLANS TO ACTION

The specificity, exactness, and questioning of rational thinking can help you carry out your plans. What is most important? When and where will you start? Who will help you, and how? If you are a person with a right-hemisphere preference, you may leave your projects up in the air, imagining that they are already happening. If you prefer the left hemisphere, you may be content to understand your plans but reluctant to carry them into action. Try to practice the following:

> *1. Relax and get in touch with a plan or a wish. Of the many that come to mind, choose one.*

2. *How do you feel about this project? Do you really want it to happen? Does it motivate you? If you really want it, go on.*

3. *Change from a relaxed to a more active posture. Search your mind for who or what can be of help. Look for the answers to the following questions:*

    —Who and what can help you?

    —When do you want to start?

    —Where, in what place, are you going to try this project?

    —How will you carry out this project?

    —What are the necessary stages in order to carry this project into action?

4. *From all you have discovered, decide: What is the next step? What will you do tomorrow? Next week? Be very specific.*

EXERCISE

PERSONAL MATHEMATICS, OR CONTINUOUS SELF-ESTEEM

We learned math in such an impersonal way that the title of this exercise may seem strange. Math was treated as something so objective that it seems almost profane to use it for ourselves. Nevertheless, many have found the following exercise helpful. It is especially useful when you need to make yourself happy.

1. *ADD the positive. Add what makes you a happy, intelligent, beautiful, gentle, or powerful person. Add your particular ways of being successful or human. Be precise and make a list, as if you were your own lawyer.*

2. *SUBTRACT the negatives. Make a list of all the things you do not know, have not been able to do, do not want to do, or do not do very well. Save this list, and take it to the next step.*

3. *DIVIDE the negatives you want to improve. You can try to deal with some points in three months, others the next semester, others never. You may also divide the negatives by delegating, sharing, or negotiating with others more capable or knowledgeable than you. Just as you divide time to reduce stress, so too can you divide your weights and burdens with others more capable than you.*

4. *MULTIPLY compliments. Make a list of at least seven compliments*

you have received. Be precise. Read them in a loud voice, listening carefully, without doubting or criticizing the judgment of the person who made each comment. Visualize them, repeat them by heart, really let them into your feelings, and, if you wish, act on them.

Take this exercise seriously and practice it. Personal mathematics can help lighten your moods and increase your self-esteem.

CHAPTER III

Giving Meaning to Your World

ASSOCIATIVE INTELLIGENCE

A*ssociative intelligence is neither the opposite of rational intelligence, nor a substitute for rational thinking. They are twin thinking processes. Rational intelligence makes connections of a sequential kind, whereas associative intelligence makes connections without regard to sequence. In certain cases, rational is appropriate; in others, associative. Both are essential to the thinking mind. A person may need to be extremely rational in order to follow computer instructions and commands, deal with money, or face personal affairs requiring exactness and conclusions. The same person may need to be extremely associative when meeting a new person, which requires catching a glimpse of something admired and expressing it in order to begin to relate.*

When using associative thinking, we make associations or links to people, places, ideas, objects, colors, concepts. Free to glimpse and unrestrained by cause and effect, we have no need to estimate, judge, or reach a conclusion. We are free to begin a voyage of discovery.

Edward de Bono broke through the barriers of rational thought with his revolutionary book *Lateral Thinking*.[1] He described rational, logical thought as vertical thinking, an appropriate image for the sequential processes involved. De Bono gave the term "lateral thinking" to the process of association, invention, and creativity. Lateral thinking became the basis for programs in creativity and mind expansion taught in business and educational programs throughout the world. The most popular process to emerge was that of brainstorming: the gathering of all ideas without interruption for criticism, opposition, or explanation. When people brainstorm, they do not discuss or consider the cause of their ideas or any possible effects. They simply give their views or thoughts without explanations. Listeners do not argue with ideas; instead, they just go on to offer more ideas. Recent split-brain research supports de Bono's presentation of lateral thinking, just as the associative, spatial, and intuitive intelligences proposed in this book complement his work.

Random Connections and Direct Perception

While logical thinking proceeds directly step by step toward a goal, associative thinking takes a leap into the unknown, with a hope for discovery but no fixed procedure in mind. As one friend, Mary Marcellus, put it, associative thinking is "a wafting" of total unconcern. Without boundaries or definitions, it is difficult to convey or give assurances of the usefulness of this process. Can you pin down the wings of a butterfly? No, but you can see the contours of its flight. You can free-fall until you discover your mind leaping from connection to connection, from an idea to a shape to a color. You may label these incomplete thoughts—or are they glimpses you do not choose to complete for fear of losing the dynamic, the originality of your perspective?

Creativity and discovery depend on the freedom to make connections, calling on them to assist us in whatever we are creating. In associative thinking, we make meaning by linking glimpses, by juxtaposing them, until in their richness, nuances, and subtlety they take on new meaning. These are the tools of every artist, every poet—juxtaposition, subtlety, nuance, freedom—as can be seen in the paintings of a Chagall or Picasso, in poems, or in other forms we recognize as art. Now we can recognize these characteristics as basic to associative intelligence available to anyone, not only the artist.

Direct perception, another element of associational intelligence, is the ability to prevent any concept, name, or image from being linked to whatever reality is before us. Its express purpose is to thwart ordinary perception. It gives us the freedom to eliminate any preestablished label. To what benefit? With no labels, we are able to look at things and perceive directly, noticing or associating with any aspect of their reality. Our creativity and desire are in charge, not the label, not previous assumptions. We are free to associate continually with aspects of reality in relation to our perception, desire, and creativity.

For example, an 🍎 is an 🍎 before it becomes an a-p-p-l-e. We directly perceive "one" of something before we can substitute the mathematical symbol "1." Every word or number is a symbol indicating something that in itself has its own existence. The experience of symbols replaces the experience of direct perception. Rational intelligence deals mainly with verbal and mathematical symbols, which are always secondary to direct experience. Associative intelligence enables us either to relate symbols or to associate directly with the object or person.

Direct perception opens the door to all the processes of the right hemisphere because to perceive directly means to be free of labels, conclusions, and concepts, which come from the analytic processes of the left hemisphere. In the words of psychologist Jean Houston, "Concept louses up percept."[2] When we are not tied to concept, we are free to engage in direct perception. We can disidentify the form from its label and allow ourselves the richness of associating with the form from different perspectives.

In associative intelligence nothing is irrelevant; nothing depends on sequence or order, form or concept. We are not tied by causes or effects. We do not engage in comparisons or opposites, in dualism, or in critical thinking. We see the complexity of that which exists, before relating to the accepted symbol. Depending on the dynamics of our connection, we decide where to focus.

Dynamics, multiple connections, direct perception, and discovery are the hallmarks of this intelligence. Just as the ability to ask who, what, where, when, why and how? is essential to rational intelligence, there are three abilities essential to associative intelligence:

1. the ability to block out concepts, labels, and conclusions in order to be able to enter into direct perception

2. the ability to process freely, making connections without reference to cause, effect, or preestablished order; the ability to search among thoughts and images in a continuous mental freedom

3. the ability to link and juxtapose associations, to connect, associate, and relate in different ways and by different means in order to arrange the forms into various compositions

The importance of associative intelligence is that in relation to the realities we perceive, we can make as many associations as we wish, as many discoveries.

Making Meaning in All That Surrounds You

In a process of direct perception, our environment continues to open itself before us. We focus or associate with what we consider most significant. We give or do not give meaning to whatever surrounds us. We can give meaning to objects or to people, animals, plants, trees, shapes, colors—anything, alive or not. It is up to us to use this process of association to create a friendly environment around us.

It is not that we are born into a hostile environment; rather, we are born into an impersonal environment in which meaning is assigned to everything by our culture, by other people who were there before us or who are now living with us as our family. Their assigning of meanings and labels to things was without doubt useful for them. We now must discover the significance for our lives or find new meaning that is friendly or beneficial to us personally. We need to convert our inheritance of an impersonal environment into a personal context that vibrates with meaning and interest for us. It is by means of an associative process that we can go about gradually making meaning in all the different areas of our life.

Nature. You can assign meaning to all of the natural world—and indeed probably must do so if we are to develop a friendly and participatory relationship with nature. Even though the tree in your garden belongs to the classification called trees, for you it may be the enormous giant who gives shade to your house and reminds you that "You are almost home!" It can accompany you all your life.

Conversations. If in conversations at home or in committee meetings in the office you tend to become bored, you may be waiting for the conclusion of what others are saying, instead of associating what they say with your own life. The associative process gives you freedom to get close to what interests you and search for the meaning it has in your life. Then, if you wish, make connections with all the things that surround you, so they can become active resources for your life.

Religion. You can also use associative intelligence to make meaning in your religion. Your church or your temple is not made only of stone, but of all the events that you have lived there and value sufficiently to remember. The statue of the Virgin Mary is not made only of painted blue-and-white plaster. The image stands before you to inspire you with your associations of femininity and kindness. As you associate with her kindness or other characteristics, she becomes closer to you and meaning deepens within you. Thus a statue of stone can be converted into a guide for your life by means of your active associative intelligence. It is your brain, your focus on associations, that converts it into something significant for you.

The Office. The computer in your office can be a cold grey box in front of which you are obliged to sit. Or, you can convert it, by means of association, into a magician who shows up at the touch of your fingers. Suddenly there appears before you the very language that, only seconds before, was hidden deeply within your brain. It was hardly visible even to yourself, not to mention the public that will see it as soon as the magician allows it to pass through the hands of his favorite assistant, the printer.

The Body. There is no end to this process of association, of converting the apparently impersonal into something new and rich with meaning for your personal life. Consider your body, that personal context wherein lives your power of concentration. You can give new meaning to the parts of your body even though they have already been defined and classified. Your right hand, for example, may be a hand of flesh and bone, or it may take on larger significance if you associate it with acting in the conscious world. Your feet can be feet, or they can be standing up in the world. Michaeleen Kimmey, therapist and healer from Connecticut, whose book on the body map is in process, has drawn associations for each part of the body. You can make your own body map, relating parts of your body either to physical functions or to how they interact with the world.

You need to understand only that these associations are your own language, language your brain has decided to use in relation to your body. This is nothing mysterious. It is your brain instead of someone else's that is doing the labeling, which may permit you to be more alert to the signals of pain or emotion. This process of association and interpretation does not exclude the conventional process of labeling and interpretation by a medical doctor. It is rather an additional process that can alert you to the language of your body before you need help. By making associations with your body, you encourage and enrich your body-mind relationship.

The Planet. It is this same process of active association that inspires us to reach for the moon and the stars in search of guidance in our daily lives. Light particles and the big white sphere that illuminates the earth at night have for centuries illuminated the minds of men and women. Throughout history in every culture the sun and the moon, heaven and earth, the finite and the infinite have inspired human associations recorded in diverse forms of art and religion. Now the image of a blue-green planet suspended in space calls us to new associations as well as to a gathering together of associations from diverse cultures.

There are many forms of history: the history of countries, of cultures, of wars, of art and science. Archetypes are history recorded through persons rather than events. Connecting with archetypes through associative intelligence will allow us to reach beyond our particular culture in order to gain a greater appreciation for life on this planet. Archetypes are human history, history recorded through human form and therefore available to us as a human resource. They are the enduring patterns of associations recorded over time and now available for our guidance. Archetypes are configurations of energy drawn from the experience of great cultures that have captured the essence of energy lived throughout human history. In the works of Joseph Campbell and Jean Houston, leading philosophers and psychologists of history and mythology, we find recorded the major archetypes or wisdom figures of Eastern and Western cultures, of Greece, Egypt, India, China, Indonesia, and indigenous populations. It depends on us to select among archetypes for our information and enrichment. With whom do we identify? Are we going to learn from Isis of Egypt, from Persephone of Greece, or from the American Indian trickster Coyote? We can allow ourselves to associate and be enriched by such diverse feminine archetypes as Demeter, Gaia, and White Buffalo Woman, by the masculine energies of Zeus and Job, Merlin and Parsifal, or by the compassionate love of Kwan Yin and Buddha, the seductive love of Aphrodite and Krishna, or the intense human love of Jesus.

As historic representatives of the energy of our planet, archetypes can serve as guides to illuminate our way into the future and help us to avoid mistakes already made throughout the long course of human history. Eventually we will have a history of archetypes from all cultures. The great stories and wisdom figures of the world will then be available for our association without reference to our place of birth. They will not replace the richness of our own heritage; they will offer us the additional possibility of associating with the thinner vibrations of all history. Both local history and planetary history will then be available to enrich our perspective.

Science. Can associative intelligence be useful for science? Why would anyone put aside concepts, conclusions, and definitions in favor of direct perceptions? Why dismember a reality that has been agreed upon and constructed over centuries? The answer: in order to penetrate again, to enter into newness, for the purpose of insight and discovery. Invention comes from a new hypothesis, a new way of seeing. The French mathematician, Jules Henri Poincaré provides an excellent example:

> For fifteen days I strove to prove that there could not be any functions like those I have since called Fuchsian functions. I was then very ignorant; every day I seated myself at my work table, stayed an hour or two, tried a great number of combinations and reached no results. One evening, *contrary to my custom*, I drank black coffee and could not sleep. *Ideas rose in crowds; I felt them collide until pairs interlocked*, so to speak, making a stable combination. By the next morning I had established the existence of a class of Fuchsian functions. . . . I had only to write out the results, which took but a few hours. [italics mine][3]

By sitting in his working chair every day, Poincaré was in his old routine or customary way of seeing. By changing his habit, he entered a new way of seeing in which "ideas rose in crowds," and he "felt them collide"—an excellent description of associative intelligence.

The scientist most often arrives at a hypothesis by means of exploring multiple connections by connections or quantum leaps rather than carefully constructed sequences. The hypothesis is a guess until it is veri-fied later. The scientist must look into the unknown, catch glimpses—arrange and juxtapose these glimpses, just as the artist does. The journey toward hypothesis is free association. Of course scientists report only those hypotheses they are able to verify. We rarely hear about the scientific theories that did not work out. Associative thinking is common ground for both the scientist and the artist. Indeed it is useful in all creative think-ing, without regard to profession.

Education. I deplore that associative intelligence is not taught in schools and in universities. I am reminded of a young student who came to me after he had been asked not to return to his college the second year. The student, Robert, was neither an artist nor a poet. In fact, he wished to become an engineer. Although an engineer needs the capacity to visu-alize three-dimensionally, the college required heavy course work in math-ematics and strong performance in rational thinking. Robert had been known to stutter, to have more to say than he could get out of his mouth sequentially. Probing further, I discovered Robert had other right hemi-sphere characteristics: the capacity for large glimpses, a sense of timeless-ness, a love of religion, a desire to see the whole before he was willing to study the parts. I set up a series of right-hemisphere study techniques, quite different from those taught to Robert or any other student in schools and colleges. After writing to request permission to return to college "on trial," he made the Dean's list at the end of that year. I believe that many such "failures" in schools and colleges could be reversed if a clear under-standing of this intelligence existed in students' and teachers' minds.

What are these right-hemisphere study skills?
1. Look at or "read" any pictures before beginning to read words.
2. Read and learn any material in boxes or knockout quotes.
3. Make your own connections between the illustrations and text.
4. Start at the end, not at the beginning. Learn the summary by visu-alizing the summary on the screen of your mind. Then make it become active and alive by relating it to your own experience so you will remember it later.
5. After reading the text of a page or column, visualize it before go-ing on. Discover how to link it with something you already know.
6. Make connections between yourself and what you see or hear in

class. Remember, instructions can only be said sequentially; it is up to you to visualize what is being told. It also helps to check afterward if you understood what was said.

7. Feel comfortable with free associating and make use of it. For example, begin your action of studying wherever it pleases you, and skip around inside the text, rather than trying to proceed sequentially.

8. Participate in class by taking the initiative before being called on. In that way you have time to prepare your answer by making the connections in your mind, rather than being obliged to respond without the benefit of time to reflect.

These suggestions are offered in explanation of Robert's success. They are not a complete list of study skills for those with right-hemisphere tendencies. What is needed is a full course in right-hemisphere study techniques in all schools and colleges so that students may be freer to guide their minds in the form in which they work best. We can also learn that it is not a question of either-or, but rather the possibility of counting on twin mental processes, rational and associative intelligence, equal partners in the thinking-learning process.

This is crucial for those children labeled "learning disabled." My experience with students ages six to twelve indicates that many enter first grade with strong capacities in the right hemisphere and weak capacities in sequential thinking. They have difficulty with sorting into categories and with many other processes required for learning to read and do math. On the other hand, as is evident in their art and actions, their minds are full of rich images, perhaps too rich to be put in sequential order. Are they disabled? Or are they merely strong in the capacities of the right hemisphere, which are not included in either the curriculum or the teaching in grade school? I believe that we have created the illness of dyslexia and learning disabilities by the narrowness of the curriculum and the exclusion of the capacities of the right hemisphere from the early school years. Is the student incapable, or is it the school which is incapable of keeping up with recent brain research?

At the experimental Mead School for Human Development, which I founded with the help of many others in Greenwich, Connecticut, students were offered art, music, and other subjects of their choice in the first through sixth grades. Although they were reminded of their musts in reading and math, they were allowed to spend more time in sports and the arts if they so chose. By the end of the fifth grade, all students were at or three years above their grade level. On the basis of this experience I think we can eliminate the label "learning disabled" by offering students the opportunity to choose the subjects that favor the right hemisphere, while at the same time keeping before them the need to complete tasks in the left. By constraining them to go directly to the left hemisphere when it is their weaker side, we are creating the learning disability. During the early years, we should reinforce the strongest mental tendency in all students, offering them study for both right- and left-hemisphere processes.

Can you imagine what our education and society might be like if the development of the right hemisphere were equally required in our schools? Imagine if it were as important to write poetry as to write paragraphs, as essential to observe and experiment with live things of nature as to be able to read a science text, as important to do art as to do math, as important to do spatial work in early geometry as to do computations, as important to make photographs or drawings as to read books, as necessary to make associations of a nonsequential kind as it is to make connections of a sequential kind! How much have we as a culture lost by not emphasizing the development of both hemispheres?

Human Relationships. Finally, associative intelligence is the form of intelligence I believe we need if we are to relate better with each other as human beings, if we are ever truly to achieve a human society rather than just a society composed of humans. Our rational thinking with its emphasis on conclusion and its requirement of continuous doubt and questioning is inhibiting the development of a human society.

When someone meets you and tries to understand you by adding up this or that, or, worse yet, by concluding that he or she knows you, how do you feel? Don't you feel deep within you that you are more complex than any summary that can be made of you? Only you can know your own complexity! As we try to share our conclusions about each other, miscommunication becomes inevitable. Who can add up, subtract, analyze the parts of a field of such constant motion as the human being, an energy field of billions of cells? With rational thinking we have learned to identify parts of the human being; we have learned to summarize these parts and then proceed to criticize and doubt. "Is it really true that she is like that?" "Although she knows this, she probably wouldn't be able to do that."

With rational thinking, we have a tendency to believe, every time we meet someone, that the experience is complete. "Yes, I met a person who is like that and she is . . . or she does . . . or I think she could or should. . . ." We think we know the person, when what we really know are only the most obvious characteristics. Moreover, our rational mental training predisposes us to criticize, doubt, and conclude. The conclusion is judgment and a mental trap that severely limits our voyage of discovery of the other human being.

Consider the alternative: the use of associative intelligence with human beings. Where do you begin? As you look at another human being, you register a vast area of motion, an endless possibility of discovery, billions of cells. Some energy is evident, some hidden, available only for glimpsing. You ask yourself what you can find that pleases you. What do you like? What can you intuit? To what can you relate? What is it that affects you, moves you, interests you, or sparks your curiosity? You look at the other person searching for what intrigues you. You cannot know the other, measure the other, or really understand the other, but you can catch a glimpse of that person. What is there? What is happening? Your eyes, your ears, your feelings, your brains are all awake on this voyage of discovery, and it begins with a connection, with a single link. You begin with something that pleases you, with a pretty blouse, dark eyes, an idea expressed, something done, the other person's kindness or sensitivity. The process continues as you express what is going on in you and then give the other person time to respond. The two of you go back and forth in relay, relating first one, then the other, continuing to connect.

When you conclude or close your mind to what is happening, you lose this process of connecting. You can continue a relationship when you find new aspects that interest you or that you appreciate in the other. You have only to express them and wait for a response in order to continue exploring the relationship.

The point is not what kind of a person someone is, but what your relationship together will be. Nor is the point whether or not the other person is boring or interesting, but how you are together. How is the energy or communication that emerges between you? Will your communication be a communion, will it be agreeable or blocked, full or only minimum, of high quality or filled with interference? You begin the contact with a process of association, and you continue your communication looking for associations, ways to relate to one another.

You and I want to be directly perceived, freshly perceived. We do not wish to be categorized, compared, summarized. What we would love is for the other person to link with some aspect that they like, enjoy, are interested in or curious about. We like precise connections as we explore one another together.

What excites me and what I am trying to encourage is the connecting of life. What I am proposing with associative intelligence is that communication become exploration and discovery. What I wish is to reach out and associate with any aspect of another human being that interests me. What excites me is that entering into associative thinking, I have at my disposal a process to explore, discover, find some aspect that I can appreciate in every human being. When I am with another human being, I am looking for something I can enjoy. Contact with every human being then becomes exploration and discovery. To associate—notice the "social" in the word itself—is a mental process necessary to increase our human connections within society. With this tool I can appreciate something about every person, about everything. I would no longer live on this earth without it. With it, I feel safe and capable of meeting anyone or going anywhere.

In terms of personal power, nothing has been more calming, more assuring, more rewarding in my life than to know I am on a voyage of discovery—not just of mountains or of seas, but also of people. Everyone is a trip! When my rational mind goes for the jugular vein, when I see what I consider or judge to be missing in the other person, I do not have to conclude, separate, and destroy. I only have to shift away from my rational, critical thinking into an associative process, search for what I like, what I appreciate. One glimpse will do. I focus in, elaborate, express and begin a connection, a process of association that is agreeable. This came out most succinctly in a workshop in Venezuela when someone suddenly gasped, "You mean I don't have to buy the whole package." I can love the glimpses that I really like about the other and leave the rest. The first steps toward love are taken with associative intelligence.

As must be evident, I feel urgent about the need to train ourselves in associative thinking. When we attend only to rational thinking, associative thinking becomes the gift of the gifted, the privilege of the artist, instead of being available to us all. We might grant freedom to all minds by legitimizing this free process of association. We need to legitimize it and practice it during our formative years, as early as we practice our sequential sentence structures and sequential computations.

Associative thinking is associating, linking, relating, connecting with whatever or whomever I wish. Exquisite freedom is the primary characteristic of this thinking process, just as tightness and order are major characteristics of rational thinking. Its greatest application, I believe, is its practical use in human relationships. Associative intelligence can free us to make an incredibly larger number of synaptic connections, bringing to life other unused areas of our neocortical network. These new connections increase our intelligence and provide our first step toward accessing the unused ninety percent of our brain power.

Nowhere was this more apparent than in the case of Tom, a child who started in the Mead School kindergarten and did not learn to read well until the fourth grade. In his early years, he excelled in art, where he made complicated paintings and compositions in which he continually juxtaposed shapes and colors and created new forms by inventive associations. He also loved the environment center, where he involved himself in explorations and experiments. He loved to associate with anything new. When working spatially in either art or science, he had both patience and creativity. When it came to reading, there was a desire, because others were reading, but no tolerance. Although he was reminded that reading was a necessity, he also felt protected by his outstanding performance in art and science. Indeed, he managed to be sick when the yearly tests were given in the first three years.

The story, however, has a happy ending. Tom managed to be on grade level when he finally took the tests in the fourth grade. Later, at the ninth-grade level, in national testing conducted by a professional testing service, he scored in the ninety-seventh percentile in the nation in reading comprehension. I believe that Tom's tremendous success was due to his early development of associative intelligence. He associated everything spatially, which must have vastly increased the number of synaptic connections. Moreover, because of his success in art and science, he never considered himself stupid. With his high self-esteem, he eventually became interested in reading, and I believe that by then his highly developed associative intelligence enabled him easily to associate words with pictures and then words in sentences and paragraphs.

The key to Tom's success was maintaining his high self-esteem in his early years by means of associative intelligence, which gave him genuine success by the mental exercise of his right hemisphere. I only wish the story could be repeated in all the first through third grades in the nation. There is no reason to abuse children by insisting that they demonstrate the sequential intelligence of the left hemisphere instead of the associative spatial intelligence of the right. By teaching to their strengths, we encourage them to develop mental ability; by insisting on their weaknesses, we teach them weakness. They develop a fear of reading and math and a low self-esteem, which prevents them from trying.

I met Louise when she was forty, the manager of an office with approximately eighteen people whom she directed and tried to relate to each day. She was confused by their accusations that she was too powerful and too manipulative. She saw herself as intelligent, interested in the welfare of her staff, and reasonably diplomatic in making suggestions. Once I got to know her I found that she learned to be rationally intelligent as a means of surviving in her childhood. Her mother had died at an early age, her father was missing from birth and her brothers living with relatives. It was not surprising that she was trying to control her environment and those in it with her rational abilities. She was a problem solver and a manager. The possibility of making friendly associations, of using associative intelligence, was not part of her education.

When Louise began to give as much importance to associations as she gave to reason, she began to see the people in her office differently. She consciously wrote out what she appreciated about each one. She began to be more comfortable with the people around her, she saw meaning in each one, and the atmosphere changed. She herself changed from being a timid person with a tough exterior to a person who now relates with confidence.

EXERCISE

TO MAKE MEANING

Practice this exercise at any dinner gathering or office meeting. It is especially important to practice it whenever you feel yourself losing interest or in situations where you feel bored.

1. *Open your belief system to the idea that everything is interconnected, and, more precisely, to the possibility that everyone can be an active resource for you and relevant to the well-being of your life.*
2. *Restrain the tendency of listening in order to compare, conclude, criticize, doubt, or question.*
3. *When others speak, try to associate with what they are saying. Let pass by what is not of interest to you in order to select and focus on the connections you have with what is being said.*
4. *Integrate what you have selected, giving it meaning for your life. Feel free to give it your own meaning.*

What you are essentially doing is becoming aware that you can give meaning to whatever others say, as well as to their presence in your life.

EXERCISE

APPRECIATIVE THINKING

Practice this exercise with all your human relationships.

1. *Clarify your belief system in relation to the complexity of human beings. Find a way to understand that human beings are always more than their visible form, whether or not you refer to the human being as an energy system radiating different vibrations or as a human composed of innumerable cells. Find your own way of interesting yourself in all you can discover in the other.*
2. *Look at and listen actively to the other person. Search for something you hear or see that you like in him or her.*

3. When you find something you like, enjoy it within yourself and express it to the other.

Remembering what you appreciate, you can improve your mood at any moment of the day.

Synthesizing the Connections

SPATIAL INTELLIGENCE

Immensity is within ourselves. It is attached to a sort of expansion of being that life curbs and caution arrests, but which starts again when we are alone.

Gaston Bachelard, *The Poetics of Space*

Spatial intelligence implies the existence of deeper brain waves. It is as if rational and associative intelligence were on some first plane of perception, and spatial intelligence on a second, more interior level. The neocortex is a dense spatial area in which mental connections are made and extended.[1] Input comes into the neocortex from all sources: from what we know as the senses as well as from the deeper limbic system of feelings and the basic brain of action. These connections are woven more deeply into the form of words, numbers, images, sounds, colors, shapes, insights, feelings, and actions.

To date we have distinguished the various connections involved in spatial intelligence according to the sensory input. Some connections appear to the artist as visual or to the musician as auditory. There are also tactile connections, formed by touch; olfactory, formed by smells; and the sensations of taste that occur when placing a complex new treat on the tongue. The tongue receives various input, but only when the input arrives in our neocortex are we able to communicate, which we may do by word, by a deep sound of pleasure, by some visual image that seems to compare with the experience, or by reaching to take another piece of apple pie.

Some people receive primarily sounds, verbal or musical, others visual images, others fragrances. Some receive a mixture from all the senses. Synesthesia is the phenomenon of perceiving a mixture of sensory input, often described by highly creative individuals.[2] Some perceive the colors of sounds, some the colors of words, some images with colors, some feelings with sounds, and others hear words associated with images. Is such synesthesia an innate ability, or is it that creative people work harder to create, and in so doing stimulate more of their senses, which flood the axons and dendrites and produce new connections? Is it that such people are able to synthesize the input from the diverse channels of eye, ear, nose, mouth, and skin? Have they developed both sides of their brain as well as larger areas of the right hemisphere? Or is synesthesia a more developed version of spatial intelligence?

We have described the neocortex as a vast area of axons that send energy and dendrites that receive. Although scientists have associated functions with certain areas, there are also vast areas that remain unassociated. If our billions of cells are capable of quadrillions of connections, then this is the space that we must attend to. Here in the neocortex there is an infinity of space within us.

My own experience suggests that this infinity seems to relate to both outer as well as inner space—sometimes my eyes, ears, or other senses are open and directed outward in exploration of the world; other times my eyes and senses are closed and directed inward in order to give me deeper concentration and exploration within me. External space is what we receive through the senses. Internal space is within the brain.

When I look for and see, with my eyes open, I am using my visual intelligence on an outer level, and the result may be an artistic rendering of what I see or an action that is based on or at least takes into account what I am seeing. Some people process visual data rapidly and are able to take in various aspects of a complex situation merely by studying it visually. We might say they are able to size up the situation easily or take everything into consideration. Visual intelligence, however, also exists on an inner plane. For some, rich visual imagery is a thinking process. They arrive at conclusions by processing a series of internal images. An inner visual thinker may then need to communicate results to others by drawings or by translating images into words using metaphor or a varied verbal description.

Both outer and inner space also exist in the auditory sense. On the outer plane, some of us are very alert listeners, connecting and interpreting a variety of sounds. An alert listener not only hears the sound but connects it with meaning. An alert as well as active listener is able to listen over a long period of time, take in words and tones of voice, and arrive at a sophisticated or comprehensive meaning. In contrast, impatient listeners hear a few sentences and react before they have had time to find either the message or the meaning. Active listening—waiting until we hear the message a person is trying to send—forms a part of most communication courses. Good listening is not only about patience; it is about auditory intelligence—connecting inner meaning to a sound received from the outer environment. Musicians have an ability with sound that reflects both an outer and inner dimension. They hear sounds and music and are able to integrate them at an interior level. They also hear musical themes, variations, sounds, and tones, as well as their combinations, on a purely inner level without reference to exterior sounds. They translate those inner sounds into musical notation and later play the music back to themselves or hear it played back by others.

Those who hear sounds internally have an auditory intelligence that is deeper than the average listening capacity. I personally do not hear musical themes. However, when I am concentrating deeply on a subject or am in search of answers, I hear suggestions that seem to be coming from a deeper level within me. We talk about "listening to our inner voice," which seems to be possible when we seek to do so. We also have the experience of clairaudients or channeling, in which people hear voices of those they claim lived long ago. Regardless of our ability to verify the claim, it is obvious that the people doing the "channeling" go into deep relaxation, listening to and transmitting voices they are "hearing."

In these examples we have three levels of spatial-auditory intelligence, the first related to outer space and the second and third to inner space, but with different degrees of relaxation or depth. The first level, alert and active listening, depends on focus as well as a capacity for linking diverse sounds with meaning. The other two levels depend on relaxation and listening concentration. Many of us have a predisposition for either auditory or visual intelligence. That is, we prefer to see or prefer to listen in order to learn. In elementary education the debate still rages over whether children learn to read faster by sight or by phonics.

Like artists and musicians, athletes have high levels of spatial or tactile intelligence. To what extent the tactile sensations are integrated and further developed at an interior level, I am not certain. I do know, however, that children with a right-hemisphere preference rapidly develop athletic abilities in individual sports such as swimming, skateboarding, skating, and skiing. I attribute this to their ability to feel comfortable in their bodies in relation to the space around them. They are free to guide themselves spatially rather than respond to rules or other players, as required in team sports. Some synthesizing of connections must therefore be taking place at an inner level, but which we are able to recognize only by applauding their kinesthetic ability. They communicate this inner level by the movement of their bodies, which many consider a form of art, although not expressed through sound or sight.

Some of us just enjoy smells, taking in the aroma of flowers or smells from the kitchen or the perfume of a loved one. How deeply do we let smells affect us? Aromatherapy affirms that we can heal ourselves by integrating at a deeper level the essences of flowers. We know that the olfactory bulbs form part of our emotional brain system, so it is quite certain that fragrances will affect our emotional state. Those who integrate these connections in a more comprehensive way within themselves may also indeed produce some form of healing.

Whether the source is the senses or input from the other brain structures into the neocortex, what is occurring in these examples is more than connection. In rational thought we use the term *comprehension* to communicate that a deeper level of thinking has taken place—a more inclusive, amplified, sophisticated kind of knowing. The experiences of athletes, musicians, and artists indicate that we need a word similar to comprehension that takes into account the deeper processing of the right hemisphere as well as input from the other brain systems. The most appropriate term for the phenomenon that integrates or synthesizes input from the senses or the other brain systems in a way that goes beyond rational or associative thinking is *spatial intelligence.*

Our neocortex is a potential spatial network waiting to be lit up. When we play pinball, we try to direct the ball to hit as many stations as possible. In the same way, in the neocortex, we focus our attention to light up as many areas as possible. Mental intelligence will be advanced when we see learning as making as many connections as possible, rather than as trying to enhance a fixed quotient or capacity. Our quotient can change daily if we exercise the network, if we allow connections to be made from all the senses, or if we consciously direct our attention to light up one area after another. We may have more fully developed our sense of sight or sound, of word or music, of smell or touch, of taste or feel, or of body awareness. However, taking the image of the neocortex as an enchanted loom or pinball machine—whichever you prefer—what matters is to allow all kinds of input to inform our neocortex as often as possible. What matters is to send impulses to the axons and dendrites so that more synapses can be formed and synthesized. What matters is to use our concentration on the inner plane of reality as well as the outer plane: "The two kinds of space, intimate space and exterior space, keep encouraging each other, as it were, in their growth."[3]

A full rendering of spatial intelligence would require a book in itself, consisting not only of spatial-visual as described below, but also spatial-auditory, spatial-olfactory, spatial-tactile and spatial-kinesthetic intelligences, bringing together the experience of artists, musicians, and clairaudients, as well as those highly developed in the other senses of smell, taste, and touch.[4]

Spatial-Visual Intelligence

After watching the evening news on TV, few of us can remember the words, but all of us can remember at least some of the images. Television shows and films are composed of images, with words added for detail and description, I sometimes think, only because we are used to the human voice. Newscasters are chosen for their visual impact; at least, there have been few rationally brilliant newscasters who are not also visually appealing. TV shows and films are visual presentations in which thought is conveyed by image. Images require spatial presentation: the TV screen, the movie screen, two- or three-dimensional art. Words and numbers require linear presentation by writing or by voice.

The images that we conjure up internally as we read novels or poetry are often more powerful than images projected through television or film. When reading a novel, we are the directors of our own interior film, seeing images that enhance the content of what we are reading. Indeed, we have more time to invent images as we read through the pages of a book than when watching a TV show or seeing a movie.

Images were the medium of communication prior to writing. Paintings in the caves in Lascaux, France, and the rock art now being discovered in Venezuela and throughout the world reveal our earliest forms of spatial-visual intelligence. Centuries later, with the invention of the printing press, words took precedence over images. It was the book that empowered the word and rational thinking and wrested power from the world of art and music, the older forms of thinking. Television and film have now reversed the trend. Just as books once made words widely available, TV shows and films now make images more available. Indeed, the images on television often seem to have more power than the word—or is it that we spend more time watching TV than reading books?

Our education and our intellectual elite have lagged behind in the struggle between the book and television. We value and teach the word through rational intelligence, while after school, students spend much of their time in front of the TV, with images that do little to develop the subtleties of spatial-visual intelligence. What would it be like to have a visually intelligent population? What would it be like to learn how to protect ourselves from TV images in the same way we learned to protect ourselves from words in newspapers or books? Would we be able to visualize as well as reason about solutions to world problems? Would it be possible to learn to invent through continuous visual connections? Would our homes, our stores, our cities become more aesthetically pleasing if we could visualize them internally before constructing them? If we educated ourselves visually, visual richness would not be limited to the artist and the museum; the aesthetic would become the norm. What powerful feedback that would be for us: to live in beauty!

We must go beyond the struggle of opposites and raise visual thinking to equal partnership with rational thinking, to educate and develop ourselves in both, to heal the split between the artistically elite and the intellectually elite, between the museum and the library, between television and the book.

Intellect and imagination live in different parts of the same human brain. They are two processes of the same brain system, both contributing to our intelligence. In the visual process we see images either externally—as when we watch a sunset or a great film or look at a work of art in a museum or gallery—or internally, as when we imagine or meditate. We may use our capacity to visualize, to imagine, to think internally about what a project, product, or plan is going to look like, or to consider what tomorrow or next month will be like. Visualizing is another form of planning. It can be used alone or together with analysis. Analysis focuses on the evident data in the present, while visual intelligence focuses on seeing an inner picture of how something will turn out either immediately or in the future. Once I have analyzed the information I wish to present in a workshop, I then begin a visualization process of seeing how to present the exercises, what responses I might receive or adjustments I might need to make, and what the program will look like in its final presentation. The visualization process gives me a more secure feeling. It is as if I have been in rehearsal.

What are images? They are configurations of energy, just as thoughts and feelings are. In an image, energy forms itself as a picture instead of as a sentence or feeling. Images are not necessarily imaginary. Some reflect the external truth, while others are pure invention. For example, you may have an image of a house that reflects one that truly exists, or you may have an image that is imaginary—that does not exist in external reality but only in your internal reality. We have the habit of identifying the entire process of visualization with imagination, and we tend to identify images with both imagination and art. We are also accustomed to calling our internal images either fantasy or hallucination, thus negating the power of our spatial-visual intelligence.

Fantasy and hallucination can be harmful if we remain attached to them or identify them with external reality. If I have the fantasy of being Napoleon and I believe that I am, this certainly can lead me into harmful external actions. However, it would be just as harmful to think I am Napoleon as to imagine that I am. The point is to be aware that both—thought and image—are inner realities that may or may not conform to external reality. Both thought and image may be imaginary. We can know only by being willing to check both thought and image with external facts.

Socially, we are accustomed to identifying thought with reality and images with the imaginary, with fantasy. By habit we believe one is real and the other is not. What we must do, now that we are getting clear about the dynamics of the right hemisphere, is to recognize both thoughts and images as mental configurations that ought to be carefully verified with external reality. If we are interested in our mental development, it is important to rid ourselves of any rational prejudices against visualization. An image is a mental configuration as clearly as a thought is. One is expressed as a picture, the other as a sentence. Both can conform to reality or not.

Even the hypothesis, so central to scientific thought, is an image of the possible. Science, however, has the habit and the processes for verifying hypotheses until they are proven true. How many hypotheses or images does the mind project before achieving one that can be verified and proven useful? This process of continually projecting images is spatial-visual intelligence.

Images, the imaginary, fantasy, and hypothesis are all mental functions of spatial-visual intelligence, which you can honor, make real, and develop as part of your mental ability. Forming images in your mind not only can enrich your life and improve the power of your brain, but also can be used to guide you in your daily life. Images are information, real information, usable in whatever range of reality you decide to live in: the imaginary, the subtle, or the externally real. Spatial-visual intelligence is a mental process that activates your neocortex at a more profound level than associative intelligence. Use it to gain access to more information of your own being.

How can we encourage the development of a visually intelligent population? Not only by teaching art to first graders, but by extending visual thinking into math courses, history, science, literature, and English courses at every level. One impressive example comes from the Mead School experience of using visual thinking in math class. Charles loved art and sports. He was a late reader, interested in math, but not very successful. When he was in the fifth grade, the math teacher decided to teach math by means of inner visualization. No one could touch a pencil except to write the answer. She told the students that some children need to use a pencil to figure out everything on paper, but that others were so smart they could do it with their eyes closed and without writing anything. Charles believed. Apparently freed from the necessity of sequentially processing, he was able to process numerous complicated multiplication and division problems, arriving at correct answers.

I do not know exactly what inner visual planning Charles used, but I do know that in all his subjects he had a preference for the right hemisphere. I can only surmise that when he tried to write out the sequential processing involved in computation, he felt constrained or forced to use the left hemisphere, where he had developed far fewer synaptic connections than in the right. In brief, he was forced to use his duller side. Once liberated to associate and visualize numbers within his mind, he must have felt the same independence, power, and connections in the right hemisphere that he used in the Art Center and in sports. He was one of some twelve students chosen for their poor ability in math who, given the chance to exercise their inner visual processes, became successful math students—so successful indeed that they were featured on the Today Show presentation of the Mead School in 1979.

Imaging or inner visual thinking is its own form of thinking. We can enhance classroom performance, however, by making the image the constant companion to the word: "I think this and I see this." There are at least two ways of understanding any information: one processed rationally, sequentially, usually through the left hemisphere, and expressed by "I think"; and a second way processed visually-spatially, usually through the right hemisphere, and expressed by "I see." Both processes are registered in our memory. Sometimes we remember the image, sometimes the word. In relation to classroom performance, if we teach by both processes, students will have two ways of accessing their memory, or at least they will be able to use their strongest way. For right-hemisphere dominant students, this is essential; for left-hemisphere students, it can only increase their brain capacity.

I would also invite us to go beyond treating government and businesses as only patrons of the arts. They could be using visual thinking in every planning session in every office. Can you visualize what this project, this plan you are proposing will look like five months from now, one year? It is not a matter only of financial projections prepared by graphic artists, but of the capacity to visualize internally by the leaders of business and government as well as by those integrally connected with the origin of projects. "What will it look like?" is the vital question involved in visual thinking, just as "What is the cause?" and "What is the effect?" are the vital questions involved in rational thinking.

External Visualization

The creation of images to accompany thoughts is a simple way to expand our mental capacities and tap into the unused ninety percent of our brains. There is no need to end thoughts with a period when they could be accompanied by a beautiful image. Every time we say "I think," we can also train ourselves to image. "When I think about you, I see your smile." "When I learn about the French countryside, I can see . . ." By becoming aware of our speech, we can invite our minds to expand thoughts into visual images and express them in words: "I imagine"; "I can see that"; "The image I have of this is . . ."; "What I see that could really help us is . . ."; or, "It looks like . . ." Let us not say "I think" when we are really imaging. That is one of the main ways in which we distort rational thinking. When we are imaging, let us express it by saying, "I can see that . . .", "The image I have of this is . . .", "The picture I have in my mind is of . . .", or "What I see as our solution is . . ."

When we are listening or when we are thinking rationally, we can add images: "I think and I visualize"; "I hear and I visualize." What if every composition in school were accompanied by drawings? What if every time we finished reading or writing a composition, we leaned back, closed our eyes, and internally visualized the images that accompanied the thought? Our right hemisphere would develop along with our left. We would be energizing both hemispheres and continuously amplifying our network of neocortical connections.

Spatial-visual intelligence will contribute enormously to your learning and memory, as well as to the richness of your everyday life. Practice the following exercise in your school courses, in your work, or in your daily life.

EXERCISE

DEVELOPING YOUR SPATIAL-VISUAL INTELLIGENCE

1. *When you are listening to lectures, you can be both hearing and visualizing images to accompany the information. It helps to close your eyes when you begin, but you can also practice with your eyes open. When both word and image are registered in your memory, then you will be able to retrieve information either through a word or an image or both. You are doubling your memory capacity.*

2. *When you receive instructions, do the same: visualize how to follow those instructions while you are listening to the words. This is especially useful when someone is giving you street directions. Listen and visualize.*

3. *After reading any kind of text, whether literary, historic, or scientific, stop at the end of each page or chapter to image spatially what you have been reading sequentially. It helps both your memory and your enjoyment.*

4. *Before beginning to write answers in any subject, learn to pause and internally visualize what you want to write about.*

5. *Practice distinguishing between the word and the image, using phrases such as "I am thinking," or "My image of this is . . . ." This way you become more and more conscious of the two forms of knowledge.*

6. *Remember that a great deal of everyday life depends heavily on your memory: you need memory to do well in exams, memory to cope with all the details in your work, memory to associate with past knowledge. If word and image are two ways of knowing, they are also two ways of remembering. They are two ways of perceiving information, storing and retrieving current or past information, and using, building, or inventing new information.*

Practice remembering the words and adding images, or practice remembering images and adding words.

When you learn the process of external imaging, in any subject or situation, you will have vastly increased the connections and therefore the power of your entire neocortex. Everything you do will be improved because both hemispheres will be activated. Sometimes you will excel in the exactness of the word and in what exists; sometimes you will excel in the general glimpses of the image and of what can be. In both cases, you will be better developed because you will have energized yourself and the life around you with both word and image.

Internal Visualization

It helps a great deal to close your eyes in order to practice internal visualization. Although we often identify closing the eyes with religious or esoteric events, to close your eyes is really a way to give yourself a better chance to concentrate. Closed eyelids inhibit outer stimuli, which in turn frees you to go in more deeply. By closing your eyes and relaxing your body, you begin to become aware of your internal spaces and gradually of more generalized wavelengths. The more you calm yourself, the more profoundly you enter into your internal being.

You can then actively imagine, for instance a house or a friend, until it is as if you feel their presence. You can sense the image, even though the form may not yet be clear. To go more deeply into your internal wavelengths, remain in the same position until images arrive that do not come from your active will. This is the essential practice of meditation, without its defined religious aspects. Images present themselves on the screen of your mind. You continue to let them pass by without becoming attached to them. The more you remain in a position of stillness and focus on the screen of your mind without losing your concentration, the more images or colors will present themselves. Smells also may come. More profound and comprehensive glimpses occur within your inner being than are usually produced when your eyes are open.

This internal visualization forms a large part of what the religious call the inner life. Focusing every time more deeply into this internal space of thin and rapid wavelengths, other dimensions of life occur. I am sure from my own experience that focusing with love on a figure such as Jesus or Buddha or a guru or a teacher that we admire or love will also help us deepen into the thinner wavelengths. However, it is important to know that this internal space is open to everyone. You can learn to enjoy it with or without a defined religious connection. Although meditation developed more fully and became more popular in the East than in the West, it is the brain heritage of everyone, whatever one's religion may be.

Previsualization

You can also use your inner spatial-visual intelligence to prevision your day or any future event or project. To previsualize is to create images of the possible before it happens. Through visualization, you can make deeper connections that will enable you to revise or adjust your original plan. For example, you can previsualize yourself giving an important conference at work. You see yourself presenting the information, answering questions, and relating to the people who will be there. This visual activity enables you to feel secure with both the people and the event before experiencing it in your external reality. Previsualization enables you to realize what is missing and to imagine ahead of time how to change your presentation or adjust your action. Instead of Monday morning quarterbacking, it is Friday afternoon visualizing. It is seeing and playing the game ahead of time, rehearsing beforehand, adjusting, refocusing, or changing the plan completely. Professional athletes now use previsualization to win. Will thinkers use it to win more of the brain and more of life?

You may prefer to develop plans logically and rationally: "If I do this, then this will happen, which will cause us to do this. The reasons are . . . ." However, after you have logically constructed your plan, you can go on to previsualize how it is going to develop in order to become aware of either details or generalities that were not evident before visualizing the plan in action.

Previsioning the day can also be used to create a more peaceful or more effective day. You can enter the day more consciously, alert to the obvious necessities of the day, foreseeing what you can do to make it a better day, aware of what you need to adjust or where you might be more flexible. Previsualizing helps make both your body and your life less stressful and more calm.

EXERCISE

PREVISUALIZATION

You can do this exercise before beginning a project or before beginning your day. Do it also before beginning any important new work, before participating in a sports event, starting a work of art, giving a conference, or attending an important meeting. Use it for any type of planning.

1. *Close your eyes and relax.*
2. *Allow thoughts and images to pass by on the screen of your mind in order to remove from your mind anything that is not about the project that interests you.*
3. *Focus on the event or project as if you were watching a film. Visualize each stage as it evolves through different imagery.*
4. *When you arrive at a stage or an image that doesn't please you, take the time to reflect on or visualize an alternative way of doing it. Arrange the image in your mind as you discover how you really want it to happen.*
5. *Visualize everything again and allow yourself to be affected by your new "film" in order to be ready to carry it into action.*

Memory: Your Internal Film Library

Spatial-visual thinking can enable you to bring your entire past into the present. You call it memory, but is it really past if you can recover it in vivid detail and enrich your present? Memory is actually a library of stored experiences that can be retrieved as easily as you retrieve a book to be read or a cassette or film to be played.

Won't you also relive all the horrible memories of the past? Yes, until or unless you learn to select only what you wish to see. When we approached a bookcase at age two, we just spilled out all the books; sometimes we even turned an entire bookshelf over on ourselves. The same thing happens with memories until you get some experience in being selective, choosing only what you want to relive. You need to practice selecting your visual treasures. It is a matter of focusing, sometimes returning unwanted images like an unopened letter, selecting again and refocusing on the ones you prefer. It is your mind. It is your memory. It is your power of concentration and selection. You are free to choose, exactly as you would pick out a favorite book rather than one you already know is dull or boring.

With practice, you will be able to retrieve great moments of your past, and pleasure will then always be available to you in the present. If it was a lousy day today and you are not yet comfortable at home, instead of turning on your television you can return to your past and watch a great experience all over again on your own inner screen. Whenever you need enjoyment or pleasure or love, turn to the great events of your life, replay them, and feel them again. They exist to be enjoyed and savored for as long as you live.

This is more than entertainment; it is basic health. It is a way to insert your personal visual tapes to relax your body, release tension, and fill yourself with pleasure. This is your own internal visual process that is available when technology is inadequate or not functioning or when the cassettes of others are inappropriate. Remember that your own visual process may be more exact and thus have more impact than any outside source could have.

A visual guide to well-being is thus continually available in your memory library: you were born healthy and know what it feels like; you have experienced great strength, great flexibility, great health. Bring these moments and situations back to your consciousness and allow yourself to be affected by them in the present. You do not need to wait until senility confines you to a rocking chair and forces you to find internal resources in the great memories of your past. You do not need to wait until you are immobilized, unlikely to create new great experiences, before you begin actively to use your memory as the treasure-house of your mind. Through memory, all of your past life is continually available to you for retrieval in the present.

Hope

Not only can you recapture the past in order to live more richly in the present, but you can also live in the future. Hope is the capacity to visualize a better future. Then, with that visualization, that new image, your own mental processes can guide you into making tomorrow more tangibly wonderful or just slightly better than today. The mind has incredible capacities. There is no reason to limit your mental processing to exactly what exists in this moment, at this time and place. Today may actually be horrible. Hope is vision: it is the capacity to imagine and see a better tomorrow. Hope is a new vision of the future, different from what you are living in the present.

Visions are integral aspects of most religions, which have always offered a vision of a better life, whether by sitting at the right hand of God in Christianity, by returning to the promised land in Judaism, or through illumination in Buddhism and Hinduism. Every religion offers a vision of hope to inspire us. The external portrayal of these visions in great works of art, musical as well as visual, has enriched and uplifted human beings throughout history.

Spatial-visual intelligence has saved lives in the most drastic of circumstances. Whatever the form of entrapment—prison, war, illness, or the darkness of our own mind—we desperately need to give substance to the word *hope* by making it an active part of our lives before catastrophe strikes. To visual-think needs to become an active verb. We must learn visual thinking before we find ourselves in difficulty.

You can make hope come alive by training yourself in the active visualization of tomorrow, this afternoon, next week, or next year. I am speaking of more than a momentary hope to lift your spirit. I am proposing to convert active images of hope into a way of guiding your life. Sometimes your mind goes vagabonding in the future hoping for the best. At other times it falls into negative projections and visualizations, depending on the mood of the day. If you do not train your mind actively and consciously, you can become a victim, not only by accepting whatever images occur in your present, but also by taking seriously any negative visualizations of the future.

It is possible consciously to plan a future with hope, by actively constructing the visualizations you wish to make happen. Although it may be necessary to change your visualization as you go along, nevertheless it serves as a guiding star. Your brain is energy. When this energy is not guided consciously, it continues to function unconsciously—that is, without your guidance. To allow your right hemisphere to roam unsupervised in whatever vision of the future turns up in your mind could mean that in difficult periods, you fall into depression, of lesser or greater severity.

You may call it destiny or blame others, or you may begin to realize that it is necessary for you to govern your own mind actively, especially your wandering and generalizing right hemisphere.

At last count, fifteen million Americans were declared clinically depressed. Are they focusing on the harsh or bitter details of the day, projecting them as conclusions onto tomorrow and the rest of their lives? Are they victims of a visualization capacity in their brain that has never been guided, never been taught to be intelligent and life-affirming? Imagine how different it could be for those who are depressed if they had been taught that they govern their minds, that while they are free to focus on the bitter aspects, they are equally free consciously to visualize a better tomorrow to guide their actions. They can change their environment rather than being deeply affected and controlled by it. At the very least they need an intelligence process that can enable them to get free of their entrapment in details and conclusions that are not producing good results in their daily lives.

We can use spatial-visual thinking to enjoy ourselves whenever we want. It doesn't cost money—we can travel without paying for plane tickets or hotels! We can improve any reality: a little snow in New York takes us off skiing in the Alps, enjoying a warm fire in the lodge. Or we can bring in totally unconnected images. Pure fantasy, you say. Yes, and how delicious when we are bored or obliged to complete a dull task and need an intermission. Visualization gives us instant space travel. We can bypass the physical present, the physically real, for the imaginably real. Why not be writing this in my favorite café in Paris? Why stay here, harnessing and holding back my mental vibrations? I am free to focus on any mental process that will enrich me, inspire me, calm me, or help me or any project I am involved in.

The future—good or bad—does not have to be something that happens to you, something you passively receive. The future can be a state that you first project with your mind, which then happens or not, depending on many other factors. Your neocortex is waiting for you to project the images of any future you desire. Sit down at your enchanted loom and weave a design that can inform you of how to act on behalf of your own life and the lives of those around you. We can all participate in helping create a better future. To visualize the future is a capacity of your mind. Use it consciously.

CHAPTER V

Traveling to Thinner Vibrations of Quantum Realities

INTUITIVE INTELLIGENCE

W*e have arrived at the thinner vibrations of the neocortex, at the vibrations of peace visible in the face of the mystic or the newborn child. In those faces we see something we are reluctant to define but that we have named spiritual, something far beyond what we are used to calling "intelligence." It is, however, a powerful state of intelligence in which a great deal of information can be received.*

I deeply believe that intuition is a state of consciousness, intelligence, and peace within reach of everyone. I am also convinced that intuition already exists in children's minds before we send them to school. Look at the face of an infant sound asleep and you will see the same serenity that you see in the face of a Buddha or a mystic. How can this intuitive capacity of our children be accepted and encouraged during their waking hours?[1] It depends, I think, on our capacity as adults to learn the intuitive process and include it in our daily context. At least we must not put it aside and save spirituality for Saturdays or Sundays but include it as one of the mind's processes that helps us travel into infinite ranges.

What Is Intuition?

Intuition is knowing from within, knowing without recourse to logic or reason. It is "the direct knowing or learning of something without the conscious use of reasoning; immediate apprehension or understanding."[2] Intuition is used by psychics, healers, religious leaders, experimental scientists, and winners at the race track. Some call it "luck," some call it "faith," some "a special relationship with God," some "extrasensory perception." There are many ranges of intuition. An advanced intuitive is a psychic; an advanced psychic is a mystic. In between are the many ranges used by healers, shamans, mediums, channels, clairvoyants, those who are clairaudient, and those who go unnamed.

We tend to distance ourselves from the world of thinner vibrations, allowing mystics, spiritualists, or esoteric people to hold it exclusively as their own, as if it were not possible to develop this capacity in everybody. Moreover, this tendency to separate the thinner vibrations from the thicker everyday vibrations has caused divisions within major religions. In Christianity there are organized church groups and then there are mystics. In Judaism there is the temple, on the one hand, and the mystic studies of the Kabbalah, on the other. Among Muslims, there are those who go to the mosques, and the mystical Sufis. In China there is Confucianism, a philosophy dealing with the thicker vibrations of everyday life, and the Tao, path of the thinnest vibrations. In Japan, Shintoism deals with the tangible thicker vibrations, while Zen honors especially the thinnest vibrations.

Recent years have seen a surge in interest in all forms of extrasensory perception: mediums, channels, telepathy, paranormality, parapsychology—all names for new and old ways of opening the door to the thinnest vibrations. My interest is that the individual become aware of and trained in the thickest wave vibrations as well as in the thinnest. I refuse the separation between the practical and the esoteric. The thinnest waves become as practical as the thickest in certain key moments of our lives. We have to open the entire vibrational range of energy in every human being if we want to stop dividing and separating ourselves from one another.

We tend to be so in love with the intuitive process that we ritualize it within religions, often paying more attention to the ritual than to what we receive. Whether we call it religion or mysticism, devotion in the West or enlightenment in the East, we have considered the intuitive process special, sacred, spiritual, or religious. Intuitive teachings have been carried on exclusively within religious hierarchies or esoteric practices. Access to these deeper and quieter states has been reserved for the few. What is urgent is that this extremely beautiful, useful, and spiritual process no longer be reserved for the few, but rather that it become available to the many. We are all so extraordinary, so capable of realizing billions of connections.

Intuitive intelligence begins in our daily life by validating and listening to our inner voice. I have a hunch, an intuition that a friend who lives far away is sad because someone is sick. I call to check on this and find it is true. "I must have intuited this," I say, but what was the process I used to arrive at this knowledge?

Bell's Theorem suggests that quantum connections exist, that energy travels without known pathways. This helps to explain intuition, but connecting at subatomic particle levels does not yet constitute a known procedure in our everyday consensus reality.[3] Parapsychology has studied numerous psychics, people who are able to know from within, without reference to any obvious procedure. However, psychics have not been able to repeat their successes, to replicate them in the predictable manner required to be recognized as scientific. Parapsychology has, however, recorded many different cases in which psychics successfully knew and predicted something across space and time with incredible accuracy. Therefore, regardless of predictable consistency, there is no reason for us to doubt the existence of this form of intelligence as a human capacity.

Stories of scientific invention reveal that behind rational procedure, the scientist also uses an intuitive capacity. Although scientists can arrange data up to a point, they then must make a leap into the unknown, a guess or a hunch to discover what might be true. Scientists call this leap a hypothesis, which is a hunch whose feasibility they then proceed to test and verify. It is perhaps the most elegant moment for the scientist, facing into the unknown, listening for the best hunch. Perhaps the only better moment is when the hypothesis is verified and becomes a scientific discovery. We focus on scientific accomplishment as if all of it emanated from rational procedure. We hear little about this intuitive process, which fed into the rational procedure. At critical moments even medical doctors must make their best guess as to what will help. They call this their sixth sense and admit to using it when all else fails. They too must face the unknown and try to do their best to help patients.

It is time, therefore, to acknowledge the existence of intuitive intelligence and by so doing attend to its conscious education. Sarah is a young woman who could have benefited by knowing at an early age of her intuitional ability. She never valued her intuitive intelligence. Indeed, it had never occurred to her to link intuition with intelligence. She thought of herself as spiritual, as interested in humanity. Her parents thought of her as their lovely but not too practical daughter, never able to concentrate, bouncing from one interest to another—the pleasing one. Although Sarah was a graduate in social work, her parents continued to see her as their light-spirited, not very down-to-earth daughter.

When I met Sarah, she was still lighthearted, but covering over heartaches of discouragement and a low self-esteem. She had always considered herself less intelligent than her rationally intelligent sister. It had never occurred to her that she had a different type of intelligence. As she became aware of her visual intelligence, she was able to realize artistic projects, of both a personal and a commercial nature. But what became her gem, her identity and the source of a new self-esteem, was the recognition of her intuitive intelligence. The more she practiced with her hunches and verified their correctness, the greater became her strength. Her friends and in time her parents recognized this as a positive ability of their daughter. Her intuitive intelligence now guides her life and informs her art.

Even in one of my workshops on intuition, where few of the students considered themselves psychic, most were able to intuit what their randomly chosen partners were thinking about. Ten people wrote the name and main characteristics of an absent friend on a card, gave the card face down to a partner, and then focused on the absent friend. The partner tried to guess the characteristics of the absent friend. From the ten pairs, everyone got something, and eight of the pairs got the main characteristics of those who were absent.

Intuitive intelligence is potentially available to everyone. It can be developed. You are seated at the control panels. To access rational intelligence or intuitive intelligence is a matter of training yourself, of being willing to follow different instructions to access different pathways. The examples and the processes of each intelligence are there for you. You can learn to make choices among different intelligence processes. You can begin to move into your own mental freedom and your own orchestration of these intelligences, in order to receive greater information or experience greater sensitivity, whether it be of heaven or of earth.

Developing Your Intuitive Intelligence

The intuitive process is about the reception of information, a reception distinct from that involved in rational or associative thinking. This reception is at deeper and at faster speeds than images. We can characterize the intuitive process as the deeper accessing of the brain, or as reception of waves picked up by the brain. The signals often come in quantum leaps, rather than coming on any recognizable continuous waves.

The intuitive process cannot be directed, but it can be prepared for and developed. Three principles are deeply involved in developing this intuitive intelligence:

1. the belief that there are larger realities, what some of us call God
2. the belief in the principle and practice of self-observation
3. the principle and practice of attunement or at-one-ment

1. Faith, or a conceptual belief in something larger than yourself. You need something in which you place your trust, be it God, the Universe, nature, or something else. However you come to understand it, visualize it, experience, or feel it, this largeness must be trusted. The process of letting go of one's limited boundaries, of one's outer dynamics, of verifiable and visible realities, is inextricably connected with whether or not you are able to let go into something larger, which you trust to be more loving or kind or safe than your immediate boundaries.

You live in your finiteness, in your limited definitions of self, insisting on those limits unless you consciously invite yourself to soften or dissolve them in order to expand into something larger and more trustful. As long as you do not consciously interest yourself in the infinite, your brain focuses on the finite. Begin by focusing on a larger horizon, and then allow yourself to move toward it. The issue becomes your ability to trust or think your way into, feel, or experience a largeness, an all-pervasiveness, a love so exuberant it expands your limits until you lose the power of description.

How to know whom to call to or on what you can rely? asks the rational mind. Because of our predisposition to and dependence on rational intelligence, we have become accustomed to the answer that "we must have faith," by which we often mean that we must be content with not knowing. However, there are starting points other than the specific knowing. There are processes other than the who, what, where, when, why, and how of the rational.

You can begin with the concept of infinity as described by the rational mind and years of scientific investigation; or with the concepts of self and other, of environment, or of all that surrounds you, described by the social scientists; or with God, as described by religious leaders. You can also begin with the brain hemispheres of the neocortex, entering first the right hemisphere rather than the left, predisposed to generalities rather than specifics. From the first general glimpses you can proceed to seek ever larger glimpses of your universe.

In order to begin this process of search, this willingness to search, you need to have a belief system or a value system that permits you to involve yourself in a vastness beyond your finite boundaries. In most cultures this involvement in vastness has been called God and has been given to us in the heritage of great religions. Those who participate in religion have a belief system in God. Many have a desire to search, to move into the experience of this vastness. Others, however, accept the vastness, sometimes as security, sometimes as love, but hesitate to enter into the active process of intuiting, listening to, and receiving from this vastness.

2. Self-observation, of your external life and internal life. Self-observation is developing the capacity for awareness and consciousness by continuous observation—continuous because we never arrive at completion. We arrive at the "cloud of unknowing."[4] We arrive in immensity, in emptiness, in endless mystery, in spectacular visions, in color and light, in glimpses of the so-called totality.

With each of these revelatory experiences, we have a tendency to stop, a tendency to conclude that this glimpse is the ultimate experience of God. In this way we have tried to crystalize religious experience into absolutes, proposing our way or insights as the definitive way. Although it is understandable that we wish others to participate in this vastness, our tendency to absolutize has in fact separated religions and caused religious wars. By trying to establish a fixed road to travel, many have substituted the religious experience for an imitation of a way or an adoration of those who have made the journey. I believe the common territory is the intuitive process. The essential point is to love all our glimpses of God and to continue our search into infinity.

Access to the thinner, higher-speed vibrations is possible by a continuous self-observation, focusing ever more deeply into these subtle levels of the brain, picking up reflections of our own selves and others on this earth range, as well as vibrations from unidentifiable ranges. The great teacher of self-observation, Ramana Maharshi, invited his disciples to ask themselves continually, "Who am I?" and then waiting for the response, to continue to ask the same question again and again.[5] Continually ask yourself and continually observe your responses. By focusing deeply within your brain, you enter extraordinary vibrational levels.

Self-observation also applies to observation of the thoughts, images, emotions, and actions in your everyday external realities. As you succeed in clarifying and dealing with the thicker waves that form your energy blocks and hurts, you become more able to get in touch with the thinnest waves of your internal being. The contrary is also true: by focusing on your internal life first, by observation, prayer, and meditation, you can receive guidance from those internal ranges that helps you to attune, harmonize, and heal your body-mind as it operates in the thicker realities.

3. Attunement. This is being willing and able to tune your instrument, your body-brain-mind system, in relation to your observation of yourself and all that surrounds you. Attunement is caring for your human body-mind system or instrument the same way musicians care for their instruments. They not only protect them from outer harm, but before each playing, they tune the parts of their instruments in order to be able to play the entire range of vibrations. You must do the same with your human instrument of body-mind.

Practicing continuous self-observation, you activate your thoughts, feelings, and senses, thereby sensitizing yourself to life all around you. You can then attune yourself to others, listen and receive, intuit or know from within. You can practice attunement by listening and responding with greater sensitivity to other persons, animals, plants, rocks, or any other form of life on this planet.

It is you who tune in the program with your radio-mind, whether it be to God or gross physical reality, infinity or finiteness. Both always exist; it is you who choose to tune yourself into heaven or earth, generality or specifics, God or the devil, or whatever names you give to the tremendously varied energy vibrations in which you live. You do it with your capacity to select, focus or concentrate, and attune with. Attunement is becoming "one" with whatever station you are listening to. At-one-ment is a way of expressing the deep state of consciousness that can result from tuning in and receiving. Attunement is also the practice of shifting into alternate states of consciousness, alternate mental states, or alternate intelligences. Aware that it is your job to tune in, you can then choose the wavelength you wish to be on and receive whatever enters into your range.

Safeguarding the Intuitive Body-Mind

Intuitive intelligence requires certain safeguards. Intuitives or psychics, who are really advanced intuitives, need to protect themselves and especially their health. They need to be careful with their body-mind instruments once thay have been so finely developed. With such sensitivity they are easily damaged or wounded and find it difficult to protect themselves. One safeguard is the love that comes with the practice of a religious profession; another is the love we have for a teacher. Love, of course, is not limited. It is available wherever we look for it and whenever we permit ourselves to be affected by it. The safeguard is really the warmth that comes with love, as well as the feeling of security that comes with being surrounded by a loved one.

Many people, not protected by a religion or not loved by friends or a teacher, walk a delicate road and fall into mental difficulties along the road to becoming psychic. Capable of disassociating easily from visible reality, they lose themselves and are classified as chaotic, far from reality, or mentally ill. Either they have not integrated love or they have not learned the equally important process of being able to associate with finite reality. Jettisoned into one reality, they have remained there. Someone who has an experience of identifying himself or herself as Jesus or

Napoleon may become incapable of identifying with the role of student in everyday life.

By age nineteen Teresa was having visions and insights that she felt were cosmic, as if she were being embraced by the universe. She spoke words of great wisdom, which made her seem mature beyond her years. Her parents were impressed and convinced that in some way she was exceptional. She turned down entrance to an Ivy League college and decided instead to travel.

On her own and with the aid of drugs, her experiences continued. She reported seeing Jesus and receiving instructions. She announced her intuitive insights to those near her, who mocked her and disregarded her pronouncements. When she neared physical harm, her family brought her home, distraught and confused. Teresa's intuitive experiences were mixed with her strong emotional desire to act them out in her everyday environment. She was restless, chaotic, and unwilling to receive help from others, so convinced was she that she was receiving and speaking the word of God. Her emotions and actions were finally brought under control by the use of heavy drugs, until she was able to reflect on her behavior.

This is a tragic story of the negative use of intuitive intelligence, or rather insufficient and unclear development of intuitive intelligence. Unfortunately, intuitive insights can easily become absolutes. They are such overwhelming glimpses, awesome and involving—how can they be doubted? They feel right and deep. It is others who are wrong and don't understand. When intuitives develop without guidance or protection, they can easily become confused about what is reality. One aspect of reality engulfs and dominates them. When intuitive intelligence is unleashed before the development of parameter intelligence or carefully guided spatial intelligence, the individual can experience the harm that Teresa suffered.

Most people have unusual experiences of receiving, of seeing, or of direct perception in early childhood. Looks of disbelief and astonishment from parents are usually sufficient for most of us to close off access to this pathway. For those who have stronger experiences in the right side of the brain, it is difficult to maintain their equilibrium against the rejection or negation of parents. Love is lost, as well as the warmth and security that goes with it. The experiences continue, but without permission and without knowledge of how to integrate them into a system of knowledge and everyday finite reality. What would all intelligence be like if we could protect this particular pathway in early childhood?

The capacity of intuitives to read our minds, to intuit a great deal of what we are thinking or feeling, has also caused difficulty. What parents can stand to have a child reading their minds? For most of us this is a frightening experience that we repress and deny. Throughout history, many psychics have caused difficulty by misusing their intelligence. If the intuitive capacity is developed without affectional intelligence, without love, it can be used to interfere with other lives rather than attune to other lives. We call it black magic or evil. It is the misuse of power.

It is urgent that we look at the multiple approach to intelligences, and more precisely at intuitive intelligence. Many persons have become ill from not understanding or knowing how to manage their mental capacities. If this intelligence is developed without regard for a person's other intelligences, specifically without regard for those connected with love and the heart, great imbalances can result. One wonders how many people are in our psychiatric institutions with some combination of overdeveloped spatial and intuitive intelligences and underdeveloped affective, motivational, and parameter intelligences. My hope is that by looking at these many pathways into the brain, we will have a new way of looking at both mental illness and mental development. I hope that many from different professions can be enlisted in the process of looking again.

EXERCISE
EVERYDAY PRACTICE

The following practices can prepare you to experience intuitive intelligence. Try them in your everyday context or as often as possible.

1. **Something larger than yourself.** *Find a belief system that enables you to search ever greater horizons. Your bridge to outer horizons can be faith, trust in God, a belief system, or a curiosity inviting you beyond yourself or more deeply within yourself. Relate your larger belief system in an infinite to your everyday finite existence.*

2. **Wonder.** *Begin by admiring, by being able to be surprised, and above*

all by wondering. A phrase that has guided me and that I have loved is, "I wonder as I wander at the wonders of the world."

3. **Everything possible.** *Begin to trust your guesses and your hunches. Let yourself include guesses, hunches, suppositions, and conjectures in your conversation. They don't have to turn out to be correct all of the time. Allow yourself the freedom to guess.*

4. **Observation.** *Observe your mind when your thoughts are forming and allow them to come through without being complete.*

5. **Relaxation.** *Learn to relax in any context or in as many situations as possible.*

6. **Receptivity.** *Learn to receive. It is important to be able to change your energy from active to receptive, from yang to yin. It is then important to accept what you receive. Do not make judgments; do not say it is not what you were looking for. Intuitive intelligence is not about directing but about receiving. Whatever you receive, value.*

7. **Silence.** *Give yourself the experience of silence as often as is possible or appropriate.*

EXERCISE

CONSCIOUS PREPARATION FOR INTUITIVE INTELLIGENCE

Each of the following can be practiced separately. However, when you can give yourself sufficient time to train yourself in intuition or receptivity, practice them in the series as presented. Doing them sequentially will prepare you for that still point of reception where intuitive intelligence begins. Just as your training in the syntax of sentence structure prepared you for rational thinking, these exercises together with the above everyday practices form the syntax necessary to prepare you for intuitive reception.

1. **Closing the day.** *Clear your mental vibrations. The day offers you moments of happiness in which you are full of energy as well as troubled moments in which you lose your strength. Review the high and low points of your day. Focus on one thing you can do tomorrow to improve your lows, and then close this day by shifting into the high points.*

2. **Muscle relaxation.** *Make yourself comfortable, stretch, and concen-*

trating on each group of muscles from your feet to your head, expand and contract each muscle group.

3. **Breathing.** *Make yourself comfortable. Experience your breathing, passively observing its coming and going. When you wish to, begin to play with the element of breath by altering your concentration, experiencing the effect as you focus on different areas of your body. Relax, allow the breathing without your conscious direction. Observe. When you wish to, focus your breathing deeply in the belly area. Focus on an image of beauty or on feeling loved and observe the alterations of your breathing.*

4. **Prayer.** *Concentrate with your favorite prayer. The word* prayer *comes from the Latin "precarius, obtained by begging."[6] Although begging seems to be out of favor in our everyday world, it does communicate a profound limbic experience of really wanting. Therefore ask deeply and allow yourself to feel the asking.*

5. **Meditation.** *Find a comfortable position where your spine is supported. Allow words, thoughts, images, and sounds to go by. Focus on one point, in the triangle in front of your eyes. Focus your breathing into your abdomen, your chest, and the point between your eyes. Allow . . . let pass by.*

6. **Reception.** *As the screen of your mind clears, observe and receive. Trust that whatever you receive is of value and holds something for you. Search in your life for the meaning. That is the message.*

Practicing stillness, you acquire the capacity of tuning into the deepest wavelengths vibrating through your brain systems. Silence and quietness permit you to let the facts, the details, the nuances, complexities, and emotions go by, clearing the screen of your mind, until you arrive in a wider or deeper space. You are entering the thinnest vibrations of your brain. Setting aside all logical procedures, you relax and present yourself as if all the connections were possible. Allow associations and images to present themselves to you. Eventually you enter into a zone of stillness in which you do not feel or imagine or think. It is a receptivity without words, without feelings, without images. You are in an energy zone in which you can only be passive and receive. Stillness and silence will help you to arrive at this intuitional stage.

PART II

CHAPTER VI

Exploring
the Limbic Brain

In reality, our passions and our desires are as much the brain's creation as are intellect and reason. They are all brought to life in a small amphitheater of tissue known as the limbic system. Inside a collection of parts that make up roughly one-fifth of the brain's area, the cold world of reality is transformed into a bubbling caldron of human feelings. The forces of fear, elation, grief, anger and lust arise from this most primitive region of the brain that evolved long ago.

The Brain: Mystery of Matter and Mind
U.S. News and World Report

J*ust beneath the neocortex and right be-*

hind our nose lies an exquisite brain system composed of six distinct structures:

the thalamus, amygdala, hypothalamic nuclei, olfactory bulbs, septal region, and

hippocampus. Called the limbic system by Paul MacLean and his predecessors in

brain research, it is also known as the feeling brain or the brain of human emo-

tions.[1] It is sometimes referred to as the mammalian brain, because all mammals

possess a similar structure. Just as the basic brain is associated with the reptile,

the limbic brain is associated with the brain of animals.

The neocortex is composed of neuronal cells in the form of axon and dendritic structures, whereas the limbic system is composed of six cellular structures, each one having different characteristics and identified with different functions. More and more refined investigations are taking place every day, which keep offering new insights and realizations.[2] This chapter does not pretend to offer a full recapitulation of the research on the limbic brain, but shows only the main points that have given me support in elaborating the emotional intelligences. I describe here the characteristics associated in brain research with the six different cellular structures so that you will be able to trace the relationship between the physiology of your limbic brain system and the emotional intelligences proposed in subsequent chapters.

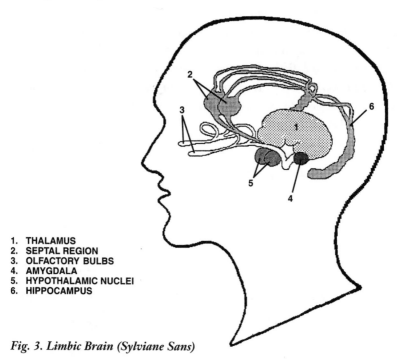

1. THALAMUS
2. SEPTAL REGION
3. OLFACTORY BULBS
4. AMYGDALA
5. HYPOTHALAMIC NUCLEI
6. HIPPOCAMPUS

Fig. 3. Limbic Brain (Sylviane Sans)

Each area is associated with at least one specific characteristic:

1. Thalamus: affection
2. Septal Region: sexuality
3. Olfactory Bulbs: smelling and breathing

4. Amygdala: oral aggression
5. Hypothalamic Nuclei: pleasure and pain
6. Hippocampus: long-term memory

The Thalamus and Affection

The thalamus, largest structure of the limbic brain, is located at the top of the brain stem of the R-system or basic brain. It "is a relay center for sensory impulses to the cerebral cortex."[3] According to MacLean, the thalamus is the first evolution of life from reptile to mammal, associated with mother-child communication as well as with maternal instinct.[4] We know that the mammal is different from the reptile in relation to family. While most reptiles lay eggs and slither away, the mammal remains near the newborn, offering nourishment until it is capable of surviving on its own.

Is this willingness to "hold with" the beginning of family? This may be the most important human question, not only about family affection but about all affection. Am I willing to be affected by you? How deeply? How long? How much are you willing to be affected by me? In difficult moments, will I slither away or will I hold with? Holding with you, near you, will I continue to allow myself to be affected by you?

Our capacity to be affected by another person, by a flower, rock, sky, or animal, by work, ideas, music, or art, by crime or great human deeds, by suffering or by joy: it is our conscious choice of allowing ourselves "to be affected by" that opens our capacity to feel. To be deeply affected leads us into wanting, into desire, and then into the full range of moods from sadness and anger to ecstasy and love. In brief, affection, the result of our being affected, can lead us into the full range of our feelings. To be affected is the doorway to our limbic brain system.

From this first and largest structure of the limbic brain and its characteristic of affection, I propose that there is a process of affectional intelligence that we can learn and practice. Without the capacity to be affected, we cannot enter the limbic system. Our limbic system will indeed keep on vibrating, but we will not be aware of what we are feeling. With affectional intelligence, we are able to guide ourselves in relation to others and the environment, continually giving ourselves permission to be affected, to feel our way, to receive signals in our emotional range about the danger or the safety, the beauty or the emotional content, of our environment. As we receive this emotional information, we learn to modulate and orchestrate our feelings, either deepening into further affection or withdrawing, as appropriate.

The Septal Region and Sexuality

According to MacLean, the septal region is associated with sexual arousal.[5] Sexuality, first registered in the limbic brain system, occurs as a mental phenomenon whether or not we act physically on these vibrations. We may think we are not sexual if we do not engage in sexual intercourse. We may even prevent ourselves from being conscious of sexual arousal. However, a glance at the preceding diagram of the limbic brain will show us the close proximity of the septal or sexual region to the thalamus. Vibrations in our thalamus easily mix with vibrations in our septal region and together form the connection between what affects us and what makes us feel sexual. We may shift our focus or concentration onto thoughts or busy ourselves with actions, but the vibrational connection between affection and sexuality is evident. The link between emotion and sexuality may indeed produce enough fear to keep us out of this emotional brain, or at least inhibit us enough to make us deny our emotional life, but the existence of the septal region within our brain system is an indication that we cannot easily bury or inhibit our sexuality without also limiting and inhibiting our capacity to feel.

To complicate matters, if we decide to limit our capacity to feel and inhibit our capacity to be sexual, we must face the consequences of restriction, inhibition, and contraction that affect not only our sexual organs, but all the other organs of our body. Sexuality is literally in our brain and inextricably related not only to all our emotions, but through the autonomic nervous system, to all the organs of our body.

The existence of the septal region within our brain is thus an indication that sexuality can influence all our so-called purely mental decisions, as well as our actions. Sexuality is not only a biological act but an emotional and physical phenomenon that sets off a tremendous energy, at times capable of dominating all three brain systems.

Olfactory Bulbs: Breathing and Smelling

The olfactory bulbs are associated with the obvious functional characteristics of smelling and breathing. We are attracted and affected by smells that influence our emotions, especially those of perfumes, foods, familiar places, and loved ones. According to MacLean, the olfactory bulbs also connect olfactory information to the hippocampus, associated with long term memory.[6]

Although smells may be stimulating, we have probably become more accustomed to judging our environment by means of our eyes and ears. Animals still use their noses as a guiding process, but most humans have all but lost their capacity to smell their way around. Can this loss of capacity in our olfactory bulbs be another indication of our attempts to close off our emotions?

We recognize breathing as a function of life: it is the first sign of life as well as the last. In sleep we continue to breathe because breathing is linked to our automatic process, which keeps us alive. However, during the day most of us still relegate breathing to the automatic processes, seldom noticing how we are breathing at any given moment or interesting ourselves in learning how to breathe consciously or effectively.

Whenever we are in intense emotional states, we breathe deeply or have difficulty breathing. In fear, tension, and anxiety, we restrict and inhibit our breathing; in pleasurable emotions of love and joy, we relax and expand our breathing. If we wish to live the full range of emotions, we need breathing intelligence: the capacity to use our nasal passages, lungs and diaphragm to orchestrate our emotional vibrations.

The Amygdala and Oral Aggression

The amygdala is associated with oral aggression. MacLean states,

> The findings that loci for chewing, swallowing, and the like are intermixed with those for searching, fighting and self-defense indicate that the mechanisms for feeding are intimately geared in with those required for obtaining food. . . . In a word, the amygdalar division of the limbic system appears to be "largely concerned with self-preservation as it pertains to feeding and to the behavior involved in the struggle

to obtain food." Several neuroendocrinological findings are also indicative that the amygdalar division plays an important role in the struggle for survival.[7]

Research by Joseph LeDoux emphasizes the association of the amygdala to fear.[8] Fear is our constrictive response when survival is threatened whether for lack of food, physical attack, or even the unknown. I believe we must no longer deny the inherent connection between our brain, our survival, our fear, and our aggression. Despite all our intellectual, artistic, and spiritual efforts to civilize ourselves by educating the neocortex, we have not succeeded. Neither neocortical analysis, nor discussion, nor even understanding directly addresses our emotions of anger, violence, and aggression. Although we enjoy thinking of ourselves as superior to animals, it has cost us dearly—or deadly. Our lack of limbic emotional education is everywhere apparent: in our cities, our hospitals, and our prisons, even in our own inherent instability within ourselves.

If we wish to become fully conscious, it is crucial to remember that the mouth is linked to the emotional brain. What we say is always colored by our emotions, or more precisely, what we say is always emotional or subjective. We can never speak objectively unless we are recording verified data. There is no mouth located in the forehead and used for neocortical speech only. We have only one mouth, and all our words must pass through our limbic brain of emotions. Therefore everything we say is affected by our emotions at the time we are speaking. Not only the words we speak but also the tones and vibrations of our voice carry the real emotional message. Emotion is mixed in with the mental message, sometimes subtly, sometimes overtly, sometimes aggressively.

VISION AND THE LIMBIC BRAIN

It is also important to realize that we never see objectively. We see only when impulses reach the occipital region of the neocortex. Before arriving, incoming impulses must pass through the lateral geniculate of the thalamus of the limbic system, as shown in the following drawing and as discussed by Drs. Eric R. Kandel and James H. Schwartz.[9]

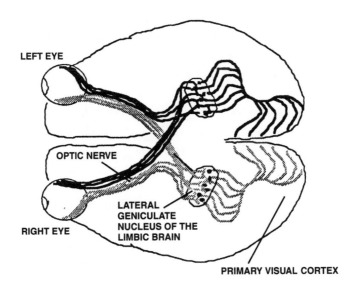

Fig. 4. Vision and the Limbic Brain (Luis Camejo)[10]

Thus sight is also emotional or subjective. Only verification can make it objective.

Hypothalamic Nuclei: Pleasure, Pain, and Chemistry

> For many years, the hypothalamus has been known as that region of the forebrain most concerned with the regulation of the internal organs. In fact, it has been called the head ganglion of the autonomic nervous system. . . . The hypothalamus has been a major target of research relating the brain to endocrine activities.[11]

> The hypothalamic nuclei serve to activate, control, and integrate the peripheral autonomic mechanisms, endocrine activities, and many somatic functions.[12]

The hypothalamic nuclei are popularly known as the pleasure-pain centers of the limbic brain. Feelings are moods, extending over a wide vibrational range of both pleasure and pain. We can be depressed one moment, happy or angry the next. Natural chemicals relating to pleasure and pain, too numerous and complex to list here, are continually being discovered in this brain, according to MacLean.[13] What is evident from the study of such chemicals as endorphins and serotonin is that natural brain chemicals extend over a range from quiescence to excitation. It is extremely important to realize that artificial chemicals or drugs also extend over this same range.

How can we gain access to our natural brain chemicals? Accepting the brain as an energy system, we can first approach emotions as vibratory states in continuous flux instead of considering them as descriptive of a fixed reality. We can then realize that emotions are vibrations that extend over the same energy range as do natural brain chemicals. When we are depressed, we have very little energy. When we are sad, we have a bit more energy; in anger, much more. Happiness is a strong vibration, excitement an even stronger one. We may have invented anger in order to experience its excitation—anything to rouse us from boredom or continuous entropy. We may have invented depression in order to experience real quiet—finally a chance to cut off the world with all its demanding vibrations. Do we have a need for both extremes? Which emotion do we need most? Which mood will make our day: quiescence or excitation?

Mood is the challenge of the emotional brain. Can we become emotionally intelligent, which means, can we use our moods consciously and skillfully to cope with life? Emotions contain information just as a thought, image, or action does. We can read the information of our feelings instead of just tolerating them or trying to escape from them. Mood intelligence is the process I propose to learn how to go into feelings, learn from them, express them if appropriate, and shift from them.

Without mood intelligence, we will have to continue to be heavily dependent on artificial drugs to regulate this brain. Cultures have always created drugs. In our culture, psychiatrists are now consciously regulating the extreme states of this brain with drugs. Street people are accessing states of quiescence and excitation with drugs, as are the most sophisticated in our society. Learning how to orchestrate moods rather than regulate them with drugs could give everyone a new mental freedom as well as a sense of conscious control of life.

The Hippocampus and Memory

Two curving structures form the hippocampus and surround the other organs of the limbic system. They are primarily associated with long-term memory. MacLean has found in his investigations that the poor functioning of the hippocampus is related to lack of memory. He also points out that for a long time other researchers have been associating the hippocampus with long-term memory.[14]

Various kinds of memory are located in different parts of the brain. We have all had experience with both short-term and long-term memory. The most obvious common experience is preparing for a final exam in school. You remember something just long enough to pass the test (short-term) but you still remember today what you really wanted to learn (long-term). Even now, reading this book, you will remember only what you really want to remember.

With visual intelligence we can access the great and pleasurable moments of our life. Knowing that they are stored in memory can add a new dimension to our life. However, experiences of pain are also registered in our memory, and most of us would rather forget our painful experiences. Indeed, we may remember certain painful childhood experiences or traumatic adult experiences only when a therapist convinces us that we may want to remember what happened in the past in order to make sense of the present. Wanting is the key to accessing our long-term memory. Knowing that our experiences are recorded and always available if we want them can give us a new freedom both about experiencing our emotions and about expressing them. We no longer need to choose between being an explosive time bomb or a repressed human being. We no longer need to express emotions as they are happening; we no longer need to fear that if we repress them, we will lose them.

We can also live them again if we take the time to access our memory, visualize the situation, and allow ourselves to feel it. We can use our memories as interior texts, as libraries filled with volumes of experiences waiting to be opened up again and relived. Whenever we choose, we can reexperience any situation, feel the emotions again, and discover new information.

When we experience a situation for the first time, we may not be able to feel it fully. We try to think, react, sometimes imagine, but usually "just get through the best we can." When decisions, especially those of early childhood and early love affairs, hurt us later in life, it is appropriate to look again, to interfere with our early conclusions, and to change those early decisions that have become limiting or harmful in our present life. Our long-term memory thus guarantees us the possibility of looking again, of changing our life decisions, until we eventually develop the quality of life we wish.

Autonomic Nervous System

Could any discovery be more important than knowing that both natural brain chemicals and long-term memory are embedded in our emotional brain? Yes. Knowing that this emotional brain system governs every organ of your body.

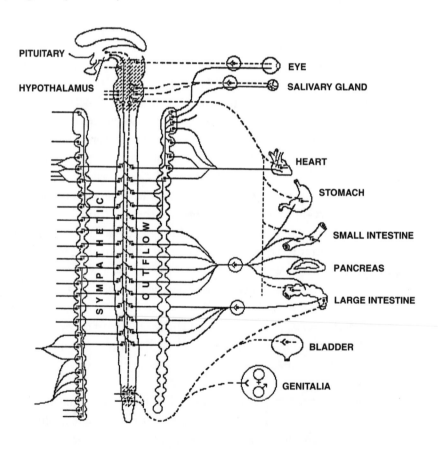

Fig. 5. Simplified Diagram of the Autonomic Nervous System[15]

This autonomic system is also called the involuntary nervous system because we do not govern our organs voluntarily. We can decide in our neocortex to open our fist, and our muscles do respond to our wish, but we cannot make the muscles of our heart or colon relax by thought or decision. Our internal organs are governed involuntarily by our autonomic or involuntary nervous system. That is, the muscles of our organs do not respond to our thought processes. The moods, emotions, and feelings—or whatever we want to name the dynamics occurring in the limbic brain system—are what regulate the expansive-relaxing or contractive-restrictive condition of all the organs of our body. Although our thoughts can affect our mood, it is our mood and not our thought that directly governs our heart and our colon.

At present a large percentage of Americans suffer heart attacks and ulcers, not to mention illnesses related to other organs. Yet we continue to talk about moody females or weak men. We cast aspersions on those who hug too much, cry too easily, or in other ways are too emotional. We don't complain about people who are too thoughtful. Could it be that we know the importance of thought, but as yet have not learned the importance of emotions? We know emotions are bothersome: they burst out, interrupting serious conversations, spoiling pleasant evenings, embarrassing us in restaurants in front of our friends. They make our children seem unmanageable. Could there be any significant reason that might justify their existence? Could it be our health?

For many years, doctors have known that the limbic brain governs emotions. They have sometimes referred to it as the mid-brain and sometimes "the visceral brain," indicating its relation to our visceral organs. The average person also knows that emotions relate to the viscera. We often experience contractions in the gut, the solar plexus, or even the heart area. Unfortunately, we refer to these contractions as tension or stress rather than understanding that they are emotions. We have mounted a medical campaign against stress as if we were fighting a new modern enemy, when in reality we are dealing with an age-old issue called emotions.

When will we take emotions seriously? Why do we even now avoid them, preferring the generalized banner of stress, suggesting relaxation, but never dealing with the full power of emotions? Relaxation will not make anger go away, although it does help us avoid it. It does not help us with sadness and cannot enable us to reach excitement. These are fundamental issues of emotions that both the medical and the psychological professions need to take seriously.

That which governs all the organs of our body deserves a better treatment. Emotions are the vibrations of the limbic brain, just as thought and imagination are the vibrations of the neocortex. Moods are to health as thought is to planning—necessary! If it were called the health brain instead of the emotional brain, it might help us to break through the barriers of our resistance to emotions.

A New Look at Emotions

Moods are not like thoughts:
    they do not begin with a capital and end with a period.
Nor are they like art:
    they cannot be framed, like a picture,
    or held, like a sculpture.
Moods permeate, more like fog:
    it's hard to tell when they begin, when they will lift,
    how thick they will get.
Clearly, we cannot access this brain as we did the neocortex.
Sometimes moods are like lightning, sometimes like thunder:
    they strike, they rumble.
If we stand in the wrong place, we get hit;
    it seems to rain before and after and during.
We are so often left to stand helpless and get drenched.

I*n any emotional scene we search for the reasons, trying to understand what happened. What caused all this, who's going to stop it, and when? We try to deal with moods by using our cause and effect training. It's a rational effort to help out, but it makes things worse: "I realize you're angry because you are . . ." "I am not!" and the mood escalates. It's as if we were sending a hot dagger into water: it sizzles and steams. In the case of hostile* emotions, rational efforts at understanding do not put out the fire. Even when we try to calm someone who is angry, we may find that person's anger turning against us.

What a bleak picture! It is clear why we have tried to suppress our emotions, why we have classified some as positive, some as negative, why we are unable or unwilling to express them. One way or another, we have all experienced the anguish of emotions, the race through past hurts and present inadequacies, the verbal sarcasm and attack, the rising tensions, and, always lurking in the background, possible physical violence—striking out, losing self-control, hurting a friend or loved one.

As a society we also consider emotions second to thought and action. We see emotions as a bothersome, unruly phenomenon that we first encounter in the "terrible twos" and must struggle with during adolescence. Emotions break up families and cause divorce. They show up in bizarre behavior, and we put people in mental institutions. They break out in violence, and we put people in prisons. We do not like emotions. They make us feel weak and out of control.

I must confess to the perfectly human wish that I could avoid the anger, hostility, and potential violence associated with the limbic brain. I am not sadistic. I also feel and hurt when people are sad and angry. Often I complain that God did it wrong. We are, however, confronted with a great physical reality: the limbic brain has been discovered, it is in each one of us, and it is chemically and physically different from the neocortex. We cannot access our emotions the same way we access our thoughts and images.

We have tried suppressing our feelings, tried avoiding, tried ignoring in favor of rational approaches. Rational approaches are fine, but they are rational, that is, processed in the neocortex rather than the limbic brain. We all know the difference between thought and emotion, but we keep on hoping that our intellect will get us through. We have also tried to contain our feelings by focusing on teaching values and correct behavior. Yet our anger has clearly not been improved by this approach: it has burst forth in violence on our streets and violence against ourselves in heart attacks and other illnesses. Our emotions lie in a deep and heretofore hidden place within our brains. In ignoring them, we have been lost in a cavern of our own darkness. Nevertheless, through research on the limbic brain and its natural chemicals, day by day a new light is entering into this darkness.

The limbic brain is a deeply interior system which we can learn to access. Emotions can be understood as the vibrations of the limbic brain, the energy which governs the health of all the organs of our body, including the heart and the guts. Knowing their central importance allows us to give our emotions a status which we once gave only to our thoughts and actions. Our new understanding of the limbic brain can help us discover the information in each of our emotions, just as we do with our thoughts, but we must remember that emotions are not thoughts. Emotions are a brain phenomenon, and just as we once learned and elaborated the thinking process, we can now learn and elaborate a full emotional process. We need a Bill of Rights for feelings in order to gain for our feelings the freedom we now grant our thoughts. This new approach will enable us to celebrate all emotions as positive, constructive forces in our lives. It can guide us toward feeling our emotions without the necessity of expressing them, thereby giving us the same interior space in which to train our feeling ability that we have had to train our thinking ability.

First Step: The Physiological Basis of Moods

CANDACE PERT (researcher on brain chemicals and emotions): To say, "I am feeling this," and to analyze that, your brain is of course coming into play. But there are many emotional messages that don't percolate up to your level of knowing them. Even so, they are used to run everything in your body.

BILL MOYERS (interviewer): . . . You're saying that my emotions are stored in my body?

PERT: Absolutely. . . .

. . . .

MOYERS: . . . So are you saying that it's the body's reaction that creates the emotions?

PERT: The body's and brain's reactions, yes. The body's everyday physiological functions, both normal and pathological, are creating emotions.[1]

Our new look at how to reach emotions must center itself in the human brain and recognize the physiological basis of all emotion. All the organs of our body are controlled by the limbic brain. New research indicates that the organs taken together form part of our autonomic or involuntary nervous system, which in turn is controlled by our limbic brain. The physiological reality, then, is that emotions, moods, feelings—whatever we want to call those dynamics that occur in the limbic brain—are what regulate the contraction-expansion condition of every organ in the body. What we have been calling emotions are really the tremendously important vibrations that govern the health of all organs. Our emotional brain is also our health brain.

Thus it is our moods, our emotions, rather than our thoughts, that govern the health of our body. Indirectly, our thoughts affect our moods, just as our moods affect our thoughts. However, many other elements, such as our actions, images, intuitions, nutrition, patterns of behavior, past history, and environment, also affect our moods. These elements are not filtered first through thought and then into moods, but impact our emotions directly. Indeed, the purpose of emotions may be to give us information that we do not assimilate through thought. Emotions are informational feedback from various systems directly into our body. Emotion is a brain phenomenon, vastly different from thought and deserving its own unique study and approach. Therefore, rather than thinking we can control emotion by thought, we need a direct approach to emotions if we wish to access their information.

The first step toward living intelligently with our moods is recognizing that they have a physiological basis within our brain; they are the language of our emotional brain. Moods are not whimsical states, selfish extras, bothersome states of bad behavior, external to our real essence. Moods are information coming from our limbic brain, just as thoughts are information coming from our neocortex.

Emotions will not end when we go to the therapist, nor when we discover the emotional impact of our mother or father on our early childhood, nor when our own children are grown up, nor when we have enough money to be happy, nor when we retire, nor when we withdraw into spiritual realms. Emotions will not end until we die. Therefore, we must identify them with our own existence and accept the physiological basis of all of our emotions—good and bad, positive and negative—in order to be able to treat them as signals of life itself and be able to search consciously for an intelligent way of processing them.

Once we have identified our emotions with our physical existence, we will be able to relate emotions to our own safety, health, power, and even creativity and energy. Revisioning the limbic brain as the second brain with its own life functions—providing information in the form of emotions and supplying energy to the organs of our body—will give us a new approach based on physiology.

Second Step: Equal Status with Thought and Action

The second step toward living intelligently with our emotions is giving them equal status with the other vibrations of our brain. Emotions are vibrations, just as thoughts and images and intuitions are vibrations. We need to bring them into that first-class family of thought and creativity. Kept apart, as second-class citizens capable of harm and violence, we are not likely to honor them, master them, or bring them into use on behalf of life.

Often people ask me why I do not just continue to use the words *feelings* and *emotions*, why I call these brain functions "mood intelligence" and "affectional intelligence." The answer is that my terms are meant to remind us that various forms of energy vibration are all that is happening inside our skulls. Vibration is the common denominator, the common language of mind. Energy is vibrated differently in our three brain structures. Thoughts, images, emotions, intuitions, and actions are all vibrational forms of life, containing information. They are different processes, but all are energy waves occurring within an area of our brain system. All vibrations are equally available for access whenever we choose to focus on them. Sometimes focusing on our feelings may save our life, as in the importance of joy and pleasure to healing. Sometimes focusing on our thoughts will be life-giving and promote our healing. When we call all brain processes "vibrations"—forms of "intelligence"—we remind ourselves to drop our singular reliance on rational thought and to transcend our modern prejudice against emotions.

Third Step: Emotions as Keys to the Interior Life

The third step toward an intelligent approach to emotions involves the process of accessing and staying with our emotional vibrations. Just as we learned and practiced thinking over many years, we now need to learn and practice the emotional processes. I discuss more fully the necessary processes of each emotional intelligence later, but I would like to make two points here that I believe are essential to taking a new look at emotions.

First, in order to enter the vibrational range of feeling, so very different from the thinking or the acting range, we need to be able to slow down. To feel is a slow process. It often cannot be done when we are talking rapidly, concentrating on content, or trying to communicate with others. We can of course rant and rage with words and feel the heat in our body. However, we cannot at the same time access what we are really wanting that lies behind our anger.

We may have a habit of speaking at a beta range of vibration, associated with the left hemisphere, or at a slower alpha range, associated with the right hemisphere. Feeling, however, is associated with an even slower range labeled in brain research alpha or theta vibration. Accessing this deeper range of feeling may require a new practice. I have called it a feeling meditation. It is different from the usual neocortical meditation in which we let go by and continually clear the screen of our mind, separating ourselves from all vibration in order to go to the thinnest levels. Here in the limbic brain, in this emotional meditation of feeling, we do let thoughts and images go by, but only in order to hold with the thicker ranges of feeling until we are affected and able to receive the information involved in our feeling.

EXERCISE

FEELING MEDITATION

Give yourself at least twenty minutes to practice this meditation.

1. *Select music that relaxes you, make yourself comfortable, and begin to listen. It is better to choose music of a slow vibration so that it does not carry you into the faster vibrations of intuitional meditation.*
2. *Visualize the situation that affects you.*
3. *Permit yourself to feel the first emotional reaction that comes.*
4. *This first reaction or this first feeling makes you feel . . . .*
5. *If thoughts enter, focus your consciousness on how they make you feel.*

6. *Using abdominal breathing, continue to go deeper, allowing one feeling to lead to another until you discover the information that feels important. You will be able to feel when you have reached a valuable message. It feels different from thinking: you will not want to continue; you will feel a satisfaction. Whether or not you later judge the message to be agreeable or disagreeable, you will be glad you found it, because it feels deep and real.*

Feeling is a practice that can give you access to your interior life and consequently a new look at emotions. Once you have practiced the Feeling Meditation, you will more easily be able to feel your feelings as you move through your everyday activities.

To go deeper into the feeling range, we also have to be willing to refuse the interference of vibrations that come from the neocortex and the basic brain. If we want to stay in a feeling long enough to receive the information it brings or to go more deeply into our interior life, we need to free ourselves of any need to come to conclusions or decide on actions based on feelings. Of course it is possible to feel and act as a result of an emotion, but often it is not advisable. If we deal with a mood as if it were the only reality that drives us to a conclusion or to action, we can make many mistakes. For example, if we feel sad we can remain quiet and be deeply involved in sobbing or crying. However, it is neither this quietness nor our crying state that can cause our difficulty. What causes a problem is rather the conclusion or actions that follow. "I'm sad because my boss doesn't give me a raise. He probably doesn't appreciate me or doesn't think I'm competent. Therefore [conclusion], I'm not going to make any more efforts. Really, now I am definitely going to change jobs [action]." The neocortex mutters on, with you imagining your boss's criticism, then defending against what you imagine, every thought moving you further and further from your own quiet, sad emotion. You feel the need to think or act and have no experience at practicing the feeling of sadness until it reveals something important to you. Or you may feel anger, but instead of giving yourself permission to feel your anger and find the message that is coming from within you, you react to external stimuli only and decide to quit your job.

In love, immediate reactions can be equally disastrous. I feel bad because a certain special friend did not call. I conclude, "He really doesn't love me," or even worse, "Nobody will ever love me. I'll never be happy again." I make judgments and create absolutes. This is how we use rational or not-so-rational thoughts against ourselves. We rush to conclusion or move into action because we do not have experience with our emotions. Either they make us uncomfortable, or we do not take the time to feel the emotion deeply enough to get its message or to understand what it is trying to tell us that might deeply affect our life. We are conditioned to think or act but not to feel. It does not have to be this way. Our feelings, our moods are states of consciousness. They belong to our private, internal world. We can learn to stay in our internal emotional world without interference. Learning to feel is learning to travel in our internal world.

Fourth Step: Feeling and Expressing Emotions

How can we express what we are feeling? The way we express our emotions depends on our training and what is permitted in our culture. Also it depends on the more developed aspect of our brain and life experience. Some people are better speakers; others see images and use metaphor to express their feelings. Art is very often a tangible expression of deep feelings. Feelings are expressed through the body of the dancer, through the body and speech of the actor, through the eyes and hands of the sculptor, through the sounds of the musician, and through the words of the writer and the poet.

Sometimes we liberate our feelings through speech, other times through actions or dreams, other times by touching or by the language of the body. Our body is the face of our emotions. The language of emotions is written not only in the movement and gestures of the body but also in the formations of the body as it has developed through the years in interaction with life experience. The body reveals our emotional experience and shows us the forms through which we have been expressing ourselves. "Life makes shapes. . . . If we could photograph our lives and show them frame by frame, we would see that we are moving sequences of varying emotional shapes."[2] We can discover our emotional history through the study of pictures of our body, our face, our shape at different periods of our lives. We can understand our emotional history not by chronological age but by the different shapes evident in the pictures.

How can we increase the freedom of expression of our body? We can become conscious of and attribute meaning to the gestures and shapes of our body. We can interest ourselves in feeling and allow the feeling to consciously move into all the areas of our body as well as be expressed by the movement of our body. Finally, we can realize that our body expresses our feelings just as language and voice express our words.

Medicine has studied the body as genetic inheritance, as an object of health, and as indispensable for movement. Now we also need to study the body as the expression of feelings. How we see ourselves affects how we feel. How we feel affects how we see ourselves. How we feel affects how we form ourselves as well as express ourselves. Our clothes may be an external expression of our body, but the language of somatics is indeed more subtle. The development of muscles, the form, the gestures, the skin, the configurations surrounding the structure of the bones—every part of your figure reveals how the language of your body was formed and shaped over time.

EXPRESSION WITH OTHERS

Whatever modality we use to express our feelings—by body, voice, words, intuitions, or signs of any kind—however we allow our deepest energy to emerge, this energy connects with other human beings. When we are in love, we reveal to the other our deepest feelings, and this evokes the other person's deepest feelings. We feel intimate with the other. Feeling deeply and revealing our feelings is what we call the process of intimacy. This process of loving and being excited stops only when we cease to deepen within ourselves, and that is what happens when we are hurting or scared or when for any reason we stop revealing and expressing our deep feeling. We begin, then, to cover up, to hide, and the energy connections disappear, reappear, and little by little disappear. We have all been in that no man's land of disconnection and boredom, where we are unable to feel deeply and afraid to reveal ourselves to others. Very often we need a heated discussion to return to our energy and reconnect with a loved one.

Instead of just experiencing a feeling reaction in immediate response to the environment, we can develop the conscious ability of deepening within ourselves by means of feeling and of practicing the many ways of expressing ourselves through words, images, dreams, and touching, through body and movement.

We also need to be aware that we cannot really hide our feelings because they are always showing in some way. The depth of our being is showing in either visible form or subtle movement. We must stop thinking we can hide from one another. Privacy is important as a political notion—it is useful to protect our vote, useful for equal rights—but privacy in the human domain does not really exist. We are inextricably linked one to the other through vibrations at a very deep cellular level, within our mind-body system and more precisely through the exposure of our basic brain to the environment.

There may be no need to let go of the subtle arts of subterfuge so intricately involved in our seductions and our gaming. However, the need certainly exists of realizing that hiding is just a game, supported by years of thinking of ourselves as separate bodies in a mechanistic system of different parts rather than in an interconnected vibratory system of energy. Feelings and their expression are basic to continuous intimacy, and they can add increased honesty and depth to our life together. In Chapter Ten on mood intelligence, I discuss how to manage and express feelings without doing harm to others.

EXPRESSION VERSUS REPRESSION

Psychologists are now engaged in a great debate about whether or not it is healthful or harmful to express feelings verbally. If we suppress negative feelings, won't they harm our body and cause illness? If we express them, will we become entrapped in them? The energy of emotions either affects us internally or is expressed externally. If we do not express our feelings, won't the repression cause illness in our body? Or perhaps momentary repression might cause us to burst out in sudden violence against someone weaker when we least expect it. On the other hand, if we express our sad or angry feelings, will others become sad or angry? Could we develop the habit of being an angry or sad person? Yes, to all of the above. The issue of emotions does indeed engage us all in this great debate of how to deal with our energy: whether it should be expressed with others or whether it can be managed internally without causing illness.

How can we express the chaotic vibrations of our anger without harming, insulting, provoking, or even attacking others? If we express too much joy, too much happiness, will others be jealous? If we express pride or jealousy, what will others think of us? We seem to be trapped between repressing feelings and harming ourselves or expressing them and hurting others.

There is, however, a way out of this trap. New light from brain research does indeed help create new possibilities. The new light is that both our pleasurable and our painful emotions are registered in the long-term memory of our limbic brain, more specifically in the area known as the hippocampus. This means that our emotional history is recorded in our brain for immediate access or retrieval whenever we really want to express it. We no longer need to be either a victim of immediate expression or a victim of repression and subsequent illness. More precisely, we can always have access to any emotional situation and express our feelings whenever we decide it is appropriate. Instant expression is not necessary. It is no longer expression versus repression. It is express when appropriate or access emotions for our personal knowledge. If we repress our emotions at a certain moment because we do not know how to express them without doing harm, we can then give ourselves the time to feel our feelings in the situation and find a way either to deal with them internally or express them.

The old choices were express and make outer trouble or repress and make inner trouble. Since we know that the information is stored in our brain, expression can come at a time of our choosing. In this way we can save ourselves and our loved ones from the terrible things we are all likely to say when we vent our feelings in immediate reaction to a situation. The threat of repression and the trap of immediate expression have both been lifted with the knowledge that our long-term memory is in our limbic brain of emotions. A new look is now possible.

Let us distinguish between feeling and expressing feelings. To become conscious of our feelings, we need to give ourselves permission to feel our emotions: to be in them, to feel free to explore them, intensify them, ride them, shift from them, or hold onto the vibration until it yields its significance or intelligence. The freedom to feel first requires the freedom to feel without the obligation of immediate expression.

I believe our emphasis on expressing feelings has inhibited our freedom to feel. Imagine you felt obliged to express *all* your thoughts. What kind of world would it be? We think continually and express only some of our thoughts. Why should we feel obliged to express all our feelings? Let us begin to access this brain more deeply by focusing on feeling first without adding the burden of conscious expression.

GUIDELINES FOR SAFE EXPRESSION

I cannot counsel anyone to express all their feelings freely. I can suggest a few guidelines that may provide enough safety for you to begin the practice of conscious expression of your feelings when you consider it appropriate or choose to do so. While you learn, you can begin by practicing in private, in small groups, and in your family. These guidelines are for safe expression either alone or with someone who has expressed willingness to practice with you.

1. Find a place in your home where you can express your feelings in private. If you really want to protect your nervous system, your home has to become a temple in which your life is sacred—all of your life, including your emotions. If you do not want to violate the world with inappropriate expressions or violate your body and harm your internal organs by repressing emotions, then you need a protected area where you can practice expressing your feelings in private without consequences.

2. It may be possible to inform your family or persons living or working closely with you that feelings are important to your health and nervous system, because feelings, not thoughts, are what are expanding and contracting, relaxing or stressing the organs of your body. For the health of your body, you need permission to express your feelings without others believing they are the target or the cause of what you are feeling.

3. Feelings do permeate, whether you want them to or not. Whatever you are feeling—be it sadness, anger, or joy—these feelings will permeate the atmosphere. Only you can be responsible for and understand the origin of your feelings. Therefore, you can clearly ask others to disconnect from seeing themselves as the cause. Your feelings are a part of your emotional history stored in the long-term memory of your limbic brain. This last moment of be-

ing angry is only the latest in a long history of getting mad at exactly the same thing. Only you can find the mote in your eye and take it out. Family, friends, and colleagues may be able to give you that freedom; they may not. You may need to withdraw to the privacy of your own room for the expression of your feelings, or else explicitly remind others each time that they are not the cause of your emotion.

4. If you explode, you can always apologize.

5. When expressing feelings, always use "I," never "you." The habit of using "you" reinforces the old idea that the other person is the cause. It always provokes conflict and keeps the argument going. By identifying your feelings with "I," you are owning them, and it is easier to ask others to let you have your freedom to feel without seeing themselves as the target or the cause. "I feel mad" is always better than "You make me angry." It is the way you have stored experience in your own brain that makes you angry, sad, or joyful.

6. You can always express feelings in the shower, your own bedroom, or any other private territory. You can punch pillows or make faces in the mirror instead of at family and friends.

7. Be careful not to use food or drink or sex as a replacement for feeling your feelings and accessing their meaning.

In short, you can:

- Feel continuously and be conscious of your feeling.
- Feel without the need to express yourself verbally.
- Express feelings through different modalities of words, art, facial expressions, body movements, or sounds. All mediums express the message.
- Express when you find it appropriate. First please study and practice the above guidelines and the exercises on sadness and anger in the chapter on mood intelligence.
- Listen and receive the expression of others. Remember not to take responsibility for what they are feeling.
- Live in a process of feeling, receiving, and responding in a resonance ever more intimate and more expansive.

Fifth Step: Shifting out of Emotions

Getting out of a mood or feeling is often a stumbling block. As long as we believe there is only one reality, then we are easily able to trap ourselves and our whole personality into one mood and only one reality. I am angry, and this is my truth. However, it is only one of my truths, one of my realities, into which I am heavily focused, and from which I am unwilling to shift. Our anger or our joy feels like US. It fills us until it feels like our integrity and OUR TRUTH. For sure it becomes our PRIDE—and we get stuck in the feeling.

We cannot become emotionally intelligent unless we have both the ability to focus into an emotion and the equally important ability to shift from it. By the very nature of emotions, they spread within us and fill us. Emotions can become intense. They have no limits and therefore we can easily become entrapped within them. It is difficult to remember the possibility of shifting from them because there is such an involvement that we feel as if our emotion is the only reality. It is easier to shift from thinking, imagining, or intuiting, because these do not fill us and permeate us as emotions do.

The nature of feeling is becoming involved and surrounded by, so our pride also becomes easily hooked as we insist on only one reality, the one we are feeling in that moment. We need to believe beforehand in the existence of multiple realities in order to help ourselves shift away from an emotion. The practice of shifting away from emotions and focusing into another brain system becomes easier and more real when our belief system includes the existence of multiple realities. There is no need for us to be victims of our emotions. We can learn to focus into them and shift away from them whenever it seems appropriate. We can consciously govern our limbic brain.

CHAPTER VIII

Through the Limbic Territory

CHARTING THE EMOTIONAL PROCESS

*O*ur limbic brain has been functioning *within us all our life. As we become conscious of our feelings, we also experience a tremendous uncertainty about how to live with them and be acceptable socially. Living and exploring the territory of emotions, most of us have had harmful experiences that have made us determined to limit our emotional life. "I'm not going to love any more; it hurts too much." "He never really loved me." "It's not worth getting angry." "Even when I feel happy, people get jealous." "Life is depressing; a great deal of suffering seems inevitable."*

What has confused us most, I believe, is the lack of guidance and the sense of insecurity that accompanies exploring the unknown, especially a territory so marked by conflict, sexuality, taboos, and family hurt. What is the emotional process? Can we know ahead of time how we got involved? Are we always vulnerable? Sensitive to everything? What makes us happy, sad, mad? Are emotions a mystery yet to be solved?

It is certain that emotions are our internal vibrations and as such are unique to the individual. But then so is the thinking process, the visual process, and all other processes that vibrate within the confines of our brain systems. Our uniqueness is how we manage the processes; it does not prevent us from identifying elements of the process. Indeed, by elaborating mental, emotional and behavioral processes, we make them more easily available and, I believe, enhance and speed up the evolution of humanity. Elaboration of the rational process has contributed to our scientific advancement. It is to be hoped that elaboration of our emotional process will contribute to our humanistic advancement.

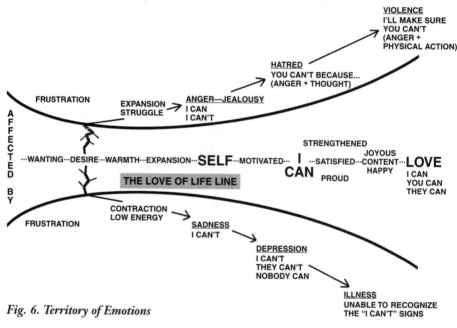

Fig. 6. Territory of Emotions

This printed map attempts to chart a pathway through the limbic territory, which you might use at least to return to safety when you sense danger or experience harm. There is a main highway with side roads clearly indicated to help you know where you are traveling and to provide some indication of what is ahead if you keep going in the same direction.

Getting Involved: Acceptance

Strong emotions seem to surprise us. How could I be so angry? What am I really so excited about? How did I get so involved? There is a process by which we can chart our emotional involvement. We become involved by first accepting the existence of anything: the presence of a person, the sound of music, the sun's setting, the existence of bills, our spouse's request for something, or the sadness of our child. Very often we pass over these daily events and people in our lives with the hope that they will not bother us. If we continue to do so, we can avoid being consciously involved. However, we will also be denying the existence of significant people and events, and they will have some effect on us. More particularly, they will absorb our energy without our being conscious of it. We will simply say we are bored or tired.

If we wish to become conscious of our emotional process, we must begin by accepting the existence of other people, objects, or situations. We then consciously allow ourselves to be affected, perhaps little by little, perhaps all at once. We may select one aspect of the situation, or we may let the whole thing bombard us. To allow ourselves to be affected, we need to slow down, to stop our rapid thought process, and to prepare ourselves to be affected. We need to shift our energy from active to receptive. If I wish to be affected by my family when I arrive home at night, I must begin by slowing down on my way home. When I put my hand on the doorknob, I must consciously invite myself to be affected and shift to a slower range of vibration that will permit me to feel.

GETTING HOOKED: WANTING AND DESIRE

Once we are affected, either we want more of the person, object, or situation, or we want to solve, resolve, or get out. The point is, once desire hits, we are already involved. Once we want to do something with what we have allowed to affect us, our limbic brain is hooked. Wanting and desiring is the vibration of this brain system. Once stimulated, only achieving at least some of what we desire brings satisfaction.

Whether we have the power to satisfy our desires produces or colors the resultant gamut of emotions. I therefore identify the emotions in terms of personal power: whether we can or cannot get what we want. To be sure, emotions vary in tone, in depth, and in intensity of vibration. To be sure, each emotion communicates information that is extremely subtle. By describing the emotional process in terms of personal power, I do not wish to diminish the great variation of emotions. Rather, I want you to grasp the importance of emotions in your life and enable you to feel safe by taking emotions out of their elusive wrappings so that you can experience them in all their variations. You may wish to follow along on the map as we continue to unravel the emotional process.

SATISFACTION OF DESIRE: WARMTH AND EXPANSION

Say we want to win the game, solve a problem, listen to our child, or get closer to someone we love. The more we are able to do that, to satisfy our desire, the more we will experience a physical reaction in our body of warmth and expansion. We feel good, and that feeling warms us and expands us, giving a sense of well-being.

EXPANSION TO MOTIVATION

The more we desire and the more expanded we become by satisfying our desire, the more motivated we become. We want to do it more, better, deeper, again. We indeed move ourselves to win other games, solve more problems, listen more carefully to our child, or get even closer to our loved one. We want, we satisfy, we expand, and this expansion continues the emotional process into motivation. Affectional intelligence began the process; now we move into motivational intelligence.

MOTIVATION TO "I CAN"

The more motivated we become, the more we move to accomplish again and again until more and more deeply we feel, I CAN. My wanting and my power are one.

"I CAN" TO STRENGTH, SATISFACTION, PRIDE

Realizing that I can, that I am satisfying my desire; I feel strong in that domain and a feeling of satisfaction emerges. To be able makes us feel satisfied, feel well within us. We may also feel proud. We were able: we wanted, we moved to satisfy our desire, we became strong, and we feel proud. Most of us have felt that in our work, with our families, or with our loved ones. It is a tremendously healthy feeling of well-being. Sometimes we say "a job well done"; sometimes we just feel good. Pride has had bad press, because sometimes instead of just feeling proud within ourselves, we seek to compare ourselves with others, concluding we are the only ones who can and that others cannot.

TO CONTENTMENT, HAPPINESS, JOY

The feelings of strength, pride, and satisfaction lead into more expansive feelings of contentment and happiness. This is an emotion we all wish to feel, but it is important to notice that it doesn't drop in from the clouds. Happiness is related to feeling satisfied, and satisfaction is related to something we desire. Joy is the expansion of happiness into a more ecstatic feeling, a delicate vibration related to happiness and contentment. The emotional scale amplifies and varies. It is up to us to concentrate into the feeling, to allow ourselves to be more deeply affected by happiness or joy, and to be willing to protect how we're affected by refusing consciously to allow in doubt and distraction. To hold the note and let it expand through our body-being is indeed to cherish emotion at its best.

TO LOVE

When we are content, happy, and joyful, we are prepared to feel love. It is as if we were wearing rose-colored glasses. By now, not only I can, but you and they can, and everyone can. This is the initial state of love. For all we try to bombard new lovers with our doubts and difficulties, they are just sure that they can satisfy their desires, and they continue to be motivated, strong, and happy. They express joy, and all their being communicates joy. It is easy to tell when someone is feeling love and loved. It is easy to understand why all great philosophies and religions preach love. It is important, however, to realize that love also does not just happen.

You are in a good mood, feeling some satisfaction with yourself when you "look across that crowded room" and find the other. You are willing to desire and want and move yourself to become even closer. You see a work that attracts you or an idea, and you are willing to desire and want. You move closer until you fall in love with the work or idea or person. Love is a feeling, and indeed the most expansive and powerful of all the feelings. I can; you can; we all can. Love is important to us individually, important to the world. Can we learn the process?

So far we have followed the main highway from acceptance to love. It is important to know this highway and to practice staying on it. When you drive off the road, remember there are signs leading you back on. Focus on the possible. Satisfy any desire. Move yourself. Look for one "I can," and you will be back to driving on the main road. Focus on something in your life that will make you feel proud or at least content. Amplify these feelings; they all take you to that most expansive feeling of love.

The Side Roads

But wait a minute: we have all fallen off this road, wandered off, deliberately driven off, or been unable to find our way back to happiness and love. Emotions are all the sounds of the orchestra. None of us has been able to stay perpetually in satisfaction, happiness, and love. Most of us have tried to limit our desires so we don't feel so dissatisfied. Some of us have escaped desires altogether or at least escaped admitting we have them by seeking refuge in the neocortical brain of thought and spirit or the basic brain of work and action. What is the process when we cannot find any way to satisfy our desire? What happens when our desire is blocked by the desires of others or by the events of our everyday life?

When we are unable to satisfy our desires, when we want tremendously but our power to achieve what we want is blocked, we respond by either a process of loss or a process of struggle. We either abandon our power or we struggle to get it back. Both processes are difficult to manage.

PROCESS OF LOSS

When we think or feel that we cannot or when we have tried and failed to satisfy our desire, we lose energy. The expanded energy of desire contracts, and we begin to feel low, bored, tired, or sad.

Bored. As you become conscious of feeling bored, ask yourself what you were last interested in that you let go of. Or, what are you really interested in? At some point you abandoned that quest.

Tired. When you feel tired, realize that you were actively involved in something. When did you begin to feel tired? What was occurring that you did not wish to enter or hold with? Where did you decide or feel that you couldn't?

Sad and Depressed. This is the deeper stage of feeling loss, the feeling of sadness. Know that there may be genuine and real loss involved. If you have reached the lowest energy stage of depression, know that you have been repeatedly sad, that you have had repeated losses. Accept your feeling response and begin to identify the losses. Know the territory. Realize that your emotional process involves an intelligent response to people or events in your world. Do not blame the world or conclude that you can never feel good again. Seek the information and use it to respond to your life. For energy and stamina, drive back to the main highway whenever possible. See the chapter on mood intelligence for responding to and healing sadness.

PROCESS OF STRUGGLE

We may have an active response when our power is blocked. We may struggle. First there are feelings of frustration: we are aware of what we want and aware that we cannot get it. Very often our feelings of frustration are directed at blaming others. We are trying, and they won't let us. We are doing our best, and they are not cooperating. Or even worse, they are out to get us; they are intent on preventing us from achieving. If this continues, we might go from a normal focus on the other as a cause of our circumstance to a full-blown paranoia.

Anger. As frustration intensifies it becomes anger. We are now committed to the struggle. Anger is both "I can" and "I cannot." It is the angst, the mixture of thinking or feeling that we can and, as we experience rejection, thinking, and feeling that we can't. If we had decided that we couldn't, we would have fallen into sadness. It is this positive struggle for life that gives us the phenomenon of anger. Anger is really a sign of life. We are at least struggling to achieve what we want rather than giving up. However, the more blocked we become, the angrier we get. The dynamic between I can and I can't continues until something is resolved. We need to train ourselves not to deliver our anger to others but to learn how to own our anger as an expression of our desire and how to manage it in peaceful ways that do not harm others. Do not deny anger, but learn how to deal with it in mood intelligence.

Jealousy. If you cannot manage or heal your anger, it may extend itself into jealousy and envy, two feelings that are really the same as anger, only focused directly on a person. I can have what she has, only really I can't, but maybe I can. The struggle continues.

Hatred. Anger forms the basis of hatred. Hatred is basically "I can, but I can't deal with you, and therefore I will isolate you. I will go to my neocortex and find the reasons you are not worth associating with." In that way I camouflage my "I can't" and satisfy myself by rejecting you. My conclusion is I hate you and therefore don't need to deal with you. Behind all hatred, no matter how many reasons or justifications may be offered, is an old feeling of anger that the person or group or country does not want to deal with or does not know how to deal with.

Violence. "I can, and I can't deal with you, so I'll make sure you can't." It is once again the same anger that the person, group, or country was unable or unwilling to deal with. This time the anger leads into the basic brain of action and bursts out in a physical expression of violence. It may be accompanied by the thought-out justifications called hatred, or it may be a direct and immediate expression of anger-in-violence.

What is most important to recognize about these side roads is that they begin with desire, which may even have reached the stages of love. Even in its earlier stages, if we are affected by something, we desire something, and we love something. But if love is blocked, the emotional process may take us directly into sadness and depression or into frustration, anger, jealousy, hatred and violence. One practical implication of recognizing that love and desire are buried beneath violence is the need not only to provide women with temporary shelters from abuse, but also to provide both men and women with education about the love and anger that is dictating their violence. It is not punishment, but rather anger education that is needed. America focused its attention for over a year on O. J. Simpson, holding its breath over the final outcome of guilty or not guilty, some waiting for punishment, others glad about his release. Did we miss the real issue that love can turn to physical abuse and may indeed end in the extreme of murder? Could we take that long experience and translate it into a national action in favor of emotional education? Instead of clamoring for justice and punishment, could we clamor for emotional intelligence?

If we are to become emotionally intelligent, we must become aware of the emotional process leading to love, or love lost falling into sadness and depression, or love blocked rising into anger, hatred, and violence. These are all variations of the emotional symphony. They are connected, and we can learn to sort them out and play them more consciously, entering into and shifting from. I am sure that there are descriptions of other emotional processes and emotional territories. All of them are welcome as we seek to enter our inner world of emotions.

I have described the emotional process only as it deals with the major responses to desire: the response of satisfaction that leads to love, the response of loss that leads to sadness, and the response of struggle that leads to anger. Love is elaborated further in the chapters on the three emotional intelligences. Sadness and anger are elaborated in the chapter on mood intelligence. Many other emotions exist that are not charted on this territory and that are described in mood intelligence under emotional scales.

Three major emotions are missing from this chart. Worry, fear, and guilt are usually considered emotions, and it is certain that there is a distinguishable feeling of worry, another of fear, and another of guilt. However, worry, fear, and guilt seem to be more related to the process of action or more accurately to our inability to act. They form part of an anxiety process that indeed can be felt but can mainly be healed by referring to the action process and behavioral intelligences of the basic brain. Please turn to the last chapter and include the anxiety process for a greater understanding of its relationship to emotions as well as actions.

CHAPTER IX

Love

AFFECTIONAL INTELLIGENCE

Perhaps Madame de Stael was indeed conscious of affectional intelligence when she was presenting her latest young lover to a group of friends at her villa on Lac Leman. She overheard one of her guests saying that the young man seemed not to have much facility with social language and immediately replied: "Ah, speech is not his language."

I remember the passionate moments of my life with excitement. I say I love passion, but how much passion will I dare to experience? Where can I find it? Do I reserve it for falling in love, or can I become passionate over a plate of spaghetti? Do I need a problem, an issue, an argument to provoke or stimulate passion in me? Or can I decide consciously when to become passionate? Am I passionate with people, with ideas, or only with traditions and values? Is it good to be passionate? Or are passionate people too emotional, too disruptive, too unstable?

Affectional intelligence is the capacity to be affected by a person, place, object, idea, or situation. The process extends from attraction to passion. It includes being able to begin and to end involvement. We govern the extent, the intensity, and the length of the affectional process. Affectional intelligence is the process of loving: to allow ourselves to be attracted, affected, and then deeply affected. When we cease to be affected by the greatness of the other, we fall out of love. To be affected is to feel: to feel deeply, to feel moved, to feel connected, or just to feel without description. We feel, are moved deeply, and don't want to characterize it any further.

People become affectionally intelligent by how they manage their feeling process, just as they become rationally intelligent by how they manage their rational process. Implicit in affectional intelligence is the capacity to select what they wish to be affected by and to what degree. They need to be able consciously to begin the process of feeling and consciously shift from it. Although people with affectional intelligence may be attracted and entrained in an immediate reaction of feeling, they are aware that this is only one of their many realities, and they are able to shift their focus and concentration to another attractive alternative. Affectional intelligence is the way out of being a victim in the external net of circumstances we call fate or destiny in the Western world and maya or karma in the Eastern.

Affectional intelligence is a key to conscious internal living in relation to the rest of the world. Just as we act and think in relation to the world, so too do we feel in relation to the world. We are born into an environment, and we learn to act in relationship to this environment. We go to school to learn to think in relation to our environment. We go to churches and temples to learn to relate to the thinnest waves of our environment. But there is no conscious learning about how to feel in relation to our environment. We let ourselves be affected by our milieu, and we try to control our emotional reactions by means of what we know how to do well: think, imagine, and intuit in our neocortex or act with our basic brain.

Nevertheless, vibrations keep happening in our limbic brain whether or not we are conscious of them. Unfortunately, we don't become conscious until really harmful events occur that demand our attention: a divorce, the loss of a job, a heart attack, or the serious illness of one of our internal digestive organs. If we are not aware of our feelings, the vibrations of contraction will continue into constriction until this provokes a physical reaction of illness or a psychological reaction of crisis. Because of our lack of emotional education since birth, we end up looking for help in the private practices of psychologists or medical doctors. True, we do need to solve crisis and heal illness when they occur. However, with knowledge of the limbic brain, we now know that formal emotional education from our earliest years would prevent a great many crises and illnesses.

Neocortex and Limbic Brain: Conscious Partnership

Your neocortex is the gatekeeper of your limbic brain. Depending on what you think is going to happen if you let yourself be affected by different emotions, you do or do not give yourself permission to feel them. You can discover which emotions you have permission to feel by doing the Gatekeeper exercise near the end of this chapter.

If your expectation when you are sad is that you will never stop crying and your world will get even worse, then that expectation is not helping you to feel sadness. If you expect to cry when you are sad and believe that crying will help relax you, then you have permission to feel your sadness.

However, if like Roger you have associated crying with feminine weakness, you are not going to permit yourself to feel sad. Roger insisted on living within very narrow parameters of his business, refusing to be affected by other people or events in his life. His business activity consumed him. He knew only how to analyze continually and tried to apply his rational approach to everything, even his children. What worked in business didn't work too well in his family, however. His children were always looking for affection, while he was always offering suggestions for improvement. It didn't matter whether he was offering advice on relationships, on math, on language, or on how to be a better son or a smarter businessman. He was sure he loved his children, but what was missing was allowing himself to be affected by them. He considered affection a sign of weakness. It never occurred to him that affection was a form of intelligence that could greatly improve the capacity of his own mind as well as that of his children's minds.

Unfortunately, this story may resonate with many men because our culture has been dedicated to classifying affection and love as a feminine affair. Men may be affectional but mainly in the context of sexual performance. However, men and women may now choose whatever is most necessary or appropriate to feel to improve their life. We don't have to keep repressing feeling or hiding from feeling if we know the secret of

selecting consciously and focusing into whatever will make our life better each day. Selection implies that we may avoid or choose not to feel a
great deal of what is occurring throughout the day. It means that we
realize we cannot let all of the many things happening around us affect
us deeply. We must select if we are to avoid continuous crisis as well as be
genuine in our feelings. We can also select the time in which we are
going to let ourselves be affected by the difficult emotions. We need
time in order to deepen into our feelings to discover their information
or message.

Every day we make our own heaven or hell based on what we decide
to let affect us. Our neocortical capacity to select wisely is crucial. It is the
neocortex and limbic brain functioning together that can free us from
simple chain reactions and enable us to govern our lives consciously. If
we allow ourselves to be deeply affected by the worst events of our lives,
we will indeed be living a hell on this earth until we finally get sick or give
up feeling. On the other hand, if we let ourselves select and be affected by
the beauty and great events that surround us, we can live paradise here on
earth. Experiment with this by doing the Heaven or Hell exercise near
the end of this chapter.

Health and Vitality

The problem related to affectional intelligence is that it can be like
opening a floodgate and not knowing how to close it. If we decide to be
affected, we can indeed be touched by all of the emotions. We usually
close this floodgate on affection, love, and passion because we have had
bitter experiences of being unsafe and feeling that we are unable to swim
in such turbulent waters. Usually we pull out of feelings with such neocortical decisions as "Never again!" "Life's too short!" "It's not worth it!"
"Who needs it?" We are learning that, indeed, we may all need it. We
may need to learn how to be affected, how to love with all of its implications, if for no other reason than for our health.

The heart is the major killer of Americans. Exercise entrains the
muscle system and stimulates the circulation of blood. However, feelings
are internal exercise! It is our feelings or moods that are continually expanding or contracting our heart, and it is our heart that is pumping the
blood throughout our body and into our brain. Thus the prevention of

strokes, heart attacks, and illnesses related to our internal organs may depend on our capacity to feel our emotions, guiding them in a continuous process of expansion and contraction.

We often fall in love, enter a beautiful process of expansion and contraction until something goes wrong, and then give up. We expand once, and then enter into conscious withdrawal and contraction, which, if we do not change, can turn into constriction, entropy, paralysis, and death. What else can we do? We can allow ourselves to be affected for even short periods of time and then shift, before going more deeply. We can also learn to continue into deeper affection and even into profound states of love if we know how to live through the moods involved and how to shift when necessary. Knowing that feeling affected is only one of our realities, we can learn to shift to other realities involving thought, imagination, or action but little feeling. We have the choice of deepening into emotion or the choice of shifting out of emotion into the other brain systems.

Indeed, knowing that we can shift consciously is one of the great reasons for being aware that we have three brain systems, each one capable of being accessed independently of the other. To feel is a choice, a freedom, a decision to enter the range of feelings, as clearly as when we choose to read a book or take a trip.

Blocked Energy and Entropy

What is the point of being affected by anything or anyone? Why not escape? Why *not* live in our heads? Health is only one reason. The quality of our life and the fullness of our energy every day is another reason. When life presents us with people, ideas, or situations that we are afraid of or don't know how to handle, we avoid them and block our energy as a result. We may be either blocking our energy or refusing to be replenished by the constant flow of energy in the universe and more specifically, around us and very close to us, as in the people, ideas or events of our daily life.

First, energy or life itself will come back into our body, and we will feel more fully ourselves as soon as we recognize what frightened or blocked us. Then we can come to some internal decision about what to do. If we chose to escape or avoid at the moment of the first experience, we can now look again and relive the experience. This time we can give ourselves the permission and the luxury of full feeling. There is neither hurry nor outside threat. There is only our internal self longing to be known.

Our emotional brain serves to detect and register information at this deeper level and will provide a blocking of energy or drag affect until it can get the attention of our neocortex or basic brain of action. The emotional brain registers past hurts in our long-term memory. Our emotional memory then cautions us against repeating painful mistakes, but unfortunately it has no verbal language and can speak to us only through fear or avoidance or simple energy blocking. It slows us down, fatigues us, or robs us of energy. The emotional brain seeks to be heard. Just as our neocortex provides a constant chatter of thoughts or images, our emotional brain provides constant signaling. If we are not hearing or heeding these signals, they will increase their effect on our body to get our attention. If we do not recognize the drag effect of blocking, the signals will increase until they make us really tired, or, if still ignored, they will increase to the pain level—whatever it takes to get our attention.

The second reason for holding into feeling is that feelings, as they deepen, do yield. Feelings yield warmth and energy in our body. Feelings also yield information, insights, images, thoughts, and profound clues to our behavior, patterns, and routines. If we can hold in and choose to be affected, we are able to notice the moments, behaviors, ideas, feelings, and people we avoid. Our deepest patterns of behavior begin to emerge. Instead of being afraid of information, we can open to it, learn from it, and open up to wider aspects of our being.

Third, if we hold with and move still further into ourselves, we develop empathy for ourselves as well as others. We feel into the pathos of life itself. We experience new thoughts, insights, and possibilities, as well as other decisions we might make, other actions we might take, to stay with the energy of the situation, person, or idea next time. We learn a deeper, more empathetic approach to guiding ourselves. We become more conscious of honoring this being who has survived all these difficulties, who has persevered until this moment.

When we have blocked our energy, how can we regain it? By finding the situation we avoided, reliving it in our mind, and discovering what we need in order to help us cope with it directly. Whenever you experience a loss of energy, look back at the day, the week, or even over your lifetime and ask the question: Where did I leave my energy? At some point you were not willing to let energy in; you were not willing to be affected by a person, idea, or event. Perhaps you were not even aware of the blocking, but your emotional brain registered disapproval or nonconnection, and the result was loss of energy. It is not that the other person or the event took it from you, which is what many of us unconsciously feel when we blame our hurts on others. It is that we use up a lot of our energy by maintaining our lack of awareness, by being unwilling to feel or be affected, by refusing to face a person, idea, or situation, whatever the "it" is. You can get your energy back by facing things now and becoming aware of what you are refusing to let affect you.

Affectional intelligence invites us to recover that moment consciously and take the time to figure out what we need in order to help us deal consciously with the situation. Learn how to recover lost energy by practicing the exercise "Where Did I Leave My Energy?" near the end of this chapter.

Although the purpose of affectional intelligence is to go into emotions, there are moments or circumstances in which we cannot stand to feel. We have learned to take pills to tranquilize us or to excite us. We have the social habit of using alcohol and drugs to change our moods. It is crucial that we acquire the natural ability to shift out of our limbic brain and focus in our other two brains, the neocortex and the basic brain. We can escape by talking too much or by distancing ourselves through images or wishes. Or we can escape via our basic brain simply moving our body toward other circumstances that affect us in a more pleasant way. Practice the "Focusing and Shifting" exercise at the end of this chapter.

Mary was attending a three-day workshop and was gradually becoming more and more frustrated with me. She didn't express her frustration, but kept withdrawing until finally she told me she was very affected by my paying so much attention to Tim. It seemed to her that I was playing favorites and Tim was my favorite. For three days she was very frustrated by my giving so much attention to him. She allowed herself to be affected until finally she realized how a pattern from her past was influencing her perception: she had been brought up in an orphanage and had come to think that everyone but herself had been given affection. As an adult this idea continued to affect her adversely. By learning about affectional intelligence, she discovered that she could consciously focus on being loved, she could allow herself to be affected by the love around her, and she could ask for love as well as love herself rather than waiting for love to be directed toward her.

It is possible to be too profoundly affected. Ann was so sensitive both to her inner and outer environment that she mostly felt the pain of the world and felt that she really didn't want to live. Her parental messages were extremely contradictory: the mother trying to lead a superficial social life and the father a rough and tough truck driver trying to adjust himself to a sedentary life of retirement. He wanted his daughter to be as tough as he was. However, her innate musical ability made her extremely sensitive rather than tough. Everything around her affected her and moved her more and more into her interior self. Clearly she had let herself be so affected that she was putting her life in danger. What helped was recognizing and appreciating her sensitivity, as well as relating it to her ability of being able to be affected. She learned that her emotions were like her music, full of tonality and resonance as well as dissonance, and that all this was normal. More specifically, she learned how to manage sadness and anger (discussed in the chapter on mood intelligence). Now she is able to modulate her affectional intelligence, enjoying the world rather than suffering from it.

Practicing the Feeling Process

Many stages, not necessarily sequential, are involved in the process of feeling. They might more accurately be described as variations of the feeling process and presented for your orchestration, as in music. However, describing the feeling process in a book does require a line-by-line itemization. Please include these stages in developing your feeling process in whatever way is most appropriate for you.

1. Concentrate in your abdomen and not in your head. The abdomen is the area in which you can most easily expand your body through using your diaphragm. Learn to breathe deeply, expanding and contracting. Inhale and expand, exhale and contract. This relaxes your body and helps you come down from the faster beta vibrations of your neocortex.

2. Stop speaking. When you want to let yourself be deeply affected, you

have to stop talking. Talking keeps you focused in your neocortex. To prevent that, focus in your emotional reaction to anything near you. If you keep on analyzing or thinking or imagining, you will not allow yourself access to vibrations in your limbic brain.

3. To begin to feel, you have to let yourself be affected. Whatever you let yourself be affected by can come from your internal or from your external context. It can be inside you, like thoughts, images, or intuitions from your neocortex or body sensations or emotional vibrations that are happening inside you. Or it can be from your surroundings—any person, object, or idea that you see or hear.

4. Focus on what you want to feel. Select from your internal or external context whatever you want to allow to affect you. If you try to let yourself be affected by everything, without selecting, you will not become more conscious, only more fatigued. It is really difficult to realize how much your body-brain system is exposed to or imagine all that is continually impacting you until either you consciously begin to let yourself feel it or it produces a clear reaction such as fatigue, a generalized stress, or specific signals of pain. Try to be sensitive to your system and select what you most want to let affect you. Make your world a heaven, not a hell.

5. Change from an active energy to a receptive energy. This change from active to receptive is easily seen in many of the Chinese martial arts. It is not obvious, but very subtle. One proof that you have made the change from active to receptive is how relaxed you feel, because to relax you usually have to stop doing whatever you are involved in. In order to change from your active energy to feeling, you have to pull back. Do not focus on anything; just open yourself to receive. The process is similar to having a phone conversation: you speak actively, then pause to listen and receive what the other says. In the same way, you shift from active to receptive energy by first focusing actively and then waiting to receive.

6. Receive and let yourself be affected. Feel what is happening inside you. Feel your mood. Avoid labels. Keep on receiving until glimpses or information appears, or keep on receiving just to enjoy the mood. This is holding with the movement of your emotions.

7. To continue to hold with your emotion, stay concentrated in your abdomen and breathe deeply.

8. To go deeper or extend the emotion, use a second process. After you have caught the mood of your first feeling, ask yourself, "How is this feeling making me feel about myself?" For example, "I feel sad, and now this sadness is making me feel . . . ." This way, you can go into a deeper process of feeling. Then you will realize that there is new information that was not clear enough to be within your reach the first time you lived the experience.

9. When the experience is about pleasant feelings such as relaxation, pleasure, or love, use your focus power to amplify that feeling in all your body. Stay in the feeling and then move your focus very slowly over every part of your body, spreading and enjoying the feeling.

10. If the feeling is unpleasant, such as vengeance, jealousy, anger, sadness, depression, guilt, worry, or fear, stay conscious enough to extract the information that it brings you, but be aware of not coming to conclusion or taking action based on such conclusions. Trust in the fact that there are many realities in your life. If an unpleasant feeling catches you unaware and you don't wish to explore or handle it at the moment, shift away until you have time to deal with unpleasant information. Remember, shift by focusing into any pleasant reality of your life, whether that be to feeling something else or thinking, imagining, or acting on something else. The chapter on mood intelligence explains how to manage your emotions, whether agreeable or disagreeable.

You can begin the practice of feeling either by focusing in the present or by remembering past situations. When you are thinking or acting and you wish to slow down into feeling, it is easiest to start by feeling the sensations of your body. Where do I feel the most? In my knee, my arm . . . .? Focus in different areas of your body to receive all the sensations that are taking place. If there are signals of pain, take the time to stop, relax, and breathe into your abdomen. As you feel, be tender with yourself and appreciative. Then very slowly, gently cover and massage the painful area of your body with the heat of your hands. It is also possible to begin feeling by asking yourself about your feeling reaction to what you are thinking or to situations in which you are involved in the moment. Ask yourself:

What am I feeling?

This situation in which I find myself is making me
feel_____ .

I am feeling_____ .

And, this feeling is making me feel_____

_____ .

Enjoy the images, glimpses, or hunches you receive. Enjoy staying in what you are feeling.

When you want to recall a situation from your past in order to live it again emotionally, visualize the situation, make it larger on the screen of your mind, let it surround you, and allow yourself to be affected. You can go back to an unpleasant situation whenever you wish new information or wish to make a new and better decision. You can also recycle all the moments of love or success that are registered in your long-term memory. As you saw in visual intelligence, you have a movie or television screen always at your disposal. You simply visualize the situation again and proceed through the stages or variations of feeling described above.

Tears as a Language of the Limbic Brain

When and while we are deeply moved or deeply affected, whether by sadness or by beauty, we often cry. In the measure that we are deeply affected, all our organs are affected, and our lacrimal glands are also affected, producing the outward signal known as tears. Tears show that we are being profoundly moved. We receive, take in, are sensitive to. As this registers in our limbic brain through our autonomic nervous system, our organs relax, our lacrimal glands relax and expand, and water comes out through our eyes.

Tears are a language of the limbic brain. They ought not to be restricted. Eventually we will come to honor them in public as a sign of human sensitivity. At the very least we need to revise our views of crying from a sign of weakness to a sign of emotional intelligence or sensitivity. We have identified tears with sadness and hurts, funerals and weakness. It is not always so. A symphony, a sunset, an act of compassion can also move us to tears.

When we teach ourselves not to cry, we are teaching ourselves to stay constricted. We are keeping the organs of our bodies tense and teaching our bodies not to relax. Men are taught that it is weak to cry. Perhaps this is one reason more men than women suffer heart attacks. We have all had the experience of giving way to tears and feeling our whole body relax after a good cry. Why, then, do we not accept crying? Perhaps we do not accept sensitivity or affection. Certainly we have not had an affectional process that included tears as a signal of sensitivity. Perhaps we think some people are born sensitive, rather than believing that just as we need a process to become rational, so too do we need a process to become sensitive. Tears are part of the process of being affected. There can be no affectional intelligence that does not permit relaxation through tears.

Security

Without the emotional brain, there is no safeguard for the neocortex or the deeper basic brain. Both run rampant, actively thinking, imagining, and acting, paying little or no attention to our feelings. This is a general description of our world at present: we think great thoughts, have visions, draw up budgets, and construct cities for a world that has never lived the emotional brain. We carry on with thoughts and actions. We desperately try to check and control our thoughts and actions by trying to relate them to standards or limits, but always unaware that we are ignoring our deepest resource: the sensing, reflecting, humanizing capacity of our limbic brain. The brain of the heart and the gut internalizes and reflects to us the human dimensions of life. Without feelings, we cannot access this information. Without this information, we cannot be secure.

"Let peace begin with me" is going to be possible only if we can learn to approach life with feelings. Unless I am able to see how I hurt myself and how I use violence with myself, how am I going to be able to move in a peaceful way with others? Will I even be able to detect how I ignore, hurt, or am violent with others if I do not find out how I ignore or hurt myself? It is clear that I can be violent with a gun in my hands, but what were the steps that led up to that violence? Did I move away from you first with my thoughts? Did I categorize you, judging you wrong or little by little imagining you different from me? At what moment did I refuse to let myself be affected by you? We must recover our feeling faculty, our capacity to be affected by the daily conditions of our lives. The limbic brain is as necessary for our personal health as it is to improve the quality of human life.

Before the world kills us, we usually do very well at killing ourselves. Our constant blocking of feelings escalates over time into numbness, boredom, accusations against others, and finally withdrawal. With a conscious decision to allow ourselves to be affected, we can begin to detect this entropy process. We can give ourselves the liberty and the time to feel and learn to read our feelings, just as we would give ourselves the time to read a book.

We can begin to make decisions that will enable us to move more safely and powerfully and sensitively in the world. As we become affected and develop feeling into empathy in our own life, the pathos of all life becomes apparent and more possible to live with. As we no longer need to avoid ourselves, we can allow ourselves to be affected by the paths and choices of others. We are able to be with them, sometimes empathetic, sometimes compassionate. Empathy and compassion are the fruits of affectional intelligence. "Conclusion" is the goal of the rational process, while "empathy" is the goal of this affectional process. It is, however, not reached sequentially, as in rational thinking, but rather by this ever-opening, ever-deepening, carefully modulated process of being affected by, integrating the information from that feeling, and entering once again into being affected.

As you develop the process of being affected by and holding with, you will be able to energize your body, motivate yourself, develop empathy and compassion, and deepen your love for yourself and others. If you have allowed life to become boring and impersonal or shut yourself away from love, you can recover and restore yourself by the increased use of affectional intelligence. To be affected by a symphony, by a gesture; to be enveloped and affected by a flower; to feel hurt when a friend is hurting; to be affected by a national problem—any one of these is to be seized with, energized by, and connected to the rest of life.

EXERCISE

WHERE DID I LEAVE MY ENERGY?

1. *Scan the screen of your mind and ask yourself: When during the day (or week, month, year) did I lose my energy? When was I unwilling to be affected? Of all that happened today, what did I most want to avoid?*

2. *Visualize a Geiger counter moving across the territory you have left behind you. You are searching for hot buried treasure, those areas of your life that have hurt you in the past and that you now automatically avoid. Look first for the period in which you had a lot of energy and then suddenly none or very little. Look closer: where, in what situation, with what person did you leave your energy? You will find a place where you were energetic, then a feeling of being down or low.*

3. *What happened in that space or time? Visualize yourself at that point and search for what it is that you don't want to feel. Now, in this moment, in the safety of this exercise, consciously give yourself permission to relive the event, this time to feel the event, to be affected by it. Notice that the physical moment, the time when you might have felt obliged to act, has gone by, and you are no longer threatened by it. Let it in again. See it and say clearly, I lost my energy when . . . .*

4. *In that situation, what I needed or wanted was . . . .*

5. *Going back to the situation, you can see now what to do to find your energy. What do you need in order to enable yourself to be affected? What would make you feel good? Imagine and feel yourself doing that. Move to act on the situation as soon as possible or else review it in your mind so it will be programmed for the next time you find yourself in the same situation.*

EXERCISE

THE GATEKEEPER

Put on relaxing music. Make yourself comfortable with a pencil and the following chart by your side.

Name of the feeling	How it feels in my body	What I expect will happen to me

1. Select the emotions you wish to experience and list them in the first column.

2. Allow yourself to feel the first emotion. To help, visualize a situation in which you felt that emotion.

3. In the second column describe how that emotion feels in your body.

4. Become aware of what you expect will happen to you when you experience the feeling, and note your expectation in the third column.

5. Repeat this process for each of the emotions.

6. Review the expectations. If the expectation does not allow you to enter the feeling, consider whether or not you want access to that feeling and, if so, how you can change your expectations. What new information or programming do you need to allow yourself to feel that specific emotion?

EXERCISE

HEAVEN OR HELL

If you choose to let yourself be affected by difficult or painful situations, by ugliness, fear, or hate, you will feel the emotional repercussions of your focus. If you select beauty, peaceful or friendly things, calmness, or love, you will feel the impact of this other choice. Experiment with this difference in the very room where you are reading this book.

1. Allow your eyes to wander around the room. You are looking for two

or three things or persons you don't like. Go into the process of letting yourself be affected by one of them until you feel what you feel about the person or the object.

2. *Now choose one you do like and would like to be affected by.*

3. *Notice how the vibrations in your body change in relation to what you allow yourself to feel. Try to become aware of what your body's signals are when you think of something you dislike and something you love.*

EXERCISE FOCUSING AND SHIFTING—

MENTAL TOOLS OF CONSCIOUSNESS

Please experiment with the practice of focusing and then of shifting. First concentrate deeply and exactly (focus), and then release your concentration (shift). The following exercise is also set up to indicate how your thoughts and images affect your feelings. (Remember that your feelings also affect your thoughts and images.)

I am thinking of_____
(a negative thought)
and it makes me feel_____

When I think of_____
(an interesting thought)
I feel_____

When I imagine_____
(a horrible, disagreeable, disturbing image)
I feel_____

When I imagine_____
(a beautiful image)
I feel_____

When I experience_____

(something painful)

it makes me feel_____

When I have a great experience, I feel_____

When I think of someone I have lost, I feel_____

When I think of someone I love, I feel_____

When I do_____

(something that I don't like)

my body feels_____

And when I think or do_____

(something I do like)

my body feels_____

CHAPTER X

High Waves
and Low Waves

MOOD INTELLIGENCE

Emotion is the chief source of consciousness. There is no change from dark-ness to light or from inertia to movement without emotion.

C. G. Jung, *The Archetypes and the Collective Unconscious*

In the last chapter we saw how affectional intelligence helps us enter into emotions. We learned the importance of selecting what we wish to be affected by in order consciously to use the affectional process to continue loving. However, in our longing and desire for the other, be that a person or a project at work, we are often also deeply affected by what we cannot do. The highs of love and full confidence in ourselves turn into the lows of I can't, of sadness, anger, and the full spectrum of emotions. Mood intelligence is the process that enables us to live both the highs and lows of all our emotions for the benefit of our health, our love, our personal power, and the richness of our life.

Purposes of Mood Intelligence

The first purpose of mood intelligence is to enable us to live the truth of our entire mind-body system rather than only the selective process of our neocortex, to have access to all the emotional information available through our limbic brain. The emphasis in mood intelligence is on *all* emotions, including those now popularly referred to as "negative." Emotions are information emerging from our inner life. The issue becomes whether the neocortex is listening or suppressing the information. Candace Pert, leading researcher on brain chemistry and emotions, gave her opinion of repression and positive thinking in an interview by Bill Moyers: "It's clear to me that emotions must play a key role, and that repressing emotions can only be causative of disease. A common ingredient in the healing practices of native cultures is catharsis, complete release of emotion. Positive thinking is interesting, but if it denies the truth, I can't believe that would be anything except bad."[1]

The truth of how our mind-body system perceives our complete surroundings, rather than only the positive selective perspective of our neocortex, is what is at stake in learning mood intelligence. Not to have access to all emotional information is to lose the signals of our reactions to the world. Information from the limbic brain differs from the kind of information we receive from the neocortex. In certain cases such as love and health, emotional information may be more important. Not to listen to emotions leaves us in ignorance of the energy constantly vibrating in our limbic brain. In daily life, the lack of emotional information can make us less energetic or effective. With the passage of time, repression of emotional information can result in illness within ourselves or violence toward others.

If we ignore our moods of sadness or anger, our emotional energy remains free to sabotage our projects subtly or, as we usually say, unconsciously. "I just don't feel like it," or "It really doesn't interest me anymore" becomes our verbal justification for refusing to feel our frustration in order to find out what is really going on.

While emotions are sabotaging our actions and our will to act, the neocortex may be looking into astrology, into destiny, or even into our own surroundings, searching for someone or something to blame for what is going wrong. The information is within us. Our reactions are already registered, and they provoke emotions in order not to be ignored. Emotions exist as internal signals of our reactions to the world. They provide a personal text that is different from either the physical or mental reactions of the basic brain or neocortex.

We have frightened ourselves away from certain emotions, especially sadness and anger, by labeling them negative. It is certainly true that if we express painful emotions we may indeed do harm to others or at least affect their happiness. However, to enter these moods ourselves, to feel them until we grasp what they are wanting to tell us, may indeed be positive, life-giving, and urgently necessary.

Why are you sad? Let yourself enter and feel your sadness. As discussed in the chapter on affectional intelligence, sadness is an indicator of information, registered in our brain, affecting our body, and blocking our energy until we pay attention. We pay attention by entering and holding with this feeling until we grasp the information. The apparently negative turns positive when treated as information, as illustrated by the exercise "What is the Message?" later in this chapter.

Mood intelligence shows us how to be involved in all our emotions, including those we are now labeling as negative. Would you limit your reading, blacklist books, or avoid certain books without exploring what books can do for you? Intellectual freedom is the struggle for the liberty of *all* information. Feelings give us access to emotional information, just as books give us access to intellectual information. We do not judge books before reading them, and we do not need to judge emotions before feeling them. Mood intelligence is to emotions what rational intelligence is to thoughts: a process of respectful travel through all information that presents itself.

The second purpose of mood intelligence is to preserve and enhance our physical health.

MOYERS: But where does this trail lead us in regard to emotions and health?

PERT: It leads us to think that the chemicals that are running our body and our brain are the same chemicals that are involved in emotion. And that says to me that we'd better seriously entertain theories about the role of emotions and emotional suppression in disease, and that we'd better pay more attention to emotions with respect to health.[2]

I believe that the continuous lack of permission for feeling and especially the lack of satisfactory experience with "negativity" is a direct cause of the high rate of strokes, heart attacks, and other organic weaknesses so prevalent in Western society. To restrict feelings is to restrict the organs of our body, and it leads to eventual weakness.

The constriction of vibrations within the body and an inability to relax, slow down, and govern breathing are all signs of stress. But what is stress? Stress is being contracted and unwilling or unable to expand. The body and more specifically the organs remain in a contracted condition that later becomes a constricted condition. I believe we feel or experience stress because we are unwilling, afraid, do not have permission, or do not know how to experience safely the so-called negative emotions. It is difficult to admit or say that we feel sad, angry, or depressed. Moreover, most people react poorly if we do express these emotions.

When you are unable to experience negative emotions, your body sends off signals of "not knowingness," confusion, and a call for clarity by rapid breathing and rapid pulse rate. "For goodness sake, tell me where to go next. What can I have permission to feel?" If you do nothing, the stress continues; you continue acting and thinking, but unaware of feeling. Meanwhile, what is happening in your body? Your organs do not have permission to slow down, to contract into sadness, or to expand into the more chaotic vibrational range of frustration and anger. They are stuck in contraction, stuck in stress.

If you live and work in your neocortex and basic brain, not attending to the feeling range, you may be fairly successful with this approach for many years. Then either suddenly or gradually, situations in your life become tougher. You are less successful and it is more difficult to keep your cool. At home or in the car you get huffy. Eventually something strong, urgent, or awful happens. Someone steals your car, you lose a loved one, or you get fired. You always thought that those events could happen to others but never to you. At last you do burst out in anger and hostility. You have finally expressed your emotions, but by now you are forty-two and your body has no experience with these vibrational ranges. Anger then becomes like a shock wave, an earthquake to your system.

I am persuaded that unless our organs—heart, colon, liver, and the rest—are allowed to vibrate, to exercise, to expand and contract over the course of our lifetime, they will gradually constrict and weaken, making it possible for tough life situations to cause us drastic harm. Feelings are the exercise of the organs of the body just as swimming or running is exercise for the muscles of the body. Our emotional gym is located within us. We need to practice feelings consciously at least twenty minutes every day to gradually build our emotional strength. We need to be reliving the great emotions of confidence and love as well as practicing the exercises for feeling sadness and anger found at the end of this chapter.

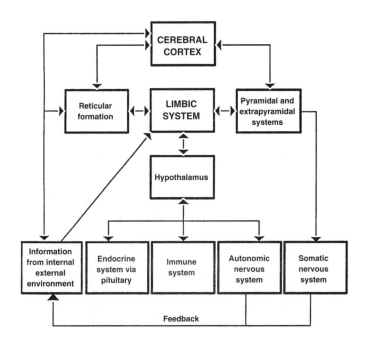

Fig. 7. Relationship of Limbic System to Immune System, Endocrine System, and Autonomic Nervous System[3]

The above diagram takes a more specific look at the connection of the limbic brain to the autonomic nervous system, endocrine system, and immune system. We can no longer permit ourselves to ignore or freeze ourselves out of either the slower or the more chaotic vibrations of the limbic brain. Both for information and for health, we need to take a new look.

The third purpose of mood intelligence is to access natural brain chemicals. In an interview by Bill Moyers, Candace Pert described the relationship of brain chemicals to emotions: ". . . the astounding revelation is that these endorphins and other chemicals like them are found not just in the brain, but in the immune system, the endocrine system, and throughout the body. These molecules are involved in a psychosomatic communication network. . . . These molecules are being released from one place, they're diffusing all over the body, and they're tickling the receptors that are on the surface of every cell in your body. . . . We have come to theorize that these neuropeptides and their receptors are the biochemical correlates of emotions."[4]

New discoveries in natural brain chemicals could fill many books. However, an overview of the natural brain chemicals, such as endorphins, serotonin, and dopamine, shows that they can all be described by locating their effect on a scale between quiescence and excitation. If this scale already exists chemically within the brain, are emotions simply the human body's way of expressing this brain chemistry? Or is it the contrary, that feeling emotions produces the natural chemistry? Or is the interaction occurring both ways?

If I am depressed and I refuse to expand or even to get angry at anything, I am depriving my brain and body of natural excitants. If I am always angry and frustrated and refuse to focus on what would calm me and give me a quiet feeling of well-being, my brain and body are deprived of the quiescent state that natural chemicals like endorphins produce.

Through medical and psychiatric experimentation, we know that we can affect and change our emotional states with drugs. Even more startling is the fact that drugs now available to everyone on the street exactly match the quiescent-excitation range of the *natural* chemicals. Heroine renders us quiescent; amphetamines and cocaine make us excited. Do we have such a chemical need for this quiescent-excitation range that we manufacture drugs to duplicate natural chemicals? Do we manufacture drugs or artificial chemicals because we don't permit ourselves access to the natural chemicals through emotions? Is feeling emotions as necessary to the human brain as thinking? When we suppress emotions, either quiet sadness or exciting anger, are we suppressing our own brain chemicals? Are we then driven to take artificial chemicals to provide our brains with the same emotional experience that we refuse to provide by feeling our emotions?

As far as we know, every civilization has manufactured drugs. There has never been a human civilization without drugs! Why? The usual answers are for medicinal purposes, for religious purposes, and for pleasure. Has there always been an innate need for the balancing of brain and body through this chemical range only now being described by brain chemists? If every human culture has produced artificial drugs, it must be that something in the human being wants to experience these diverse emotional states. If we can't get them naturally, we will get them artificially! Apparently we do not want to live without these feeling experiences of the full range from quiescence to excitation.

Indeed emotions are crucial to life itself. Studies conducted in Sweden by P. Svanborg and Marie Asberg indicate that the reduced functioning of the neurotransmitter serotonin is a biological marker of suicidal risk.[5]

Can I "turn on" or enhance the natural chemicals of my brain by practicing all of the feelings of this quiescent to excitant range? This is the question that shakes me profoundly. I believe emotions can give me access or improve the access to my own natural brain chemicals. I believe we have developed artificial chemicals to supplant, replace, or enhance natural brain chemicals because we have not known how to enter into emotional states, how to make use of them without harming ourselves or others, and then how to shift out of them. I believe we have been ignorant of the purpose of emotions in releasing natural chemicals.

Aware, now, of the necessity of these natural chemicals to our autonomic nervous system, our endocrine system, and immune system, we must actively search for the processes that will provide us full access to our feelings. I propose that mood intelligence is one such process. Mood intelligence invites us to reclaim our power by experiencing all of our emotions in order to access our natural brain chemicals, to govern, protect, and exercise the organs of our body, and to receive information for leading our life appropriately.

Emotional Scales

How can we learn to experience the extremes of joy as well as the extremes of anger? How can we become conscious of all our emotions? We need a frame of reference large enough to encompass all of them. Music can serve as one such frame of reference. Putting emotions on a vibrational scale similar to musical scales, we can take moods out of a dualistic framework of negative and positive by framing emotions as harmonics: with tonalities, depth, volume, intensity, counterpoint, atonality, dissonance, and resonance.

I think that using energy scales will enable you to appreciate all of the emotions without prejudice to those we now describe as negative. A good singer would not consider singing only half the notes on a scale. Would there be variation in music without dissonance as well as resonance? Could a symphony exist without counterpoint? Can you imagine Beethoven or Mahler without chaos, anger, or sadness, without contraction as well as expansion, with highs only, no lows? I believe that we human beings could feel the extremes of expansion and contraction similar to those of Beethoven or Mahler if we knew how to orchestrate them within our body instruments without harming others.

EXERCISE

EMOTIONAL ENERGY SCALES

Explore your moods and create your own scales of emotional energy. Relate the emotion to the energy you feel when you are experiencing the emotion. Write slow, medium, or fast to indicate the different vibrational energy speeds. You can use the notation of quiescence and excitation to indicate the two extremes of the scale, with E for expansion and C for contraction, but feel free to invent other indications as you experiment with making your own scales. I include the following scale taken from my own experience to illustrate how one scale might look.

FAST	panicky E
	mixed up C
	disturbed E
	frustrated E
MEDIUM	blocked C
	conflicted E
	worried E
	troubled E
SLOW	undecided C

Fig. 8. One Emotional Scale

Take your time and feel your own way through the following emotions. Then locate them on your personal scales according to the energy you experience as slow, medium, or fast vibrations. The following emotions are grouped together to help you begin. An additional challenge is to find a greater number of scales for pleasurable emotions.

1. *depressed, sleepy, sad, hurt, offended, put off*
2. *uneasy, nervous, uptight*
3. *empty, picky, annoyed, upset, angry, jealous, mad, violent, silent*
4. *okay, good, confident, happy, strong, sexual, great, proud, excited, ecstatic*
5. *gentle, loving, warm, tender, full, vulnerable, chaotic, blissful, open*

Or, as another person grouped her emotions:

1. *confused, insecure, tense, anxious, fearful, violent*
2. *lost, confused, threatened, uncomfortable, distant, petrified*
3. *uncertain, nonconformist, nervous, fearful*
4. *depressed, sad, annoyed, bothered, angry, offended, furious, out of control*
5. *hurt, frustrated, mad, rebellious, out of control*
6. *discouraged, unhappy, feeling bad, upset, hurt, complaining*
7. *affected, stimulated, belonging to, proud, loving, erotic*
8. *satisfied, trustful, happy, very well, united, wild*
9. *warm, close, tender, sexual, strong, ecstatic*

Now that you see how two people did it, please try to create your own emotional scales. Note that the thicker, slower, lower mood waves were grouped at the beginning of each numbered section on the scale, but where that put them in relation to each other was highly variable, unique, and personal—which is as it should be.

Mood scales are to mood intelligence what the ABCs and reasons are to rational intelligence. Making your own mood scales is the first step toward recognizing the multiplicity, richness, and variability of your feelings. Your scales can also serve as guides to make you aware of when you are reaching emotional extremes. If you want a peaceful life, concentrate on the side of the scale that says slow speed; if you need more excitation in your life, focus your attention on the fast speed.

Relating energy to emotions is basic for the development of mood intelligence. We must give ourselves time to practice our emotions in private before we release them on our family or the world as raw reaction to unexpected situations. Discovering that we really can enter emotions and shift from them at will is basic to our becoming fully conscious of our power. If there is no practice, if we just let our moods strike us, then we will be dependent on the basic learning or lack of learning that we have received from the streets, from our family, from work, and from our loved ones. Using raw experience may damage our life or the lives of others without our realizing it. With the practice of experiencing how each emotion feels, we can begin to orchestrate our body, recognizing when it is appropriate to calm ourselves and when we need to increase our excitement.

Loss of Power

You try to govern your life as well as possible: you perceive, feel, desire, act. What could possibly go wrong? Emotions are your body. Emotions are you, your power, your desires. Sometimes you achieve what you want. Other times, what you want is just not possible, whatever the reason, whatever the obstacle. Your energy is blocked; your power is checked.

When we do not get what we want, we react either passively, which can lead to sadness, or actively, which can lead to frustration and anger. Some people have permission and feel comfortable being sad. Others feel anger more easily. Some of us have a preference that may become a repetitive pattern: we are usually sad or usually mad. In general there is more permission for a woman to react with sadness when her desires are blocked and more permission for a man to become angry. We also inherit from our families a preference for reacting passively or actively.

Figure 9 shows the emotional reaction when desire is blocked. We can react actively and feel bored, frustrated, or angry. From that state, we can easily go to the extreme of hatred, which is a combined mental-emotional state, or to violence, which is a physical-emotional state. When desires are blocked, we may instead react passively, feeling sadness, which can extend itself to the extreme state of depression.

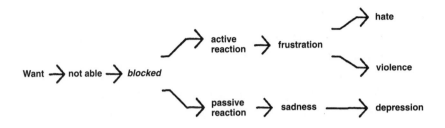

Fig. 9. When Your Power Is Blocked

The opposite extremes of contraction and expansion carry different names according to the professional orientation of the person who is dealing with this emotional phenomenon: depression-excitation, manic-depressive, passive-aggressive, yin-yang, or quiescence-excitation. I have selected the words *quiescence-excitation* from chemical research because they seem to me less prejudicial, less affected by different cultural and professional biases than the other terms.

If you become stuck in one extreme, whether it be in excitation and anger or in sadness and depression, it may mean that you do not have the natural chemistry that helps you to change. Or it may mean that you do not have the experience of how to shift out of extreme emotional states or do not know how to value the information they hold for you. In brief, you may lack either chemical equilibrium or experience in shifting your emotions. You may wish to consult the medical profession, which is now usually treating the extreme states involved in manic-depression with various types of drugs. However, if you do not have a critical chemical deficiency, you can still learn to experience your emotions in order to be able to manage your own equilibrium and increase your natural chemicals. Moreover, if eventually you need the help of a doctor and of prescription drugs to help you avoid dangerous extremes, you could choose both: consult with your doctor while at the same time learning how to manage emotions, especially those related to your power being blocked.

Being stuck worries us all. We think of getting stuck in anger or sadness, of losing energy and never being able to change. There are indeed millions of Americans stuck in clinical depression, and we don't know how many more stuck in anger and excitation. Depression is the known illness that results from getting stuck in contraction. However there may be other illnesses related to contraction, such as chronic fatigue syndrome in which a person feels continually tired.

Which illnesses relate to getting stuck in the extremes of excitation? We know that cancer is a condition in which cells cannot stop multiplying. Is that a condition of excitation? Could it be that cancer of the lungs is related to a continuous state of excitation produced by smoking, for example? Could it be that the cells involved in the breast are in a state of excitation and cannot relax themselves? Research of Redford Williams and others at Duke University in North Carolina indicates that the excitation known as anger is a serious cause of cardiac illness and heart attacks.[6]

A person's internal emotional condition is a factor of health. The energy states we are calling emotions are internal factors that contribute to the physical development of serious illness. Given the relationship between the limbic brain and the immune and endocrine systems, a patient's emotional condition needs to be taken into account when we are studying illnesses. We expend millions of dollars searching for viruses as the cause of many unexplainable illnesses. The common cold is a virus that takes us out of our life of excitation, imposing rest and quiet. It may be that other viruses also serve to take us out of excited moods. It may be that the body cannot stand the same interior stuck condition of either endless excitation or endless quiescence and produces the conditions in which a virus can grow. To quote Bill Moyers and Candace Pert:

MOYERS: As a Westerner, I think of illness as being caused by a bacteria or a virus. If I pick up a bacteria, I'm likely to get sick.
PERT: Well, of course your immune system responds—but, just to take one example, viruses use these same receptors to enter into a cell and depending on how much of the natural juice, or the natural peptide for that receptor is around, the virus will have an easier or a harder time getting into the cell. *So our emotional state will affect whether we'll get sick from the same loading dose of a virus.* You know the data about how people have more heart attacks on Monday mornings, how death peaks in Christians the day after Christmas, and in Chinese people the day after Chinese New Year. *I never get a cold when I'm going skiing.* Another example: the AIDS virus uses a receptor that is normally used by a neuropeptide. So whether an AIDS virus will be able to enter a cell or not depends on how much of this natural peptide is

around, which according to this theory, would be a function of what state of emotional expression the organism is in. *Emotional fluctuations and emotional status directly influence the probability that the organism will get sick or be well.* [italics mine][7]

When we are feeling good or excited about life or what is going on, endorphins or other peptides are filling the receptors, allowing little chance for viruses to enter the receptor cells. If we cannot go skiing every day to prevent colds, we can become deeply aware of the importance of our emotional states. That means either living on the main highway, the love-of-life line of the emotional territory map, or learning what to do when we fall into the emotions of sadness or anger.

When we are stuck in either quiescence or excitation, our mood is converted into our reality. People advise us to be either more animated or more balanced, but it is difficult to follow their advice. Many courses on handling stress teach us to relax, and this is very important for those who have an addiction to excitation, but for those who are addicted to sadness and contraction, only antidepressants and other mood-lifting drugs are available. I suggest that we need to teach ourselves how to fluctuate, how to move along a continuous range from expansion to contraction and back to expansion. We need both, the answer of relaxation and also the answer of excitation. It is the experience of the complete range that will free us from being stuck and open us to feel many different emotional realities.

Orchestrating the Quiescent-Excitation Range

Mood intelligence involves living all our moods. Sometimes we enter into the emotion to feel what it wants to tell us. (See the exercise "What Is the Message?" later in this chapter.) Sometimes we need or wish to shift from a mood (see the exercise on "Focusing and Shifting" in the chapter on affectional intelligence). Mood intelligence involves both entering and shifting, but it also involves a more subtle and continuous orchestration of our emotional energy. Using the quiescent-excitation range as a reference and guide, we can orchestrate our moods by consciously choosing ways to produce either a feeling of calm or a feeling of excitement.

There are many ways to influence our experience of emotions. There are many ways to shift from one emotion to another. Food, sexuality, desires, thoughts, actions, art and music, plus any artificial chemicals or drugs that we take—all influence our emotional state.

Food. It is impossible to enjoy a good plate of pasta without feeling more calm and impossible to eat chocolate or meat without feeling more animated. Judith Wurtman, researcher at M.I.T. in Boston, writes about the subtle connections between different foods and our chemistry.[8] Japanese researcher Michio Kushi, expert in macrobiotics, has classified different foods as "yin" and "yang" as they correspond to passive or calm energy and active, outgoing energy.[9]

Breathing. Breathing also affects emotions. We can calm ourselves with abdominal breathing or excite ourselves with rapid breathing.

Relationships. Attraction to another person excites us and invites love and sexual feelings. Love encompasses both great excitement and deep serenity. Loving someone or something sometimes excites us, sometimes calms us, sometimes both. If we succeed in loving both to excite and to calm ourselves, we won't need to overeat to calm ourselves or take drugs to excite ourselves. Neither will we need to catch a cold to give ourselves rest or become a victim of illness that results from too much excitation. To love is to be in excitation with someone or something and also to be in rest with. We can enter into an expansive-contractive process, which includes both the excitation of orgasm and the quiescence of rest. We can consciously love either our selves or another person, a creature or an idea, an event or an object, guiding ourselves through the quiescence-excitation range. To love is to be willing to contract ourselves when we are expanded and to expand ourselves when we are contracted.

Thoughts. As seen in the chapter on affectional intelligence, our focus on pleasant or pleasurable thoughts makes our body feel expanded, and our focus on disagreeable thoughts makes our body feel contracted. To use the neocortex to doubt or criticize ourselves continually makes us feel down. Perfectionism can be terrible because it prevents people from ever feeling themselves expanded, even when they do something well. Their insistence on always doing better and better robs perfectionists of satisfaction and prevents them from feeling good before going on to the next objective. They continue and continue, yet there is always more to do—a proven formula for continuous contraction and stress.

Actions. Actions also produce emotional reactions. Some actions make us feel good, others bad. Generally, what we know how to do makes us feel good, while what we don't know how to do makes us feel bad and often confused and afraid. When you want to help yourself to feel good, what actions might help? Consider sports, hobbies, fixing up the house, any of the arts you enjoy, gardening, working in the environment. Know the actions in your daily behavior that put you in a good mood. Program your actions and enjoy each activity more by consciously allowing yourself to be more affected by it. Know that when you are too bored or too calm, it is time to try something more difficult. Know also that when you are too frustrated, it is time to pause and look for something to do that calms you.

Even the happiness we say we value so much consists of variations of contraction and expansion, tranquility and enthusiasm. Happiness is a word and a concept we try to freeze with our neocortex. We need to remember that as an emotion, happiness is a movement that contains the two points of the emotional scale, quiescence and excitation. When we are aware of the range of moods, we can better program our actions. We can help ourselves by consciously orchestrating the day, by consciously giving time and space to activities that calm us and those that excite us. Instead of being a victim of whatever happens in our environment, we can plan our day with activities that help us feel happy.

Art and Music. The fastest way to change our mood is to shift attention to someone or something beautiful in our environment or to play music and allow ourselves to be affected by the sounds.

Everything that deals with action, thought, sexuality, breathing, nutrition, art, music, or artificial drugs registers emotionally in our limbic brain and affects our natural chemistry and consequently our moods. Moods are like a thermometer for following the highs and lows of our internal chemistry. We can read our emotional temperature and guide our daily actions, thoughts, images, art, music, relationships, sexuality, breathing, and nutrition in order to guide our moods and feel better. We need only to remember that this thermometer registers both ends of the mood spectrum: quietness and excitation.

Practicing the Two Extremes: Sadness and Anger

Mood intelligence requires familiarity with, practice, and mastery of the two extreme reactions to the loss of power: the passive reaction represented by sadness and the active reaction represented by anger. I do not believe we can manage our own health until we learn to master both sadness and anger. *I do not believe there can be an end to violence until we learn to master both sadness and anger.* We can talk about health and peace, but these are words without meaning unless we can achieve health and peace within ourselves.

If we are truthful about our feelings, we all fall off the main highway of love, of feeling good, of being motivated and happy, into the side roads of sadness and anger. Just as there are the high waves of love and happiness, so too there are the low waves of sadness and the chaotic waves of anger. Realizing that we are energy systems, we must also realize that we cannot freeze energy into a perpetual high state. What rises in excitement must relax into quiet. We cannot prevent energy, but we can ride the waves and avoid being stuck and drowned if we learn the secrets of these waves. It may help to suspend the labels sadness and anger, to suspend the classification of negative, and begin a new approach to these internal states of consciousness that occur as a true feeling reaction every time desire and power are checked by external events.

To live these low emotional energies and learn that they too can inform and enrich our lives is indeed the high calling of mood intelligence. Can we become more intelligent as a result of living our sadness and anger and doing so without causing harm to others? That is the challenge!

This section includes many exercises designed for you to practice sadness and anger in order to give you conscious experience with these two extreme moods of passive and active energy. You can practice alone or in a group with people you trust. Please feel free just to read the text found before and after the exercises and then return to practice the exercises when you have the time.

SADNESS: THE CHALLENGE OF THE LOW WAVES

Sadness always represents some kind of loss. This loss may be of power or potential, of a person, place, thing, or idea, of satisfaction or status.

Sadness implies that we have loved deeply. It also implies that we have thought that someone or something belonged to us and that the situation would go on forever. Sometimes we can even imagine we possess something or someone and then experience sadness over an imagined loss.

Often we don't recognize sadness or express it with other words: "I feel disappointed"; "I feel unwilling to"; "I don't want to"; "I'm bored with"; "I don't know what's happened to me, but"; or simply, "I feel so down today. I have no energy." These are steps toward sadness, or they are being used to prevent ourselves from admitting sadness.

The basis of sadness is the loss of some kind of power: "I can't"; "I'm not able to be"; "I'm not able to have it"; "I can't love him or her"; "I can't love it," in relation to something specific or general. "I can't" implies that I have loved something and lost it. Now I am no longer able and I feel sadness. To realize that sadness is about loss may help us deal with this emotion and even its deeper variation of depression.

Kathy had two sons and an alcoholic husband. She decided to become a nurse against the wishes of her father, who was a medical doctor but did not approve of her entering his profession. He believed that a woman's place was in the home. Nevertheless, Kathy studied to become a nurse, graduated, and fought for a good position in a major hospital. She was successful for a while until she felt herself forced to resign because of escalating opposition from her family. After losing her professional standing, she tried once again to adapt to her role as wife and mother. By the time I met her, she was on medication for depression. She had tried to give up the medication several times but finally accepted that there was no other way out of her depression.

I explained to her that sadness and depression are normal feelings caused by a state of loss and that it is possible both to get into them and to get out of them just as one does with other emotions. Treating depression as an emotion rather than as a fixed category of illness opened up a new perspective for Kathy's life. She understood that the loss of a profession that she had desired made it normal for her to be both sad and depressed. She would have to be cold and unfeeling not to have had this reaction. Thinking of depression as an illness both scared her and made it seem logical to her that she needed to take medication. When she began to consider herself normal rather than sick, she began to feel her feelings and gradually gave up the medication.

This kind of success may not happen in all cases. I am not trying to deny the category of clinical depression, but I am trying to indicate that depression is intensified sadness and that we need to give people a chance to deal with their real sadness before resorting to medication.

EXERCISE

WHAT IS THE MESSAGE?

It is important to stay with any emotion until you grasp what the feeling is trying to tell you, and this is especially true with sadness. Give yourself permission to enter sadness consciously by practicing this exercise.

1. *Slow down, focus in your abdomen, and breathe deeply.*
2. *Feel the difficulty of the loss, what it means to you. Feel the "I can't"; feel your inability to act. Feel the sadness, the loss.*
3. *What is this feeling wanting to tell you? Feel and wait. Don't analyze; just stay in your feeling.*
4. *Hold with the sadness until you relax or until tears come. Hold with the tears and sadness as information emerges. Allow the tears to relax you.*

EXERCISE

FEELING AND SHIFTING OUT OF SADNESS

It is also important to know how to get out of sadness. When you are already inside the feeling of sadness, remember that you are in "I can't"; you are not in your power. For that reason, you must condition yourself beforehand to how you want to react. Choose one or a combination of the following strategies to use when you want to shift from sadness. Program these strategies into your memory in order to be able to use them when appropriate. You might also post all the strategies on your refrigerator door or somewhere in your home to remind you of things you can do to help yourself when you are feeling sad.

1. *Give yourself something that makes you feel better. Love yourself. Be gentle and caring. Give yourself something specific to encourage yourself.*

2. *Receive from others and the environment. Be affected by others. Allow them to inspire you. Notice what is great about them; identify with them. Let yourself be affected by any form of beauty, be it music or art, a human creation or the natural beauty that surrounds you.*

3. *Reach out. Ask for love, a hug, or attention of some kind. Express the difficulty and consciously ask for help from a friend, a professional, or someone able and wanting to give love and attention. Don't wait and unconsciously expect others to help. This causes resentment, and most of the time others cannot know what you are wanting or expecting from them.*

4. *Postpone it. Set aside time really to take in the loss and sadness. Do the exercises on healing sadness.*

5. *Engage in a routine or a ritual. Shift to what you love to do that doesn't stress you.*

6. *Remember a moment of love, competence, strength, or fullness from your internal store of memories.*

7. *Wait for the "I can's." Shifting to "I can" too quickly will repress sadness more and more, and this may cause further stress.*

Follow your strategies step by step until something appears attractive or possible.

Very often people are reluctant to believe that it is important to give time to feel sadness. Sadness, of course, does not feel good. It feels sad and we don't like it, so avoidance is understandable. However, when there is real loss, the body and all of its organic systems need time to recover.

Carol was in her late thirties when she lost her husband. He had been sick a long time, and everyone was relieved when he finally passed away. Carol did what many try to do, return to a "normal," active life. She didn't want to follow any of the suggestions for feeling and shifting appropriately out of sadness, especially the idea of waiting for an "I can" rather than insisting on it. Waiting for "I can" means giving yourself permission to feel sadness and loss of power rather than deciding that you can be powerful under all circumstances. Sadness is really an intelligent response to loss. Pretending that you are not sad is emotionally stupid.

Carol decided too quickly that she had suffered long enough and immediately began to enroll in courses that were mentally and physically demanding. She adopted a positive thinking, optimistic attitude, but what was hiding just below the surface was an old pattern of "I can manage anything." The world praised her optimism and even her new marriage six months later, but her emotion-management skills were put to a severe test when she did not find happiness in this marriage. Within another six months she was ill with cancer, and there was no time then for her to rest her immune system or to intervene effectively in her lifelong pattern of "I can handle everything." I cannot say she would not have gotten cancer if she had taken into account her feelings and given herself time to feel her sadness. I can say that her pattern and her effort to be positive stressed her system, as they had done at other serious and sad moments in her life, such as the death of her mother and then her father as well as the serious illness of her brother. Through it all she played the "tough guy." Unfortunately, the concept of being emotionally intelligent came too late to help her.

We can all benefit from taking a gentler approach toward sadness when things happen to us or to our families. Sometimes, when serious consequences are averted, our immediate reaction is to be happy or at least relieved. However, we first need to experience the sadness and loss. Such was the case with Mirna. Thieves had held up her daughter at gunpoint and taken her car. Of course Mirna was happy that her daughter's life was spared; she saw her task as convincing her daughter that she was okay. However, first she needed to help her daughter with her feelings of sadness for the loss of the car, as well as with the fear and the shock that her emotional brain must have registered during the ordeal. She also needed to take time to experience her own feelings about her daughter's misfortune. Thus both Mirna and her daughter could have benefited from the suggestions in the exercise for feeling and shifting out of sadness.

It really is possible to feel the depth of sadness and to learn how to heal it. You would not let a physical wound fester year after year until it kills you; you must not let an emotional wound continue to harm you, to rob your energy, or to weaken you until you become susceptible to serious illness.

To heal your sadness, you have several options:

• You can focus on the thought of loss and let it prolong a feeling of sadness, or you can focus on the feeling of love for the lost person or situation until it produces a warm feeling of love.

- You can focus on the feeling of wanting what you lost until it produces desire and the urge to struggle into action.
- You can focus on the feeling and recognition of love until it produces inspiration toward more life.

Explore these different ways of healing sadness through the following exercises.

EXERCISE

THOUGHT OF LOSS VERSUS FEELING OF LOVE

1. *Scan your life for a situation of great loss.*
2. *Focus on the loss. Allow yourself to visualize the full situation again. Feel the loss.*
3. *Visualize the person or any aspect of the situation where there was love. Feel that love.*
4. *Experience the differences: go back to the feeling of loss and feel how loss feels. Then feel again the love and feel how love feels.*
5. *Honor yourself for loving. Dwell on any gifts you received from the loving. Feel the loving whenever you want to. Be affected and continue to be affected by the loving. Keep on loving what you already love. The choice is yours: will you focus on loss, or will you focus on love?*
6. *Whenever you fall into loss, now be aware that you can shift to love.*

EXERCISE

SADNESS INTO WANTING

1. *What am I wanting that I think I can't have now?*
   What I lost was_____
   and what I wanted was_____
2. *Allow yourself to see the "I can't," then look for one "I can" or several "I can's."*

3. Feel the struggle between the "I can't" and the "I can."

4. Feel the wanting.

5. Stay in the wanting until you receive new insights or thoughts that can help you achieve what you want.

6. Feel the wanting until it moves you to action.

EXERCISE

SADNESS INTO RECOGNITION, OR HEART BURIAL

You can want what you lost and feel deeply enough to want to struggle again to have it. The love, the wanting, encourages you to struggle for more life, as in the exercise "Sadness into Wanting." However, sometimes you have lost a person. The process is then more subtle and involves an awareness of your deep loving and your desire that the great aspects of that person continue. This exercise is more appropriate in that situation. It is a ritual that involves a process of acceptance, reflection, and recognizing and honoring the great aspects of life.

When your sadness is over the loss of a loved one, I like to call this exercise the Heart Burial.

Give yourself time alone with beautiful music.

1. See the situation of loss.

2. Feel the loss again.

3. Shift to your feelings of love for the person.

4. Within your feelings of love, remember the great characteristics of that person, drawing from your personal experience.

5. Find some way to symbolize those great aspects, and place those symbols in your environment to remind you of love and to inspire you to more life—OR

6. Place one or more of those great characteristics of the other person in your memory and your heart.

7. If you wish, be willing to cultivate and embody one or two of those great aspects in your own life and thus assure that the best of the other will continue to live on this earth through your conscious appreciation and love.

ANGER: STRUGGLING BETWEEN I CAN AND I CAN'T

Anger is our active reaction when desire or power is blocked. We cannot get what we want and are frustrated. This feeling can be internalized until we become sick, or it can be externalized into shouting, mild actions against others, or outright violence.

It is not always easy to recognize either our own anger or that of others. Because of different brain preferences we express anger differently. The following list can help you recognize better your own anger and that of people near you. It is important to be able to recognize the more subtle faces of anger, both to be able to heal yourself and to respond more adequately to others.

* A person with a preference for the left hemisphere expresses or hides anger in disagreements, rapid conclusions, rationalizations, justifications, and disapproval backed up with a long list of reasons.
* A person with a preference for the right hemisphere becomes disoriented and chaotic, uses absolutes, incomplete thoughts, generalizations, and evasions.
* A person with a preference for the limbic brain often hides anger in internal explosions, illnesses, silence, sadness, depression, physical symptoms, susceptibility, resentment, and withdrawal from others.
* A person with a preference for the basic brain can experience physical imbalance, bang into things, have accidents, or get into compulsive routines or displacement habits such as smoking, drinking, eating, drugs, or repetitive speech. People may either go toward the presence of others, as in groups or gangs, or turn completely away to isolation.

Once we have learned to recognize the many variations of anger, perhaps the most necessary skill to learn is how to defend ourselves from other people's anger rather than increasing it by our own hostile reaction. When anger is explosive, we all have the habit of defending ourselves. We call it survival, and it is indeed primordial. However, as a survival tactic, it is like throwing more fuel on the fire. "I did not, and what's more, it's your fault because you . . ." Hardly a way to stop a fight! With centuries of experience trying this method, by now we should be able to verify that it does not work. It neither calms the other person nor limits the field of battle. Quite the opposite. When we respond to aggression with aggression, be it verbal, emotional, physical, or any other form, we only increase the war.

The discovery of long-term memory in the limbic brain means that all of the frustrations of your life are registered in your own brain. Every new frustration is added to what is already there. The frustration of the moment is the latest in a long series of frustrations. Every one of us has a history of anger. It is no longer necessary to deny anger: a surgeon can put electrodes in someone's brain and discover it. Therefore, we all need to know how to defend ourselves from this human normality. First, we need to recognize anger by any of the methods listed above or by hearing an angry tone of voice.

Practice the following exercise to learn to defend yourself. Practice it as often as you would a martial art. It is an emotional art and deserves your repeated practice if you wish to be able to rise above your conditioned survival reaction to anger.

EXERCISE

DEFENSE AGAINST ANGER

1. *Notice the thunderstorm coming. Tell yourself, "I've gotten through before and will again. I can't stop the thunder or the anger or change this angry person."*

2. *Shift back to yourself. Center yourself and repeat to yourself constantly: "I am well. I am well. I am not the real target. I am well. I am well. I am not the real target. I am well. . . ." The purpose of this repetition is to strengthen yourself to withstand the attack.*

   You need to BE WELL to handle anger. If you start from a place of fear or get filled with your own anger, the attack and the anger will increase. The point is to prepare yourself, to remember that you are only the most recent trigger of the other person's anger. The real cause or target is buried under the many other times that the other has been frustrated by similar situations as recorded in his or her long-term memory. It is that memory that increases the pressure. You can hear it in an angry tone of voice as distinct from a usual tone of voice.

3. *Shift your observation to the other but remain grounded in yourself. Repeat internally to yourself, "He (she) is hurting and wanting." Do not say this out loud. The other person can't hear it just now. Remember, the definition of anger is not getting what you want. You may wish to offer an explanation, an apology, or help.*

4. *Shift back to yourself. Actively consider what you can do and what you cannot do.*

5. *Shift to the other. Express specifically what you can do and what you cannot do. In response to a parent's anger: "I can't change the grades the teacher already gave me, but I can try to get more help next semester." Emphasize what you can do, and continue to repeat the process until there is a softening around what can be done.*

EXERCISE

SHIFTING AWAY FROM ANGER

When you are angry and do not wish to express it or feel it at the moment, learn to shift away from it. Knowing that anger is fully recorded in your long-term memory, you can learn to make a later appointment with yourself for a time when you can safely feel your anger, explore it and heal yourself. When you wish to shift away, use any of the following strategies—but long before then, I hope you will have chosen one favorite method and practiced it until it is automatically available to you.

1. *Find and shift to an "I can." It is not a solution, but any "I can" will engage your attention. When you feel too angry to manage yourself, slowly look for and shift to any simple, small, easy "I can." Especially good for traffic and airport delays.*

2. *Shift to a routine or ritual. When frustrated, search for an activity that will entrain your energy, such as a hobby, sport, or meditation. Washing dishes also works—or chopping wood, raking leaves, even cleaning closets.*

3. *Look for a quiet room for feeling and expressing to the walls or to yourself, for holding with or healing yourself if there is time.*

4. *Use nonverbal expressions. Avoid expressing the content of your anger to avoid getting more deeply involved. Use sounds without content,*

growls, or any grumble of dissatisfaction to release your tension.

5. *Request a truce and time to consider. You probably need it to find out what is really bothering you and what you are really wanting.*

6. *Express your confusion. "I am not sure what is going on with me"; "This doesn't feel good"; and "I don't know what hit me."*

7. *Express your anger with a no-fault provision: "It's not your fault"; "I always have difficulty when . . ."; "This has happened to me before, and I get . . ."*

I believe that no-fault insurance, which was invented by the automobile industry to save the cost of constant court litigation over accidents, is one of the great ideas of our age. I wonder how long it will take us in the human industry to discover how much no-fault insurance will save us in hurt feelings and disintegrating relationships. Now that I know my anger is caused by my own history of anger and is only ticked off or stimulated by others when they bang into me and bend me out of shape, I am ready to take out no-fault insurance for all my human relationships. I hope you will seriously consider doing this, too.

EXERCISE
EXPRESSING ANGER PRIVATELY

I mentioned previously the importance of expressing anger in private rather than dumping it on the other person. Each one of your brains can help you express your anger. Your left hemisphere with its exactness over details can construct a legal case in your mind, or you can simply write a letter without sending it. Your right hemisphere can help you find what bothers you by imaging all the absolutes against the other person: "She always . . ."; "I will never talk to you again. . . ." Your limbic brain helps you feel again more deeply, allowing tears, complaints, grunts, or groans. Your basic brain can take you into action, allowing you to hit pillows, shout things over and over, or pace up and down.

Why all this activity? To what end? To relieve your constricted energy, to get anger's corrosive effects out of your body as quickly as possible. Catharsis, as it usually is called. But beyond that, there are four objectives that I consider to be the real reasons, if not the only valid reasons, for expressing anger privately:

1. *to find how your anger can be hiding or covering over what you really want; to search for what you really want*

2. *to discover the patterns of your anger involved in the moment; to learn your own anger patterns*

3. *to see, hear, feel, find anything positive that you CAN do; to know that anger is a struggle between "I can" and "I can't" and to search carefully to find an "I can" that will help you pull out of the struggle with a positive action in your favor*

4. *to allow you to exhaust yourself until you want to be still and go inward to heal your anger (see next exercise)*

For me these four points are as precious as gold. I believe it is really unfortunate to waste my energy shouting, screaming, or hitting pillows to discharge energy, without at the same time learning what I really, really want and seeing what I can do about it.

When I know what I really want, rather than just what triggered my anger, I may be ready to express my frustration to the other person. When I know something that I myself can do about my anger, I am no longer a victim; I am no longer dependent on the actions of the other. Now I am able not only to express but also to hold with through a process of negotiation.

EXERCISE

EXPRESSION WITH INTENT TO NEGOTIATE

- Be sure you want to express the anger. It may or may not be in your best interest. Just as you don't express all your thoughts, you don't have to express all your feelings. Be sure you wish to hold in and negotiate with the other person. If not, you might just as well express yourself privately. No one wishes to hear your dissatisfaction unless you are at least willing to look for alternatives!

- Begin with an "I" statement, not a "you" statement. An "I" statement demonstrates that I own the anger and the other person is not the cause. A "you" statement fuels the fire, makes the other defensive, keeps the war going, and results in argument and disconnection. Know how you would like to start. Train yourself to begin with "I." Several possibilities are: I am sorry, or I don't mean to burst out at you, or I'm angry . . . I'm having a hard time . . . , or It's not your fault . . . I just can't stand it when . . . .

• To express your feelings

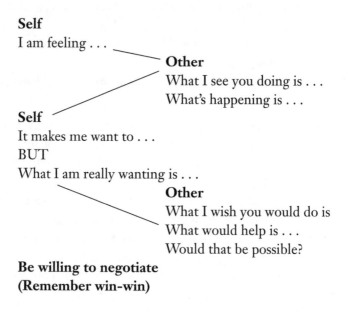

Self
I am feeling . . .

Other
What I see you doing is . . .
What's happening is . . .

Self
It makes me want to . . .
BUT
What I am really wanting is . . .

Other
What I wish you would do is
What would help is . . .
Would that be possible?

**Be willing to negotiate
(Remember win-win)**

There is some anger that we carry as wounds for many years. It continues to cause us harm and disturb our relationships. Liza had refused to see her father for five years, and when I met her she had no plans ever to see him again. Her anger with him no doubt had a long history, but the event that most infuriated her and was primary in her memory was the time he had taken sides with her brother and thrown her out of the house, labeling her and not her brother the cause of the turmoil. Liza had decided never to forgive him. Even though she continued her relationship with her brother, she decided that her father's actions were unforgivable. Her brother's appeal for reason and understanding fell on deaf ears.

At some level Liza realized that this wound was very deep and that she had carried her anger for too many years. As she was taking my course on Self Care, she felt she might as well try the exercise on healing her anger. As she returned to the experience, she found that she was no longer interested in action against her brother but that what she deeply wanted was for her father to recognize her efforts in school. When she discovered that the choice was either continuing to hate her father or being willing to give herself recognition for her efforts, she decided to do the latter.

For the next month she practiced giving herself recognition and became convinced that it was possible to heal the old wound. She felt differently. She then sent a postcard to her father, who answered with another postcard. She took the next step of inviting him to dinner, and the communication has been open ever since. I might add that she must have done an excellent reprogramming in the second part of the exercise, because she now takes the initiative in recognizing her capabilities and has even gone on for a doctorate in psychology, which gives me some assurance that she will know how to protect her power in the future. (See Part Three of the following exercise.)

If you wish to heal any long-standing anger, give yourself time to do the following exercise. It is really more of a meditation and is best done in three parts with rest in between and beautiful music to accompany you. After you have practiced this often and have memorized the sequence, you will be able to apply it easily and frequently as you go about your daily life.

EXERCISE

HEALING ANGER

Part One: Getting the Gift

1. *Make a conceptual shift from "You are the cause of my anger" to "I am the cause." This situation is triggering something in me, in my emotional history. It reminds me of previous situations where I felt hurt because I couldn't get what I wanted.*
2. *Ask "when" and not "why." Instead of asking "Why am I mad?" ask, "When did this happen before in my life? This reminds me of . . . ." Roll back your tapes of recorded memory. You may stop at any situation that seems appropriate, but often the earliest scenes with your parents are the most poignant. Because of our need for their love, early memories of not getting what we wanted often contain the most hurt*

— 159 —

or anger. Whatever situation you select, make sure it is similar to the situation in the present that makes you mad.

3. *Visualize and feel the earlier situation again. See it, enter it, and be affected by it until you reach empathy with yourself, until you are with the pathos of that situation and care that it is this human being—your self—who is hurting, until you can feel empathy for yourself.*

4. *What were you really wanting? While you are feeling yourself in the situation, look for what you were really wanting.*

5. *Will you give it to yourself now? Are you capable of giving it to yourself now, or do you want to continue insisting that the other person give it to you? You are now against the wall: either continue being angry at the other for not giving it to you or decide in favor of giving it to yourself. In cases where what you desired may not be possible in your present reality, your gift to yourself can be something similar rather than exactly the same object. It can be something as general as recognition. Are you willing to give yourself recognition in the near future? In what area of your life will you give it? This is the key: if you don't give it to yourself, the other person will remain guilty in your mind for not having given it to you. The neocortex will continue to think that way and the limbic will continue to feel anger. Either you end the vengeance by giving to yourself what the other was not able to give or did not give, or you continue in resentment and anger rather than healing.*

6. *If you are willing to give yourself whatever the other did not give to you or did not do for you, ask yourself: when, where, and how will I give myself that or do that for myself in the next weeks and months? Plan carefully, and honor any promises you make.*

7. *Until you can act on your promise, close this part of the exercise by visualizing and feeling yourself giving it to yourself.*

8. *The more you realize that it was your anger with the other that led you to discover something that was missing in your life, the better you will feel about him or her.*

If you succeed in giving to yourself now what you wanted then you will feel good. The purpose of Part One is to heal your limbic brain. Please go on to Part Two to reprogram the decision you made in your neocortex.

Part Two: Inner Energy Battle

There still remains the necessity of reprogramming your thoughts. Your decision in response to that early anger—chosen most likely when you were small and weak—may be inappropriate for who and what you are today. However, it is still locked in as an appropriate decision until you make an effort to program in your mind another decision. It is as if we took photos in our child mind which will remain active until we make new ones. I do not believe we actually replace old decisions, but I do believe we can program on top of them. (See the chapter on pattern intelligence.)

Part Two consists of an energy battle with the other person in which you have the opportunity to decide again. Then when a similar situation arises, you can meet it with your more recent and consciously considered decision.

1. *Give yourself time and make yourself comfortable. Although the situation you wish to heal may have occurred when you were very young, now you are an adult. You have a different body and mind and a great deal more knowledge. Visualize yourself now as a fully empowered adult, even though you are about to discuss a situation that occurred long ago.*
2. *Visualize the face of the other person and imagine yourself face-to-face with him or her.*
3. *Begin an internal dialogue between the two of you. Permit the other person to offer an explanation or defense, but this time, it is necessary that you win the battle, that you resolve the situation in a way that feels right to you. It is urgent that you explain to the other person how you want him or her to act differently with you. This is an internal energy battle, the other person's will against your will, and you can't give up or leave it in a state of confusion.*
4. *Continue until you arrive at a resolution, a win/win, with each of you gaining something from the other. When you succeed, you will feel warm and good. You will feel a change of energy.*
5. *Go back to visualize the recent situation that caused your anger and visualize yourself responding based on the new dialogue you have just experienced.*

The purpose of the energy battle is to reprogram yourself. What you were dealing with was not the other person but the conclusion you had reached about the other person in your mind. The photograph you took of the other person in that situation has remained registered in your memory ever since. If you succeed in reaching a new decision, a new program within you, you are going to be able to react well with similar persons and situations in the future. Then, whatever triggered your anger, sending you on this long healing journey, will have helped you, because you will have succeeded in discovering the cause of your hurt and anger and of doing something about it. You will have succeeded in replacing dependency on and anger with the other by loving yourself through the very specific act of giving something to yourself that others could not or would not give you. The purpose of anger is to diagnose exactly where you need to give yourself love. No doctor can reach into this level of memory within your limbic brain and heal you. Only anger can provide so specific a diagnosis of where you are hurting and wanting. Only you, willing to explore your own anger, can find your hurts and become the healer.

Part Three: Managing Your Power More Carefully

Anger is your emotional reaction to loss of power. It is a signal to alert you that you care about being powerful in a particular situation or with a particular person. Power is energy; it is the life force within you. Anger shows you exactly where the obstructions to your power or life force are located, where you felt yourself or believed yourself to be powerful before you were blocked.

1. Ask yourself what activity you were engaged in when you got angry.

2. This activity will tell you where you have invested your power. Although you may feel weak at the moment because you are unable to continue, remember that it was your activity and your power that got interrupted and made you feel frustrated and angry. Identify the activity that was making you feel powerful. You may need to complete the sentence: "What I care about that got interrupted was . . . ."

3. Close your eyes in order to concentrate and reflect. Think about and visualize how you can better manage this particular power in you that you care about. How can you do a better job of caring for this particular activity? Do you need help, more time, more sensitivity, more planning, the willingness to avoid obstacles? How can you protect this specific power?

When you realize how deeply you resent having your power obstructed, you may also be more aware that you do indeed care about your power and need to manage it better. Instead of focusing on how the outside world is offending you, you may begin to focus on taking conscious care of yourself and what really matters to you. Anger can show you what you really care about. Your reaction of frustration can serve as an alarm, signaling that you have not carefully protected your power. It may now be possible for you to manage your power differently, to move around obstructions, and above all when you feel yourself frustrated, to take your frustration as a checkpoint and consider how to move through the obstacle rather than reacting by going more deeply into anger.

At a workshop I was leading, there was a knock at my door and Robert's wife pleaded with me to come to her room. Her husband had "lost it"; he was murmuring to himself, gesturing, and reaching over his head as if trying to communicate with unknown beings. After I showed considerable empathy and identification with him, he began to talk with me about his life. Although his wife knew his story, she sat patiently nearby, listening as if for the first time. He spoke of being unwanted by his mother. Unwed, she had fallen in love with his father, an important figure in the town. The mother preferred her lover's attention and did not want to embarrass him with the birth of a son. She hid Robert at her parents' home and returned to enjoy her love affair. What message must Robert have received in those first seven years of life? "I'm loved but not wanted." "My father is powerful, but I can't be his son." "My mother loves me but doesn't want me." We will never be certain which of these messages he received. What is certain is that the more he told me, the angrier he became, starting to shout and wave his arms. He saw his wife and slapped her. He grabbed her, and I tried to stop him. His violence was increasing. I held his arms until I could get myself and his wife out of the room. It was a long and difficult night. Eventually Robert accepted pills that calmed him—at least temporarily. He received more help and once again has a calm and gentle exterior, holding down his professional position at a university. Who will know that under this calm exterior lies violence waiting for another chance?

I tell this story to indicate that anger stores itself in memory, that hurt does not disappear, that it waits, curled up behind the intellect, or crashes out in violence when it finds a weaker victim. It is therefore only our conscious decision to heal our ancient hurts that will eliminate our inner violence.

If we would dedicate enough time to healing our anger instead of blaming the other, we would change the balance of war and peace in favor of greater peace. If we would know that anger exists to show us where we need to give ourselves love, we would be able to heal ourselves by continually nourishing our own life. Blame and scapegoats would disappear. If we would know that our anger is a signal that we need to manage our power differently, we would indeed become protectors of life. We would have risen to the greatest challenges of mood intelligence.

CHAPTER XI

Lighting Your Own Fire

MOTIVATIONAL INTELLIGENCE

Well, why else do you think you behave? Everything you do is run by your emotions.

Candace Pert

The motivated person is on the move, continuously desiring, slowing down sometimes, a shuffle here or there, but intense, deep, certain. Sometimes we look through our neocortical lens at a person like that and shake our heads, saying, "I don't know how she does it. She just keeps on going. Never lets up." We think she should rest a while, be more balanced, be interested in something else. Our negative jabs reflect our jealousy. Even while we criticize, we long to know her secret: What would really get us going? Really motivate us? Propel us to a job well done, to success, accomplishment, enjoyment, and love? We are all pretty sure that if it is not pure luck, that it has something to do with being motivated.

Motivational intelligence is the capacity to recognize what we want and what moves us to action. It is being able to guide our life in relation to our wanting and desiring. Using motivational intelligence means being aware of what moves us and being able to guide what moves us. Just as we use rational intelligence to guide our life through a process of reasoning, we can use motivational intelligence to guide our life through a process of desiring.

It is certain that if motivation is about moving ourselves through life, then all three brains must somehow be involved in that process. We may process our visions and dreams through the right hemisphere, but without some exact goal setting and specific details from our left, we may never realize our dreams. It is also true that if our goals or desires run counter to our values or the deepest conditioning of our basic brain, we may never be able to motivate ourselves, no matter how hard we try. Although all brain systems are helpful, I believe the secret to motivation is love, desire, wanting, and the passion we associate only with the limbic brain. Wanting and desiring are popular terms that identify the basic governing vibrations of the limbic brain.

Am I conditioned to want something, or do I really want it independent of my conditioning? "You can't want what you haven't known" is an oft-repeated phrase. What I want to draw attention to is the vital connection between patterns and wanting (also discussed in the chapter on pattern intelligence). At an early age my basic brain began to be conditioned. More precisely, patterns were registered in my memory then which continue to affect my nervous system today. I may continue to act through many years of my life, or all of my life, following these patterns. They may determine my wanting, as all behaviorists will argue and as I agree. However, we can also want independently of our deepest conditioning. What is important to me is that we can focus on this wanting—this unique phenomenon of the emotional brain—to enable us to guide ourselves away from conditioned patterns. Although those patterns might have helped us survive, they may now be outdated, even harmful to our life.

The most important function of a therapist or helping professional may be to awaken this wanting, this desire to live in spite of the patterns that are determining the harmful behaviors that made someone first seek help. Therapists may indeed be wasting their time and their patient's if they cannot perceive and access the deeper wanting of the person seeking help. Rollo May referred to this deep wanting as "intentionality," the discovery of the real intentions or the real wanting of the patient when the session begins.[1] In search of the real wanting, sometimes the therapist intuits, sometimes asks, or sometimes focuses into the dynamics of emotion. To know that wanting exists independently of the repetitive process involved in conditioning can encourage us to be affected by desire and pleasure while we work on the longer process of overcoming early conditioning.

Our patterns can thus affect our wanting, but our wanting can also exist independent of patterns. Even more important, it is our wanting, desire, and passion that we need to encourage in order to give ourselves the strength to live and the strength to untangle ourselves from debilitating patterns and go on to form new patterns that will help us.

From Wanting to Love

Perhaps the greatest contribution the limbic system can make to life is freeing us to acknowledge the importance of wanting and desire. By this wanting and desiring, we enter deeply into connection both with ourselves and with other life. Our desire to eat keeps us alive; our desire to love and be loved by others also keeps us alive. Wanting is basic to motivation. "What do you want?" "What really excites you?" "What gets you into motion?" are the stuff of the limbic brain.

If it is true that it takes all three brains to motivate us, if it takes the goal and the dream of the left and right hemispheres and the supportive values or patterns and routines of the R-system, why then have I dared to identify motivational intelligence with the phenomenon of wanting and desire in the limbic brain? The answer: I believe that unless we want in life, and want powerfully enough to learn what we want in very specific terms, we will use our other brain systems to enervate ourselves gradually, de-motivate ourselves, sabotage ourselves, and finally destroy ourselves. When we are not conscious of our desires, our neocortex can find reasons or images to justify our retreat from life or from life forces that might nourish us. For those who have inherited a pattern of depression from their family or culture, their basic brain may be doing this without their conscious neocortical awareness. If we are not conscious of or do not know the importance of wanting, we can gradually lose interest in our business, our home, our family, our loved ones, our friends, and, eventually, our own life. The answer is to fight back, learn the importance of desire, and carefully invite it back into our life. The fight begins by convincing the neocortex of the relationship of wanting to the sane and joyful management of our health and our life.

I believe we have not paid attention to, honored, or understood the phenomenon of wanting and desire. With the discovery of the limbic brain system, we may finally see that wanting is a key phenomenon of life. It may even be the master phenomenon that governs various phenomena in the other brain systems. We understand if we want to understand. We perceive if we want to perceive. We dream if we want to dream, hear or see or remember only what we really want, smell or eat or make love if we want to, act if we want to.

We can also bury our wantings. By not admitting them, we prefer to be unconscious that at some level we are always doing what we want to. The limbic brain carries on without our conscious participation. If it did not, we might not be alive. We have only buried our excitement, because we are more conditioned to saying that we were working all day or helping others or obliged to or doing the only reasonable thing—and so forth. We have buried the most valuable phenomenon of wanting because it sounds more acceptable in our culture to say "I was busy" than to say "I was doing what I wanted to do." We value and honor our busyness, but not our wanting.

To try to find out what you want, you will have to go searching for what really excites you. You will have to study yourself consciously to find what you are wanting, what makes you feel excited and expanded, what starts you trembling with excitement, what stirs you into motion. The knowledge of what excites you and what has always excited you becomes the match that you keep on lighting to illuminate your fire of wanting. Wanting is the fuel for motivation. Only this fuel can keep you motivated or keep you really in love with life.

Wanting is the constant vibration of the limbic brain. Thinking is to the left hemisphere and imagining and intuiting are to the right hemisphere what wanting is to the limbic brain. When wanting diminishes, so also the vibrations of the limbic brain diminish, with consequent effects on one's health and interest in life.

Wanting is, I believe, the deep fire within us to which Pierre Teilhard de Chardin alluded in his *Toward the Future*:

The day will come when after harnessing the ether, the winds, the tides, gravitation, we shall harness for God the energies of love. And, on that day, for the second time in the history of the world, man will have discovered fire.[2]

Wanting is the slow, burning fire that leads us ever more deeply into all the emotions. If we learn how to stay in and move through that fire, we arrive at love, at personal love as well as compassion. If we put out the fire of wanting, we will never harness, neither for God nor for ourselves, the energies of love. It is only insistent, burning desire that enables us to blow on the fading embers when love begins to die. It is only our desiring of love that can keep love alive. We have honored love and compassion. We now must honor the process of wanting and desire, so inextricably connected with love and compassion. We cannot afford to be unclear about desire. Life is at stake, and desire is our fuel.

Obstacles to Desire

I believe that the greatest obstacle to motivation is our lack of clarity about wanting and desire. As we try to live our desires, we get into conflict with others, we experience painful moods, and often we give up. Mood intelligence will help a great deal, but I believe that until we truly encounter this enormous emotional frontier of wanting and desiring, we will not be able to live life fully.

There are many obstacles to feeling our desires. To want is a phenomenon that has been inadequately described with words. If someone asks you, "What do you want?" you might admit to some fantasy or mention some hidden desire—or perhaps answer that you don't know. In workshops the usual answer is, "Sometimes I want this; sometimes I want that." These doubts and glimpses are characteristics of the right hemisphere of the neocortex, not of the limbic brain. Wanting in the limbic brain can be felt in the body; it is gut level.

Another problem is that wanting has been commercialized by advertising. The continual visual seduction of TV ads bombards us, trying to make us want what we see. It is doubtful, however, that the responses that we call desires are at a deep gut level, or even at a heart level. We may say we wish we could have, but rarely feel "I am really wanting." Often, if we have to ask twice if we really want something, it is enough to make us abandon our desire. It was really only a wish, an impression or attraction of the neocortex.

Other people may easily make us forget our wanting or persuade us it is not convenient. We prefer to change our minds instead of staying in our gut. We butterfly from wish to wish, refusing to feel deeply that of which we so freely speak and imagine.

Neither is action always a clear indicator of desire. Sometimes actions indicate what people are wanting; their desires may have moved and motivated them to act. However, we can also want something deeply but dissipate our energy of wanting, whether by means of our right hemisphere dreaming about it or by means of our left hemisphere planning it in so much detail that we never get around to acting on it. We can also dissipate our desire in the well-established rituals or obligations of the basic brain that cover up our passion or permit us to avoid what we are really wanting. Many of us awaken in middle age to discover we have been hiding our deepest desires under our rituals of work and family. We call it a crisis, but it is only a wake-up call finally to include in our life what we are really wanting.

There are many ways of hiding wanting without realizing that is what we are doing. Wanting affects the entire body, and when we are no longer able to obtain what we desire, we somatize—we put our body into a state of semi-sleep. Wanting can easily be diminished and avoided until it becomes a very unclear dynamic which sometimes we admit as wanting and sometimes we do not even recognize.

With our neocortex and especially our rational mind, we often conclude that what we want is not something intelligent. "Why want it, when I know I can't have it?" concludes the neocortex. Seems reasonable, but what about the struggle for and with life? What about staying in our wanting, holding with the desire, and receiving, rather than avoiding the reality feedback? Instead of staying in the process of wanting, we make hasty judgments. Instead of holding with the wanting until we become successful, we decide success really does not interest us. Instead of continuing to love someone, we decide it is not worth the trouble, that it would be better to look for someone else. In this way, we can go on leaving pieces of our heart and gut strewn across the pathways of our life.

We prefer to make judgments instead of living through difficult feedback. What we want becomes less important than what we estimate, judge, or intuit is possible. Everything becomes more important than being able to succeed in what we want. We focus on the result instead of focusing on the process of living without trying to calculate the results in advance. We get fixed on the object of loving someone or of having money rather than involving ourselves in the process in order to achieve that result. In this way we frequently wander into a maze of little streets, losing the main highway. We need to give importance to the *process* of wanting and to how to motivate ourselves to live the entire process in order to arrive at the desired result.

Very often the fear of failure reduces our enthusiasm and is the hidden reason we cut the process of fully living our desire. We need to know that to fail is not a risk. It is a necessary part of the process of going forward. The scientific process is an example of a well-developed ritual that not only values and reports failures so that others can learn where not to go, but also presupposes that someone will continue the journey, certain that there are many alternatives.

However, if you are not a scientist, you have not been taught this ritual, and even scientists fail to associate this process of continuous wanting with their personal lives. Scientists reading this book may even feel uncomfortable that I have identified their highly neocortical scientific process with the limbic process of wanting and desiring. Why? Why do we feel uncomfortable with our wanting? To insist on our desire is frequently called "being egotistical." As children we were taught it was selfish to want too much. "Too much" was never clarified. Sometimes it came with guilt-ridden phrases such as ". . . when you know we can't afford . . . ," "Your father works day and night and you want . . . ," or "Other children don't have that." Parents or other care-givers alluded to children in faraway lands, while we had our eyes fixed on the child next door who did indeed have what we were wanting.

I am angry when I see how we have conditioned ourselves and our children to hide this life-giving phenomenon, teaching them that it is selfish or egotistical to want instead of teaching them appropriate ways to get what they want or at least to feel excited about what they want. When we stop wanting, we die. Most of us know of terminally ill people who have stayed alive a month or even several years because they wanted to see a loved one or wanted to witness an important event. In spite of that, when people say clearly "I want," we think they are selfish; when they say "I don't want," we think they are spoiled. It is our concept of the ego along with its negative sisters, selfish and egotistical, that has been keeping us from taking a positive look at desire and discovering how it can help protect and nourish our life.

Accusations of being selfish and spoiled are often supported by religious injunctions to serve others rather than ourselves. However, I believe that when we cast aspersions on wanting as being selfish or anti-religious, we are going counter to a life phenomenon that constantly nourishes creation. Indeed, desire is basic to all creation.

A person's deepest desire and longing is a profound religious as well as material issue. Jesus was a passionate seeker, clear about what moved Him and about what He wanted on this earth. He wanted to rid the temple of the moneylenders, and He did it. He wanted to enter Jerusalem, and He did it. He wanted to heal the sick, and He did it. He continued wanting to unite people with God, even at the cost of enduring suffering from His captors. He wanted to be a witness to God, and throughout the process of His death and resurrection, He never stopped His wanting or abandoned His desire. Are not these magnificent examples of desire?

Even Buddha, whose followers often invite us to give up desire, was a passionate seeker. He desired more than the rest of us: he desired to know the absolute nature of reality until he realized it. You may argue that he found the absolute only when he sat down under the bodhi tree, but I have to ask: Was it the passion burning within his being that so opened the cells of his brain that he was able to experience absolute reality? If he had been born under the tree and never moved, never longed for the truth, would the experience have been the same? I believe not, because I believe his limbic brain would never have been affected and his organs never touched, and without the heat generated within the body and cells of the brain, one does not see the light.

When the neocortex looks at an experience, speaks about an experience, and followers continue to explain the experience, I believe that what we hear is not the original experience as it was felt and acted. The three-brain systems allow us to distinguish this: the thought emanating from the neocortex; the wanting, a matter of the heart, governed as we now know by the limbic brain; and finally, the efforts of the disciples to repeat the experience, the repetition of the deepest basic brain. Therefore, in order to understand the religious depth of wanting, it is necessary to focus on the heart of Jesus and of the Buddha as well as on their long process of wanting and desiring.

We also have difficulty with wanting because it is linked in our minds with pleasure. We want pleasure; pleasure feels good. But—isn't it forbidden? Isn't it hedonism? Pleasure was loudly rejected by the Calvinist roots of Christianity as well as by the hard work ethic of the American society. Religious and social values seem to bar the way. Again we are caught in the trap of staying in only one reality or one brain system, the basic brain of values and obligations.

We need not choose between hard work and pleasure; we can have both hard work and pleasure. Our limbic brain, and more particularly the organs of our body, need the expansive relaxing state that we call pleasure. As we saw in the chapter on mood intelligence, if we do not produce pleasure naturally, we may, or are regrettably likely to, produce pleasure through the artificial means of drugs. Pleasure needs to be revisioned as life-giving rather than as hedonism, greed, or laziness. This revision is possible when we realize we are guiding ourselves through three brain systems rather than one. We do not need to let our neocortex make an absolute of its approach to life, nor stay indulgent forever in the limbic brain of pleasure, nor abandon our deepest basic brain's need for the order and repetition that work can provide.

Perhaps our greatest difficulty with wanting is thinking that we have to satisfy all our desires. I believe this is what makes us quiet children when they say they want something. We think we must satisfy them. The same is true as adults. We do not like to hear a loved one, wife, husband, or friend express a want, because we think we should satisfy it. Instead of calling the other spoiled or thinking we have to satisfy their endless desires—we could honor their wanting and then encourage them, or help them to do the work to get what they are wanting. This is the deep change that we all need to make in order to be able to honor our own desires and those of others.

Wanting and Satisfying: Dynamic Twins

Wanting never ends. It is a key process that lasts all our lives. To want is forever; satisfactions are temporary. Wanting is the name given to the emotional process of expansion that functions continually in the limbic brain. Satisfaction is the name given when we temporarily close around success. We achieve something we were wanting and feel satisfaction, a sense of well-being. Satisfaction is a twin process that needs to accompany desire. Instead of discounting desire, welcome it and look to see how it can be satisfied. Satisfaction is the stopping point or resting point in the process of desire.

There is, of course, the problem of never being satisfied. You wanted a new suit, you saved up, and you went to buy it. Now you criticize yourself for not being satisfied with the suit or for wanting more than just a suit. You ask yourself, "Will I never have enough? Will I never be satisfied?" It is normal and important to continue wanting, whether it be a new pair of shoes, a new hairstyle, or a tie that sets off that new suit— whatever. Although it may be normal, it has often proved difficult to handle dissatisfaction. What to do, then, with this phenomenon of dissatisfaction?

- Realize that every time you satisfy a desire you can rest and celebrate instead of criticizing yourself for wanting more.
- Use your neocortex to select the desires that are within your budget or that are otherwise possible for you. Also, use your neocortex to establish your priorities, always referring back to your limbic brain to check if that something is what you really want.
- Use your basic brain either to rest or to act on something else.
- Remember that the twins of wanting and satisfying will last forever and that they indicate that your emotional being is well and quite alive, dynamic and in motion. Healthy, in fact!

Wanting is continuous; satisfaction depends on possibilities. Just as we learn to continue our thoughts until we reach conclusion, we can also learn to continue our wanting until we reach some form of satisfaction. Satisfaction is to wanting as conclusion is to thinking—a form of temporary closure.

Also, while many of our thoughts never end, we do not criticize ourselves for continual thinking. In the same way, many desires can be felt and even expressed without being satisfied, and we do not have to criticize ourselves for wanting.

What we can know clearly is that we do not need to act on every desire or rush to satisfy all of them. A desire is an emotional indicator. Wanting and desiring are indications of our profound involvement in life, and they show us what we have allowed ourselves to be affected by. As the emotional signals that they are, they tell us what we want, what we love. When our wanting is neither pleasant nor life-giving or when it gets too expensive, we do not have to continue wanting.

Unless we are trapped in an addiction (which can require special attention, discussed in the chapter on pattern intelligence), we can withdraw from any desire by lowering the volume, just as we do with music. In this emotional process of wanting, we need to diminish our vibrations by focusing less and less on the object of the desire we cannot satisfy or no longer wish to satisfy. We need to use our neocortex to give reasons for diminishing our interest and our basic brain of action to get ourselves to withdraw from the object of desire. Before we pull out on desire, however, we must check to see if there is not something that would give us satisfaction or if indeed we still really desire—at heart level or gut level.

Also, we can put our rational intelligence at the service of our emotional brain. For example, if I know something is not good for me or notice that I do not feel good doing something, I can then decide not to go any deeper or not to keep on going. We govern the process of allowing ourselves to be affected, of entering into something, of going more deeply, of satisfying our desire, or of pulling ourselves away.

Practicing Motivational Intelligence

Four key processes are involved in motivational intelligence.

First Process. Engage in feeling what you want, wanting it, and letting the wanting move you. Be careful not to lose the process of feeling in order to follow a preestablished plan. We sometimes exchange the feeling for the plan. We can lose our feeling by imagining or focusing on an eventual goal. Motivation is then converted to stress because we override our feelings and give priority to new mental visions.

Feelings can help you be efficient because they give you real and immediate feedback. Instead of using only your neocortex to develop a plan and then continuing nonstop toward the goal, it is important to interrupt in the middle of a project to ask yourself what you are feeling. What feedback are you receiving, and how does it make you feel? At this new point in the project, what are you wanting now? Then you can use feelings to readjust your plans rather than ignoring them, which can lead to hurt, wasted motion, or subtle sabotage. Knowing what you really want can save time, money, and heartache. When you know what you're feeling or wanting as the project continues, you can invite your neocortex into more accurate, more efficient, and less illusory planning. If you cannot feel the subtleties of what is occurring, you will proceed without the information that feelings can offer. By feeling the blocks, you will be able to move around them or through them. Within those blocks may be the necessary power as well as information needed to complete your project successfully.

The key to this process of motivational intelligence is to feel what we want, experience the desire, and live our longing. Sometimes we think that is painful. Sometimes it feels painful and we immediately shift to thinking about doing or thinking about wanting, moving away from experiencing our wanting at a visceral level. Wanting then becomes intellectualized or postponed or framed as goal setting. However, the truth of experience is the same here as elsewhere: we know how to want only by the experience of wanting. We need this experience of wanting to be able to motivate ourselves.

Second Process. The second process involves observing what makes us enthusiastic and more specifically observing what excites us. In order to motivate ourselves consciously, we need to keep ourselves in a good mood. We have to know how to move ourselves within experiences that excite us. To motivate ourselves consciously means to excite ourselves consciously. Therefore, we need to know whether we get excited by situations, people, food, drinks, ideas, music, sexuality, challenges, art, sports, hobbies, weather, recognition, flirting, compliments, or rewards. What is it *exactly* that gets us excited? We have to observe our own reactions to life in order to know that consciously—otherwise we will be a victim to trial and error or unconscious experience, which will eventually exhaust us.

Desire is a deep, passionate, unclear feeling. Noticing or observing is a keen, subtle observational skill. To feel and to observe are two very different abilities. You need to watch and observe your body to see what gets it to act. What makes you pick up the phone, take a plane, write a book, or see clients? What gets you to do an action again and again? It is as though the neocortical mind must hover above the fire and watch what makes it flare up. Only by observing our bodies very closely can we notice what stimulates us to move: good company, someone in need, money, a compliment, God, status, making love, childhood dreams. As we pick up clues to what excites us, then when we want to continue to be excited and motivated, we use these clues as matches to throw again and again on our fire.

For example, if you respond to compliments, you can ask for them. Tell yourself you are wonderful; get anyone else to tell you you are wonderful. You don't need to shift into your neocortex to doubt the compliment or decide if it is objectively true. Just give it to yourself. Feed the flames to keep your fire alive, to get yourself to continue living.

This, I believe, is the secret to conscious motivation: being willing and able to notice which matches work and then using these matches continually to light the flame. To be able to stay in the wanting, in the longing, in the desiring through the vagaries and the difficulties as well as intensities of life, we need to feed the flames so the fire will not go out. First we need the matches, the knowledge of exactly what excites us. We then need to use these matches to stay in the heat and desire and passion.

EXERCISE

THE MATCHES

To find your matches, begin with observation. Put yourself in a relaxed state in which you feel free to observe yourself from a distance. Be prepared to forestall any type of judgment or prejudice against what you observe and to focus on the details of what makes you enthusiastic or what excites you.

1. *If others want to make you happy, how do they do it? Do they act in a specific way, say something, or show you something? Visualize yourself first in the presence of a loved one, then with a friend, and then with your children. Visualize yourself in a bad mood, and then observe how each loved one knows how to return you to an enthusiastic state of mind. What methods do they use?*

2. *When you are in a bad mood, how do you recover? What do you know how to do for yourself to motivate yourself again? "What makes me feel good is . . . ."*

3. *Review the events of the last two weeks. Focus carefully on the happy moments. What is it exactly that moves you in your home, in your work, in your free time? In that period, what did you most enjoy doing?*

4. *Review your life in search of the gold: what did you do tremendously well? What excited you in the different stages of your childhood? When you went to grade school? To high school? In your family, your adolescence, and your university? Continue to look for the excitement. Move to your first job and your present one, your best vacations and your most recent ones. What moves you in your relationships and your loves?*

5. *Review all that you have written and, accompanied by music, give yourself time to feel each notation, enjoying the best of your life.*

6. *Select five things you could give to yourself in order to get yourself excited. They need to be things you can initiate without the help of another person. These are your matches. If the day is not going well, you can use one of your matches to motivate yourself and assure yourself that you can always end up having had a good day.*

7. *Write your matches in simple language so you can remember them and then memorize them in association with each finger of your left hand. Or, you can write them on little pieces of paper and put them in a real matchbox. Put the box in a specific place of honor to remind yourself that you never again need to be the victim of a bad day or week or year! It is a matter of lighting the flames of your own life and being sure that each day is guided by what motivates you.*

Others may make great efforts to motivate you with little or no results. Only you can know what truly excites you. Really, it is always you who knows best how to motivate yourself.

Third Process. The third aspect of motivation is to find some way to identify our life with all life.

What is the fire that we are trying to keep alive? It is life itself. It is energy or whatever concept we use to define energy: God, work, love. Life is energy in some form. We need to look at this deeply, because it is exactly life itself that we are questioning when we are not motivated. When we doubt or question life, what we experience is a loss of energy. "There's no reason to do anything, no reason to move or act today. Besides, I don't feel like it. I don't want to do anything!" With our neocortex we can doubt and question any aspect of life in front of us. With our deepest basic brain we can wrap life into a package of obligations. Our energy gets buried under a series of endless tasks and "shoulds" we must complete. The neocortex doubts life, the basic brain builds walls around it, and the limbic brain just gets worn out.

How can the limbic brain help? One way is to free the limbic from its neocortical and reptilian cousins that are insistently pursuing it with doubt and obligation. Free the limbic brain for what purpose? To fulfill its role in relation to energy, to life itself: to encourage us to feel like being, to feel like doing, to feel good or bad or ambivalent or angry or loving whenever and wherever, until we can penetrate these moods and discover what we really desire, what we are really wanting. To feel is a sacred dimension of life. When we have no desire or wanting, we are in danger of losing life itself. Without desire, we give in to entropy, to the closing in of energy on itself. We do not want to use our matches, we refuse to motivate ourselves, we allow the fire of life to go out.

This is why the third aspect of motivation is knowing the nature of life: life is energy itself. When we refuse to rouse ourselves, we refuse to participate in life itself. Many times that is exactly what we may feel like doing: we are mad at life, we grudge, we hold out, or subtly we sabotage. Herein lies the importance of mood intelligence: to develop the capacity for travelling into our emotions and shifting out of them. Knowing that emotions are our intelligent reactions toward life, we can travel into them, find their information, and then use them to put ourselves back into the mainstream of energy.

That is why we need to know that we are energy and find some way to identify with that mainstream. The secret is knowing that we are one with the river, one with life, one with energy.

I am energy. I am life. Every time I deny life, I lose energy. I lose vibration and warmth. To be alive is to be hot; to be the oxygen-burning furnace of life that we truly are. The farther we get from the fire, the smaller our flame and the colder we become. If we identify ourselves with the river of life, we can move with it, live our moods, and use our matches to keep ourselves in motion—staying warm, passionate, excited, staying truly and vibrantly alive.

What would finally make the difference in life? I believe it is this: the identification of our life with all life. It is not to declare or think or feel ourselves separate. If we identify with energy, we will feel that we belong, that we are "a member of," and will be continually accepting and receiving energy.

Fourth Process. The last process of motivation is to be disposed to fall in love with life.

It is sufficient to be in love with something or someone, whatever that may be. What I love is what moves me most deeply. Any love affair will do. Any love affair means with any person, place, thing, animal, idea, object, work, or leisure. I repeat: any love affair will do. It is our way of saying yes to life already in existence—honoring what is here, approaching it, penetrating, surrounding, and integrating ourselves with it. When we do this, new life is born in many forms, and these forms continue in the motion mainstream of life. By making love with life, we give birth to new life. Life is motion, and as motion continues, we continue; we exist differently in ever-renewable forms, penetrating, surrounding, and continually making love with life. Intercourse every day is the answer to motivation. Intercourse with any aspect of life will do.

We first knew Elizabeth as the person who spent eight days of our course reclining in a hammock at the edge of a group all properly seated in chairs. She prevented anyone else from taking over her territory. We noticed her presence only when she would raise her hand from time to time and lift her head to ask a question. She always seemed sensitive, intelligent, and happy, so I concluded that she must be a very peaceful person. Much to my surprise she is actually a powerhouse in everyday life, continually on the move, helping other people, and creating new ideas for the school she has directed for many years. Everywhere she goes she brings her enthusiasm for change and actually adds her support to make those changes. For her, everything is possible and indeed possible right now. She carries on with enthusiasm, but deep within is a tremendous love of life. She is not only in love with the life of her school and the students within it, she is also in love with new ideas, with her country as well as travel, with beaches and picnics and laughter and theater. She does not think consciously of how to motivate someone; she is motivation herself. She is always lighting one of her many matches and speaking up for life. If I could I would export her.

The purpose of motivational intelligence is the sustaining of life. It is a most sacred love affair. To love life is to love our deepest connection with creation. To understand that our body is the sacred form in which we have been entrusted to live our life gives motivation its sacred dimension. Motivational intelligence is to guide ourselves and sustain ourselves in this deep river that is life itself.

CHAPTER XII

Emotional Intelligence and the Openings of Your Body

With your eyes you take in light
With your ears you take in sound
With your nose you take in oxygen
With your mouth, plant and animal life
With your genitals, human life
With your skin, all that surrounds you.

W*ith each opening we are exposed to other life. We are in resonance, dissonance, contact, and connection either at higher speeds and more subtle vibrations of light or increasingly more dense vibrations in the form of human life and our environment.*

All these variations of life interact with us. They affect us, move us into different moods, and motivate us. These openings let in "the stuff" that impacts our emotional intelligence. How sensitively or intelligently do we handle what we see, hear, smell, breathe, eat, make love with, or surround ourselves with? Can we modulate, moderate, manage, or orchestrate how all this input affects us? Do our moods depend on what we see, hear, or eat, on how deeply we breathe, whom we are making love with, or in what environment we find ourselves? Will we motivate ourselves by falling in love with sight, with sound, with plants and animals and humans, with all that surrounds us as well as the air we breathe? Our emotional intelligence is a composite of all our answers to these questions. Emotional intelligence is how deeply we allow ourselves to be affected, how rich and diverse and appropriate our mood responses are, and how well we can move ourselves through life motivated by the life reaching us through these many openings. Affectional, mood, and motivational intelligences can now be applied in relation to each of these physical openings that connect us to the world.

For thousands of years we have been studying the eyes and the ears. At least a million books have been written about perception. We have been thinking and drawing conclusions about the world and reality based on how we SEE it or how we HEAR it. But what about the other openings? What about how we FEEL it? We can relate to visual intelligence and auditory intelligence, but what about oral, nasal, or sexual intelligence? The mouth, the nose, and the genitals are deeply connected to the limbic brain. However, we call what we do in this brain "feeling" instead of "perception." From there comes an important distinction: we honor perception as something intellectual but deny feeling, thereby denying the three openings that are continuously perceiving the world and giving us emotional feedback.

The nose is connected with the limbic brain through the olfactory bulbs, the mouth through the amygdala, and the genitals through the septal region. Our inability to handle sensitively these three openings is causing at least three major problems in our society: cocaine sniffed through the nose; alcohol and tobacco taken through the mouth; and the genitals responsible for over a million children born to unwed mothers as well as AIDS, a virus transmitted primarily through sexual contact.

It is time to look beyond our eyes and ears and focus our attention on the development of our intelligences connected with the nose, mouth, and genitals. The emotional intelligences of affection, mood, and motivation are a beginning, but we need more specific attention in relation to these three physical openings. When combined with the repetition phenomenon of the basic brain, these openings are behind the issue of addiction, whether it be drug or alcohol addiction, sexual addiction, or the crimes committed to maintain those addictions.

What we put in these three openings either excites or tranquilizes us and affects the chemistry of our brain. Whether we are conscious of our emotions or not, we are affected. To determine just how affected you are in relation to each of the openings of your body, answer the questions in the following awareness diagram.

	Affectional	*Motivational*	*Mood*
MOUTH	Do you care about what you eat? Have you ever suffered from bulimia or anorexia? Do you have an eating disorder? Are you a compulsive eater? Picky?	Do you really love what you eat? What are your favorite foods? What foods make you happiest? Do you want to eat? Are you a gourmet, a lover of food?	Do you eat when you're mad? Drink when you're sad? Drink to make yourself feel happy?
NOSE	Do you have allergies? Sinus, asthma, or breathing difficulties?	Can you change your state of mind or emotions by breathing?	When you are happy, how is your breathing? When you are sad? Scared? Mad? Making love?
GENITALS	Do you let yourself be affected by the other person? Interested in making love? Do you have any sexual difficulty? Obsession?	Do you want to make love? Do you love making love?	Do you make love when you're sad, mad, angry?

The purpose of the questions in this chart is not to score your emotional sensitivity or intelligence. It is rather to invite you to become aware that you are sensitive. Many of the disorders and even addictions related to these openings are indications of a person's sensitivity. What does that mean, and what can we do with it? We can become much more aware and indeed alert to what we are doing with these openings either to make us happy or to cause us suffering. We may even be able to heal what doctors are as yet unable to cure. For example, I now take any irritation of my sinuses as an indication that I am oversensitive emotionally or blocking something related to my emotions. I look for what is going on within me—anger, sadness, loss of energy—and try to attend to it, as I have indicated in the chapter on mood intelligence, or I ask myself what I am letting affect me so deeply that I am blocking my emotional system, or I wonder what I am really wanting that I am not giving myself. For almost a year I blamed my airplane trips and sudden change of climate in Venezuela for my sinus problems. Now I understand that although these may be influences, pills will not prevent sinus problems. I have become more alert to my sensitivity and more gentle with myself as I move to do something with this emotional information.

As you see by the questions in the above chart, each of the emotional intelligences can serve to make you aware of what is going on within you in relation to these openings. Each of these intelligences also indicates what to do about it. For example, you may be too deeply affected by pollution in the air, by something going on in your love life, or by something you are eating, seeing, hearing, doing, or not doing. Whatever it is that is affecting you so strongly that you are overloading your system needs to be modified. Perhaps you have become too intense about your love or perhaps not intense enough. How is your love life affecting you? Does it need modification? That could mean using your neocortex to select out what is harmful or not absolutely necessary to love about your loved one. It could mean allowing yourself to love more deeply.

Affectional intelligence covers a scale from initial affect through all the ranges to profound affection. If we are affectionally intelligent, we are aware of what is affecting us and willing to modify it before it becomes harmful.

Mood intelligence means not only being aware of our moods but knowing what to do at least with the two extremes of sadness and anger. It is not emotionally intelligent to let ourselves fall so continuously into sadness that we become addicted to depression or to be so continuously angry that we become jealous, hateful, or violent. The minimum of emotional intelligence requires knowing the secrets of healing sadness and anger before they take a serious toll on our life or the lives of those around us.

Motivational intelligence means being aware of what we want and of wanting and moving to satisfy at least some of what we are wanting. If we ask ourselves what we are wanting, we probably either don't know or are unconsciously denying. There is so much that all of us want and have learned not to admit because we believe we cannot have it. We also may have tried once or twice and then given up. We may have come to a logical conclusion that the effort of trying is not worth it. We ought not to be either surprised or offended by the word *denial* or by our own unconsciousness. All of this needs to be respected. However, the problem is that the wanting may continue to exist within us because it is either biological—sexual or nutritional—or psychological—a deep longing for love or recognition. The latter is not to be ashamed of or regretted, either. Indeed, some people are imprinted from generations past to seek recognition. Others still long for love not only because it is a biological-psychological necessity, but because they have been hurt many times as they sought to meet this need. If we really hear our longing, it will lead us to heal our past hurts and may even motivate us to find again a loved one. Our continued longing is our sensitivity and our emotional intelligence. By doing something about our longing, we may improve our health and even save our life.

If you find that any of your three openings are causing you difficulty or illness, be aware that your emotional system is jammed, overloaded, or in some way not functioning well. Look to the three emotional intelligences to check your awareness, and then use them to discover what you can do about it. You may need to consult a therapist or medical doctor for assistance, but first be willing to use your own emotional intelligence to help yourself. Use intelligence before illness. Your continued alertness and willingness to be emotionally intelligent is the best prevention. Once the signal becomes illness, be willing to ask for help.

Let us take a more specific look at each of these openings in order to see how we can become more emotionally intelligent with them. Although I am commenting on each opening separately, together they form an interconnected emotional system. For example, difficulty with the nose or breathing may indicate that there is an eating or sexual overload, difficulty with the mouth may indicate a breathing or sexual issue, and difficulty with the genitals may indicate a problem with eating or breathing. We can see our emotional system as a whole, or we can look more specifically at each opening as an indication of what is going on within the entire system.

Mouth

We know eyes are connected with the intelligence of seeing and reading and we train them consciously. We dangle mobiles over our infant's crib to engage his or her mind through the medium of the eyes. We also train the ears to hear sounds and make distinctions, at first related to the parents, later to instructions in elementary and secondary school and lectures in the university. In brief, we are trained to become intelligent by means of the eyes and ears.

What do we do with the mouth? For certain we are overjoyed when the infant's mouth closes around the nipple and draws milk deep into its belly. We are assured that this life will survive. Our consciousness begins and stays at the level of survival, however. We never seek to teach this mouth to make distinctions about taste or about the connections between taste and life. Every other object a child sees we invest with meaning: notice the rattle, the book, the rug, everything that is in the room. With food, we divest it of meaning and desperately try to get the child to accept everything, to make no distinctions, to eat it all "because it's good for you." We teach a child to distinguish objects, to distinguish sounds, but never to distinguish food. When children do naturally, it irritates us, and by the time they are six or seven we win a passive-aggressive stare as they look out at Us-the-Authority, insisting that the child not voice any distinctions about food. First a survival pattern, then an authority pattern— how can our connection with food become intelligent?

The pattern of food for survival continues. As we try to liberate ourselves from the authority pattern in our adolescent years, we do indeed experiment with food, finally permitting ourselves both selectivity and exaggeration. Later we sometimes enter into a "balanced" way of eating under our own watchful adult censorship. In mid-life we adopt diet approaches as authority substitutes for ourselves or our parents. As our chemistry changes, producing effects in late middle age, we finally give in to our overeating, cheating and repenting, often haunted by guilt and followed by the authority voice of "I know I shouldn't, but . . . ." The battle over eating returns in our late fifties or early sixties, this time accompanied by real illness or at least severe warnings from the Doctor authority.

Is not this continuous reliance on authority an abandonment to ignorance? Is there no intelligent approach possible? If we can become intelligent with objects, as in art, with words, as in logic and linguistics, and with sound, as in music, is there no way we can become intelligent with food?

FOOD AND AGGRESSION

The link between our aggressive emotions and our mouth has many practical implications. When we are angry or frustrated and do not feel it is safe to express our anger, or when we feel incapable of breaking through our frustration, we may turn to food to satisfy or calm our aggression. We may even eat food to prevent ourselves from becoming physically or verbally aggressive. Food tranquilizes! It gives us a sense of well-being, or at least a feeling of relaxation and pleasure. It is a tranquilizer that is available, socially acceptable, and conditioned in us since birth.

Feeling good by eating goes back to our first reactions to life. When babies are born, they begin to breathe, cry, or yell and then search for food. The mouth quivers and expands as it lets out its first sign of frustration, and then closes calm and satisfied as the milk enters and soothes. Was it on the first day of life that a pattern was formed: first the frustration—I can't get what I want—then the yell, the mouth reacts, then the food enters, and calm at last? This primary pattern of satisfying frustration by using the mouth helped us survive. It may also have laid the foundation for our pattern of using food to satisfy our emotional frustrations. We eat when our power is blocked: I want, I can't get what I want, other means fail, food satisfies, it feels good, and I am relaxed. We eat to calm our anger. Our initial desire is replaced by wanting food. It may take too much effort or more power than we have available to satisfy an initial desire, but we have enough power to go to the refrigerator and satisfy our desire to feel good by eating.

How can we distinguish between food to survive and food that is used to calm our anger? I believe we need to be able to recognize our desires, recognize when our power is blocked or frustrated, and be able to satisfy our wantings and heal our anger by means other than food. We need all three emotional intelligences to become aware of what is affecting us, to heal our anger, and to motivate ourselves by satisfying our desires through as many healthy means as possible. If we have become harmfully overweight, we might need pattern intelligence to interfere with our addiction and parameter intelligence to guide us to a new conditioning. We can take a first step by linking the mouth to emotional intelligence and learning to become aware of what is affecting us. To quote the title of Jack Schwarz's book, "It's Not What You Eat, But What Eats You."

Smoking and drinking are two other ways we have used the mouth area to calm ourselves. During the day, smoking serves. When we are irritated, anxious, worried, frustrated, or in the grips of any emotion we have not been accustomed to feeling or not had successful experience feeling, we can respond to the tension of the trigeminal nerve system surrounding the mouth as well as any patterned aggression by resorting to the safety of a cigarette. Having done this thousands of times and associated it with relaxation from whatever we are engaged in, we have become conditioned to relax at the signal of a cigarette. What can we do instead? Learn abdominal breathing and practice it throughout the day, especially in moments of tension. Occupy the mouth with objects that are not known to produce lung cancer.

The cigarette has served during the day, whereas alcohol, not so conveniently packaged, has been the choice of the night. To arrive home and have a beer or a scotch makes everything all right. Certainly it does relax the muscles and just as certainly the mental association with happy hour does signal the body to relax. Where people are on the range of relaxed to drunk is an issue of health. What is certain is that by using the addictive method of alcohol, they have removed the possibility of becoming aware of their feelings. They are burying, covering over, or killing off their emotional reactions to their day. They are not interested in becoming emotionally intelligent. This may be because of lack of experience with emotions, bad experience with emotion, or a belief system that feelings have nothing important to tell us. Just a reaction, no real information that would be valuable for our life. During the day we may have to live in our mental and action brains, passing over our emotional experience. However, I am convinced that our emotions are our interior life; they hold information vital to our desires and ability to enjoy and lead a satisfying life. What to do? Fifteen minutes reflection before we take a drink or have dinner would permit us to access our feelings. Throwing ourselves on our bed to find out what is going on inside our belly would do a lot more for us than filling our belly before we know. If we are tense or constricted, a long shower releasing our tension would also give us permission to express our feelings in private as we search for their meaning. The information is then available to us, we are relaxed, and we can proceed with our evening and the food and drink of our choice.

SPEECH AND AGGRESSION

Not only is our mouth used to take in food, cigarettes, and alcohol, but it is also used to express ourselves verbally. The same pattern of aggression may emerge in our speech as in our eating. All of us have had the experience of suppressing difficult emotions, biting our tongue at work, or swallowing angry words at a social event, only to find ourselves exploding in anger at unexpected moments with family or loved ones or those weaker than ourselves. These are obvious examples of oral aggression.

It may be that the mouth is patterned with aggression from our mammalian history. A lioness does not go shopping at the supermarket, reading her list and studying prices, in order to feed her cubs. She goes out hunting, aggressively searching for food and killing it. Look at the location of the amygdala, so close to the thalamus; it is almost a part of it. It is easy to imagine that aggression is inherent in affection. If the lioness had not felt affection, would she have been aggressive enough to kill in order to feed her cubs?

Whether this mammalian pattern is what still influences us as we shout and attack each other verbally is difficult to trace. What is certain is that we are verbally aggressive. In searching to become emotionally intelligent, we need to realize that aggression is related to our limbic brain. Any proposal for emotional intelligence will have to take into account the influence of the amygdala on the emotions as well as the multiple uses for the mouth to nourish us, to express aggressive as well as loving emotions, and to provide verbal expression from our neocortical brain of reason and imagination.

How shall we cope with this connection to our emotions? First, we can become aware that the mouth is associated with aggression. Second, we can learn that what we put in our mouth may be to calm our frustrations. Third, we can know that everything that comes out of our mouth is colored at least by our mood and perhaps by our aggression, whether intentional, subtle, or repressed. Once we are aware, it then becomes important to learn how to orchestrate our moods. More specifically, it becomes important to put ourselves in good moods and not blame other people for our bad moods. Mood intelligence is being able to get in and out of all moods. Oral intelligence may be about putting ourselves in good moods before we eat or speak, rather than speaking or eating to put ourselves in a good mood. The development of an oral intelligence could be crucial to unraveling those connections between the desire to live ourselves and the need to threaten others when we become frustrated or angry. The mouth may be as crucial to emotional intelligence as the eyes and ears are to both visual and auditory intelligences.

Nose

Once we take that first breath to prove we are alive, we seem to be satisfied. From then on, rather than exploring the expansive-contractive power of breathing in relation to life and all emotion, we either go on automatic or use breath to indicate a reaction to emotion. We constrict our breathing in fear, causing irregularity in our heart rhythm and blood flow. We constrict into sadness, declaring ourselves to be hurt and helpless, rather than slowing our breathing into a softer, gentler rhythm to match the sadness. We wait for fate or events to pick us up and increase our energy, rather than knowing consciously that we can expand our breathing and arouse our own selves to help us feel better.

This inability to engage in the expansive-contractive processing of breath leads to a condition we have labeled stress. Stress, as already mentioned, is being constricted and unable or unwilling to expand, through breathing or any other means. Stress is a serious, all-pervasive indicator of our inability to deal appropriately with our emotions or modulate our ways of living.

The Relaxation Response by Herbert Benson clearly points the way.[1] When we are stressed, Benson tells us to relax. How? The practice of breathing begins the process of expansion and enables us to open up and be affected by realities less immediate than the ones that are pressuring us. Breathing releases us from whatever tension we are thinking about, imagining, feeling, or acting out. Breathing relaxes us.

Breathing does much more. It increases the oxygen flow to different areas of the body, depending on where we concentrate and how we expand and contract with our breathing. Breathing is inner massage. By directing our breathing we can relax not only our muscles, but also our internal organs, especially the areas around the stomach, pancreas, and liver—all potentially constricted areas because of their connection to the digestive process. Deep breathing or concentrating in the abdomen while allowing the breath to expand and contract the entire area relaxes the muscles and affects the blood flow to the intestines, as well as relaxing the entire body. By concentrating, we can also direct our breathing to other areas of our body, such as the throat or heart, either to keep them healthy or to strengthen them if they have become weak. If you have a family history of illness or weakness in a particular area of the body, conscious breathing into that area is a wise preventive practice.

The lung area may have become constricted through years of shallow breathing, years of smoking, or both. If people who smoke had learned the variations of breathing in their early years, they may never have constricted the lung area to such an extent that it became insensitive to smoke. For them, smoke inhalation became a substitute for oxygen inhalation. Not smoking may rid them of serious carcinogens, but it does not provide the positive expansive remedy that a conscious breathing program can provide.

Breathing is a much greater phenomenon still: it directly affects all emotion. We have all experienced our rapid breathing as we become sexual. We have experienced hyper-breathing when we are excited, slower breathing when we are sad, chaotic breathing when we are afraid. Knowing this, shall we just passively identify breathing with emotion, or shall we take the initiative and enter into learning the process of breathing, just as we once learned the processes involved in thinking? Breathing could become a human art that we all learn just as we learn how to write.

Breathing enables us to vary the depth and intensity of our emotions.

Yogis have known how to use breathing to control not only emotional states but also blood pressure and heart rate, two physical indications of one's emotional state. Through breathing yogis may also have been reaching sexual states while calling them by another name. The close proximity of the olfactory bulbs to the septal region makes me wonder if the meditative state of yogic bliss may not more accurately be described as a sexual state—in thinner vibrational ranges. Sexuality may not require a partner; it may require only deep affection, sexual arousal, and the capacity to modulate the vibrations involved. Yogis have already developed an intelligence of breathing. Simply because this knowledge has been associated with Eastern philosophy and a religion different from ours is no reason for us to ignore this knowledge. It makes an important contribution to human life. Our examination of yogic texts is an urgent first step in the development of breathing intelligence.

Breathing intelligence may be as necessary to emotional intelligence as verbal intelligence is to rational. We know that the mental effort of articulating words accompanies and enhances rational thinking, just as the articulation of numbers enhances the mathematical process. In brief, breathing is to emotional intelligence as words and numbers are to rational and associative intelligences. By intensifying their visual capacities, artists thereby increase their visual intelligence. By increasing their auditory capacities, musicians increase their auditory intelligence. If we seek to be emotionally intelligent, we may need to develop our breathing intelligence in order to intensify, vary, subdue, amplify, and change our emotions.

Genitals

The need to revise our approach to the sexual openings of our bodies is as great or greater than our need to reconsider the sensitivity and complexity of the nose and mouth. The parent-child struggle to train our genitals to function regularly at appointed times and in appointed places dominates the first three years of our life. The first great trial for parents is cleaning the child, which as soon as possible turns into the first great battle of will, confusion, guilt, and obligation. It is little wonder that even though Freud ferreted out toilet training as basic to adult sexual relationship, most of us block this early memory of struggle with our parents and our genitals. Shall we be conscious or unconscious of our genitals? When shall we start, and what shall we do with our early history?

Control, regulation, obligation, desire to please parents, plus guilt over inevitable failure are the heritage of our efforts to deal with our genitals. This is hardly a favorable heritage to begin the process of love seeking and love making that extends throughout life. Yet this is the heritage with which we begin our adult sexual lives. To this we add the early childhood injunctions against touching ourselves "there" and threats of madness and craziness, used to prevent young adolescents from exploring the pleasurable sensations associated with the genitals.

The presence of the septal region in the limbic brain and its association with sexual arousal makes it clear that we cannot hope to access fully or make use of this limbic brain system without elaborating more clearly and more consciously the full power of sexuality and its inextricable relationship with all emotion. If we are to become emotionally intelligent, we will need to become sexually intelligent.

It is hard to imagine where to begin. We have linked sexuality with pleasure, with crime, with disease, with identity, and with birth of new life . . . but with intelligence? We have tried sex education but are not clear on whether courses should contain only biological description or whether they should include a variety of other topics such as sensuality, morality, fatality, disease, choice of partner, choice of gender, examples of sexual behavior, pornography, sexually appropriate age, sexual abuse.

We have no agreement on appropriate sexual behavior or on appropriate sexual partnership: heterosexuality, homosexuality, bisexuality. Cultures, religions, and ethnic groups are locked in combat over what they see as the key to all morality. As if this were not enough, the outcome of sexuality is all too often life that cannot or will not be taken care of by the mother, the father, or society. We are deeply divided over whether to prevent the conception of life or end life before it is born. We face struggles between the life of the mother and the life of the baby. We have the technological capacity to prevent life, but no agreement over using the technology. Sexuality has been submerged in a battle of life and death. With the presence of AIDS, this battle between life and death has been intensified and extended beyond mother and child to include all teenage and adult members of the community. In all this darkness, government seeks the path of least resistance, more aware of the vote than of providing leadership. Religions clash and science defers, launching periodic statistical studies.

Meanwhile, over a million babies are born every year because of unprotected sex to unwed mothers reluctant or unable to take care of them. Thousands of lives, if not more, are ended before the babies can be born. Other thousands, if not more, die every year because of unprotected sex between adults affected by the HIV virus. How much death do we need? How much ignorance before we will find out how to be intelligent with our genitals? Perhaps the genitals are the last remaining organ of the human body to be covered with so much obscurity. Perhaps they are the last frontier. Perhaps if we declared them a national disaster we would appropriate sufficient funds and muster sufficient leadership to do battle with this confusion and darkness.

Sexual intelligence cannot be developed by one researcher alone. So intricate are the interweavings of the neurological, biological, behavioral, cultural, and spiritual factors that only a concerted foundation or national effort to bring together the specialists involved can produce an intelligence that really can reach the public. However, I am interested in life and in love with life, and throughout this book I have been speaking up for life. The issue of life is too critical to remain silent, so I would like to offer certain basics that might serve to open dialogues in search of greater consensus. You might wish to agree, disagree, or add your comments as you read each point.

First, the genitals are physiological openings, just like the other openings of the body. They need to be disassociated from our long history of ignorance and associated with present-day knowledge.

Second, when contact is made with these areas, tremendous energy results. That energy is so powerful that it is extremely pleasant and addictive, even after one experience.

Third, the energy vibrating throughout the genitals is also the most powerful energy. Under the right conditions it produces the connections that create life.

Fourth, from infancy, touching the genitals produces an energy that is pleasurable.

Fifth, between the ages of ten and thirteen the pituitary gland opens, causing an "explosion" in the limbic brain that changes brain chemistry and causes the physical growth of hair and breasts, which we identify with adolescence. A person feels different, the body and brain are different, and a dominant energy is released, producing a drive or attraction to sexual, genital contact with other human beings. At that age genital contact with another of the opposite gender can create life.

Sixth, there is no adequate verbal explanation to prepare an adolescent for the power of that sexual attraction or contact. There are full-blown descriptions, warnings, injunctions, and threats, but no way to experience what is being talked about so much. Safe sex has not worked for millions of unwed mothers because they could never imagine they would be so overwhelmed. I believe the only true safe sex is autosexuality, which would at least prepare them for the power of the energy attraction they are likely to feel. By autosexuality, I do not mean stimulating oneself to release tension. I mean the capacity to make love to oneself, lovingly, sensuously to explore and learn about one's own body. In that way adolescents may both be more prepared to love another and be more able to wait and to choose an appropriate partner.

Seventh, being willing to love oneself is appropriate not only for teenagers but also for adults who for various reasons find themselves alone without partners. If the choice is between being dependent on the presence of another to love us or loving ourselves, the choice needs to be in favor of our own well-being and health.

Eighth, endorphins are the pleasure chemicals of our limbic brain and important to sustaining our health and preventing disease. Pleasure is vital to health, and sexuality is a primary form of pleasure. I believe that sexuality needs to be available to all ages without the threat of creating life that we cannot care for, without the threat of endangering others' lives by passing on the HIV virus, and without the threat of years of loneliness in which we abandon our bodies because we are dependent on others for pleasure.

Beyond these basic points, we have available the application of our three emotional intelligences to guide us. With affectional intelligence we become aware that indeed we are attracted and affected, but we do not need to declare ourselves in love and ready to go to bed. We can know to expect to be attracted to and even affected by others, but we do not need to conclude that this is our "true love." How many marriages have been broken because we were expecting to be faithful all our lives and then are suddenly tremendously affected by someone else? We conclude the new person is our "true love," break our parameters with our spouse, and marry the other, only to discover too late that attraction and affection can happen often, can happen deeply, and can continue to happen throughout life. We need to be able to use our affectional intelligence to tone down our emotions if it is not appropriate for our life to follow this feeling into action.

Affection does not need to be a surprise. It needs to be practiced with many people, with all forms of life, with our friends, our work, our art, our family, our nation. It needs to be treated like music: listened to, turned up, expanded, turned down, and even turned off. Lower the volume when the attraction affects the genitals and you do not wish to continue to intercourse. Lower the volume and shift to parameter intelligence. We know how to limit the food we eat because we have learned how to pay attention to the signal that we would be uncomfortable if we went on eating. We stop being affected by the food in front of us. We can also learn to shift from the energy affecting our genitals in order to protect ourselves.

Affectional intelligence will also let us select what we most love about a person. If we are able to concentrate on and be affected by the qualities of a person without being affected by our image of how that person would be in bed, we will be able to be affected by and love many people without endangering the relationship that we have chosen for our family. We need to liberate our ability to love. I believe the key is in affectional intelligence and in our ability to guide this intelligence with the selective and awareness capacity of our neocortex.

Practicing all the emotional scales can give us a freedom with emotions that is basic to emotional intelligence. Experiencing the many variations of feelings is like learning to read words. Eventually we put words together into paragraphs and books. With experience we can put feelings together into body enjoyment, body music, and body symphony. Being affected by the many aspects of the other will nourish us rather than destroy us. Can you imagine listening to Beethoven's Ninth Symphony and then asking, What shall I do with it? Music is for listening, for enjoying. Feeling is for feeling and enjoying. Be affected by the variations. Free yourself from the need to act on feelings; free yourself to feel feelings. Then you will become involved in the subtleties, nuances, and distinctions that have always been the hallmark of intelligence. You will become emotionally intelligent.

So dark has been our history around sexuality that few of us have survived without trauma or at least major hurt. The experiences of sadness, loss, impotence, violation, frustration, and anger are registered in our personal histories. We now have available at least the basic rudiments of mood intelligence, and in particular we know how to heal the scars left by sadness and anger. To be intelligent and enjoy sexuality, we will need to heal our past, experienced when we were unknowing or unable to protect ourselves. It is not emotionally intelligent to carry our hurts from past loves into our present loves. The result is blame for lack of enjoyment, pressure, guilt, and projection on the other what is part of our own history. Mood intelligence invites us to take responsibility for all that happened in our past sexual experiences and to convert that hurt into love for ourselves, so that we may be fully available to love again.

Motivational intelligence honors desire and respects our wanting and longing for love. Desire keeps us alive. It is a basic, expansive vibration, and it affects our genitals as surely as it affects our heart or mouth. We want to eat, we want to love, we want to breathe, and we want to feel the tremendous energy in our genitals and lower part of our body. We have, however, a long history of denying that we desire this sexual energy. Of course we have found it dangerous: it can break hearts, destroy homes, create babies, and even expose us to death. All this is true. However, what is also true is that the genitals exist. They circulate energy, block energy, and store energy. When the lower part of our body is not relaxed and expanded, it is contracted. If constricted, the energy creates distortions in other openings, trying to be calmed by eating or activity. My point is all that energy wants to circulate, filling and balancing the body. We want to feel that energy of the genitals. We want sex, whether we admit it or not. Even more important, if not governed consciously, the energy from the genitals will explode, dominating not only our eating and our activity but our moods and desire for life. Motivational intelligence honors the existence of wanting and says that some of our wanting needs to be satisfied. Motivational intelligence not only recognizes that desire is basic to the limbic brain but insists that we must be responsible for moving and motivating ourselves through life. We must catch our own internal flame to carry forward this life creation we call ourselves, but also to preserve this fire in order to share it with others.

The search for sexual intelligence must go on if we are to become emotionally intelligent and consequently able to protect our health and realize the tremendous capacity of human life to love and connect with all other life. We have united around great physical causes such as cancer and AIDS. We need now to unite around this triple physiological threat that is affecting our behavior and ripping apart our society. We are choosing up sides and shooting each other in well-organized battles over abortion. Sexual crimes are pitting citizen organizations protecting their neighborhoods against the courts for releasing first-time offenders. All this instead of combining our efforts in search of sexual intelligence.

Obesity shortens life; so do alcohol and smoking. Alcohol and drugs take not only the user's life but thousands of other uninvolved lives. The drug problem is a consumption problem; it is an emotional brain problem. Our efforts to regulate incoming drug traffic look good, but they overlook the fact that it takes a human brain to want drugs and to act and steal to get them. We are spending billions on drug traffic and alcohol regulation that might better be spent trying to develop an oral-nasal intelligence that would provide alternatives and regulation at the level of human consumption.

Such battles will continue to destroy our society until we recognize and unite around the cause of the problem—the three openings leading into the central limbic brain system. If we are not educated, these openings will be far more destructive to us than people who cannot read or write.

The comments in this chapter are only sketches, meant to draw our attention to both the need and the possibilities. Perhaps also these sketches can serve you, the reader, enabling you to take steps in your personal life and the lives of your children before waiting for larger solutions.

PART III

CHAPTER XIII

Crossing the Threshold of the Unconscious

INTO THE BASIC BRAIN

I am not a suspended, rootless thing in the world,
I am earth of its earth and breath of its breath.

Nikos Kazantzakis, *The Saviors of God*

T*he deepest brain is about the earth. It is about stability and security. It is about acceptance of life as it presents itself. It is about life and about preservation and creation, not in finished form, but in continuum. We are in the continuum. Life or basic wave-motion energy goes on without us and also with us as we emerge into existence.*

In the formations of the basic brain we make our first appearance as human life. This is our first brain of basic rhythm, of motion, of reaction and action. This brain exposes us to the earth through our skin, which no longer slithers on the earth but which nevertheless clings to whatever is near. If we notice the ways we invent to be on earth, we become conscious of our being. We notice our efforts to be secure by making tribes and nations and families or at least couples; to control and dominate by using our work, our children, God, and finally ourselves; to become part of or to participate by using any means possible, be they social or antisocial, positive or negative, criminal or good, freeing or possessive, original or addictive. We wrestle in diverse ways to become.

It is in this first brain that everyone tells us we are enough, God loves us as we are, nature is, and we already belong. Again and again human life keeps appearing and keeps not being able to hear this sound closest to the earth, this ground of being. It is here in this first brain when the other brains no longer function that we are still alive. What form of consciousness is here?

- the continuous beating of the heart
- the continuous breathing of the lungs
- the continuous expansion-contraction of this brain

Continuity, at the very least, is here.

What to Name this Brain

It is difficult to find an appropriate name for the deepest brain. From the perspective of evolution it is our first brain. It was named the R-complex by Paul MacLean, because in physical formation it is similar to the brain of reptiles. It is, however, also described in medical texts as part of the central nervous system. Although our deepest brain is similar in formation to that of reptiles, and although some of the basic activities of this brain seem very reptilian—such as repetition, imitation, and deception—there are also subtleties in this brain not conveyed by these words. Especially when we take into account the link between this brain system and the entire spinal cord, including the afferent-efferent nervous system and extending to the openings of our skin, the name nervous system brain would seem to convey the much larger implications than I believe are involved. R-complex, first brain, or nervous system brain all work—but I have decided to resolve the difficulty by calling it simply the basic brain, because it seems to me basic both to the other brain systems as well as to the subtle management of energy. When relevant, however, I use all these names interchangeably.

We may be either conscious or unconscious of the energy that we call our self or the energy that surrounds us. However, life goes on with or without our consciousness. This basic brain continues to filter energy in any state that we refer to as unconscious: whether caused by physical damage to the brain, the normal rest periods of sleep, or just lack of awareness. While there is life in the body, it is because energy is still passing through this basic brain system. To access this energy we need at least the following abilities:

- the ability to enter into the rhythms of what is happening
- the ability to create parameters and to dissolve them when they are inappropriate
- the ability of neutral observation of ourselves and all that surrounds us
- the ability to move toward and away from, in tandem with life closest to us, which is freedom in this deepest brain

Characteristics of the Basic Brain

Paul MacLean defines the basic brain as the R-complex, including the brainstem, the reticular activating system within the brainstem, and the basal ganglia surrounding the brainstem. "The . . . brainstem and spinal cord constitute a neural chassis that provides most of the neural machinery required for self-preservation and the preservation of the species."[1]

The main structures involved in the basic brain are the brainstem and the spinal cord, which serve as a channel for impulses and information between the outside environment and the basic brain; the reticular activating system within the brainstem, which channels information to the limbic brain and neocortical systems; and also the basal ganglia, which provide motor function, as well as the storage of basic memory of sensorial patterns.

BRAINSTEM AND SPINAL CORD

The spinal cord filters incoming vibrations into the brainstem and therefore is essential for the full understanding of human behavior in relation to this brain. The spinal cord extends the length of the back and conducts impulses from the skin or outer world to the brainstem.

Along the spinal cord extends the afferent-efferent nervous system. Figure 10 shows the afferent system relaying impulses from the openings or pores of the skin to the spinal cord and then to the brainstem. From within the brainstem, these impulses are then available to be sorted through a group of fibers known as the reticular activating system and passed into the limbic system and then to the neocortex. Impulses are then returned through the efferent nervous system to the muscles for action in the outside world.

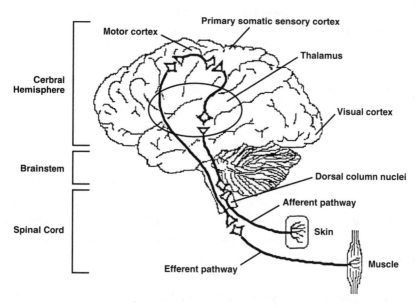

Fig. 10. Afferent-Efferent Nervous System: The Skin-Brain-Action Circuit. From Eric R. Kandel and James H. Schwartz, **Principles of Neural Science,** *2nd ed., Appleton & Lange, 1985.*

Notice that our spinal cord links us to the outside environment by means of the afferent-efferent nervous system, which is continually receiving impulses from our muscles and skin. Also notice that our skin is covered with pores, which are a system of openings constantly exposing us to the world. Although we are used to thinking of our skin as a covering for our body, almost as a form of defense, it would be more appropriate to see our skin as our interface with the environment. Our pores are the eyes of our body. They are the openings that permit energy to come into our deepest brain, just as the nose, mouth, and genitals are openings into the limbic system, and the eyes and ears are openings more directly related to the neocortex. All openings are, of course, interrelated within the three brain systems.

What is implicit in this description is that we are constantly exposed to each other and to our environment. The connection between the outer world, our skin, and this deepest brain provides a physiological basis for Thomas Merton's comment "We are already one."[2] It also helps explain the "collective unconscious" proposed by Carl Jung that affects so deeply our interior life. We can try not to be affected by others or not to think about them, but in the basic brain we cannot keep them out. Collectively, we are all connected, whether we become conscious or remain unconscious of our connections.

Information from our environment enters at least as far as our brainstem without our conscious consent. Only as it passes into our limbic system do we become conscious of this information as feeling, or later as thought or image or intuition as it enters the neocortex. It may well stay "unconscious" until it appears as information in our left or right hemisphere. Our surroundings and the people near us are continually conditioning us. The entire context in which we live and work is informing our brain through the pores of our skin in the same way that a symphony informs our brain through the openings of our ears. We can infer that we need to look at the content of our immediate environment just as carefully as we would look at the books we are reading, music we are hearing, or art we are seeing. Our surroundings are continually impacting us.

Our basic brain is affected not only by the surroundings in which we live but is also, at the same time, affecting and creating the context in which we live. The importance of context in our development brought me to conceive of parameter intelligence, a search for the parameters that define and circumscribe the context or different environments of our life, such as our home, our work, our relationships, and our health.

Given that we are constantly being imprinted by our environment, there are certain questions involved in consciousness. At what point are we actively involved in accepting this imprinting? Or are we conditioned in an unconscious manner by this imprinting? Do we participate at this deep level? For sure, this deepest brain participates and in some way converts incoming impulses into information, but how can we become conscious of what we are receiving or what this brain has already received? It is exactly this process of how impulse converts into recognizable information that we seek to bring into enough awareness to permit our conscious participation.

One obvious first step for consciousness is to focus on this process of reception from our environment through the openings of our skin. Consciousness then involves observing, studying, and taking into account that the context in which we live did not just happen, nor was it predetermined. Rather, it is the result of continuous impact-imprint-acceptance-reaction to the people, places, and information of our environment. Our deepest brain has been recording, registering, and storing in memory different combinations of information since birth.

To be behaviorally intelligent, we need to be willing to observe our interactions from the point of view of an observer and not from the point of view of an owner of that behavior. We need to be a fair witness to this interesting combination of complex interactions that has gone on all our life and that is influencing our behavior today. With such neutrality we will then be able and want to study our childhood experiences with the same curiosity and acceptance that we might use to study any history, whether it be of a family or of a nation.

Ask yourself what occurred in the past that influenced your development and is affecting you today. Rather than focusing on your mother and father and what they did or did not do in your childhood, focus on what you probably concluded under those conditions. Do the same with early imprints from your culture, your religion, and your education. What did this organism probably decide? You need to take into account the stimuli and your responses, as well as the conclusions or reaction-decisions of your basic brain, if you want to change your behavior. If not, your heritage serves as a network of resistance against any new desire from your limbic brain or any new decision by your neocortex. This network of resistance is why willpower alone, however strong or well intentioned, does not do much to change behavior. Pattern intelligence was conceived as a way to discover the early links made as a result of the continuous exposure and interaction of this deepest brain with its context.

RETICULAR ACTIVATING SYSTEM

The reticular activating system is found within the brainstem, as is shown in Figure 11.

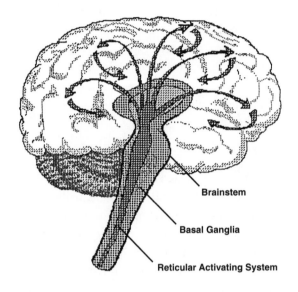

Fig. 11. Reticular Activating System[3]

Gatekeeper to consciousness, spark of the mind, the reticular formation connects with major nerves in the spinal column and brain. It sorts the 100 million impulses that assault the brain each second, deflecting the trivial, letting the vital through to alert the mind. The mind cannot function without this catalytic bundle of cells. Damage to them results in coma—the loss of consciousness.[4]

One hundred million impulses assaulting the brain each second! What happens to them? They enter at least as far as the brainstem, then through the reticular activating system the energy may pass into the emotional or limbic brain and then into the neocortex, as shown in Figure 11.

When these impulses are registered in our emotional brain, we begin to feel or allow ourselves to be conscious of what we are feeling. When they are registered in our neocortex, we begin to think, imagine, relate, or intuit. It is also possible that we do not become conscious of much of the incoming energy until later. At night, entering into the deep relaxation of sleep, we may allow ourselves to access more information, which may appear in images or verbal messages we call dreams—the most subtle language coming from this brain.

The energy may also show up in sudden realizations or unexpected awareness. It may be that some weeks or even years later, when we are engaged in a totally nonassociated activity, all of a sudden we "get it"; we have a realization, an "a-ha!" moment. Somehow, we have given ourselves permission to access the information that was already stored within us, forming it in a new and meaningful way.

BASAL GANGLIA

The basal ganglia are formed around the brainstem and include the caudate nucleus, the putamen, and the globus pallidus. Damage to certain parts of this area may result in inability to control motion. Although we believe we control our actions and although we want to control them, we have to count on the participation of the basal ganglia of our basic brain. As described by Richard Restak in *The Brain*, we can decide to write our name and want to write it, but in order to act on this decision and desire, our basal ganglia have to be involved.[5]

MacLean emphasizes that the basal ganglia are involved in far more than motor activity, however. Instead of waiting for the results of additional brain investigation, I decided to probe further based on studies of human behavior. I asked myself: Could it be that the basal ganglia store certain data that are learned as instinctive reactions for the protection of life? Could it be that the first data of stimulus-and-response are stored in this brain as patterns, which then continue to direct our behavior? Could it be that impulses basic to life stored themselves as sensory patterns, available for automatic retrieval?

For example, we learned to walk as a child in interaction with our environment and by means of responses to stimuli. We stored the pattern of how to walk, and now we walk without thinking about how to do it. In the same way, we were impacted by various kinds of behavior, rather than just motor behavior, from people in our environment, and we learned to act in response to what was happening. Our reaction to the stimuli could have been either imitation or a contrary reaction. All we know is that we were exposed and that our basic brain registered our reaction. Therefore, the sensorial memory, message, or pattern, whatever we wish to call it, is registered in our basic brain.

Even though reptiles may access these patterns directly through their reptilian brains, perhaps humans can retrieve these instinctual patterns only upon command from the neocortical centers in collaboration with desire from the limbic system. Or perhaps it is here in the basic brain that all patterns are stored and may, on a more subtle level, be activated through stimuli from the environment—even without conscious agreement from the neocortex or limbic system. We have all had the experience of deciding not to take another drink or piece of cake and believing we did not want to, when the drink or cake was in our hands before we realized what we were doing. We say "it just happened." We have decided many times that we will not react, even if the other person makes us furious, but somehow or other something happens and we do react.

Something in ourselves is stimulated by something in the other. Until now we have called this lack of specificity "the unconscious" and in that way felt ourselves free from knowing our own behavior or even free to blame the other person, the situation, or life itself. Now, knowing about our basic brain, we can become conscious that what is stimulated is that message or pattern that we have stored in our own memory.

Instead of blaming the other or hiding ourselves from our own memory as if it were an unmanageable darkness or shadow, we can take another look at this memory and find ways to form new decisions. When we are not able to make a new decision, at least we can become conscious that the root of a specific problem lies within ourselves and not in the other person. The other is only a mirror that stimulates us.

The existence of sensorial patterns stored in the basic brain also explains the process of addiction, in which we are all involved, if not with alcohol or drugs, then with habitual and repetitive behaviors. I believe it is important to realize and to admit that we are all addicted to something. Indeed, positive addictions can be very helpful. The issue is to become conscious of the addictive process and to choose addictions that will favor our lives.

We have been concentrating on the motor memory of this brain rather than on our patterns of behavior. I believe we must search in the basic brain to discover the roots and the repetitive subtlety of our patterns. For us to become conscious at this level of imprint and addiction, I propose the use of pattern intelligence.

Energy and the Basic Brain

As I began to search for how characteristics of reptiles could be useful to human development, I felt stuck in a certain predetermined limited vision. By associating the basic brain with stimulus-response vibrations, I felt trapped by the interpretations of behavioral psychology and by a scientific focus on stimulus-response. I resorted to my other favorite activity: viewing the human brain through the lens of new physics. I had learned from physics that there is no separation between matter and energy. There is only energy, and all energy is vibration. Therefore, this deepest brain must also be energy in continuous vibration.

If all reality is energy, the energy is available to our sight sometimes as a wave, sometimes as disconnected wave forms we call particles. All wave forms are vibration. Intensity, variation, or amplification of a wave produces what we call thicker or thinner dimensions, high waves, low waves, or the cresting of a wave. The rise and fall is the wave in continuous motion. I began to reflect on the wave form as being characteristic of this basic brain. What if we were to view human behavior as a wave form? How would pulsation start? If it continued in repetitive form like the waves of the sea, what would this produce in human learning? If life were repetitive pulsations of energy, how would learning take place?

There emerged in my mind a chart (see Figure 12) in which the center is read as a wave that moves toward and away from, illustrating the basic movements or behavior of a learner. The horizontal lines suggest the energy of learning moving in repetitive wave forms, each wave representing a more intense phase or accumulation of learning. Again and again the force of motion and repetition carries us. We continuously receive sensorial feedback, which moves us forward in the learning if favorable and moves us away if unfavorable. I conceived the wave as neutral energy in continuous and repetitive rhythm.

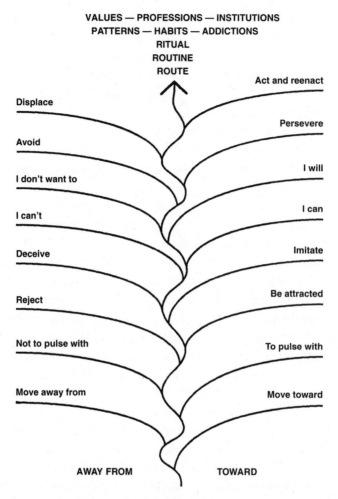

VALUES — PROFESSIONS — INSTITUTIONS
PATTERNS — HABITS — ADDICTIONS
RITUAL
ROUTINE
ROUTE

Act and reenact

Displace

Persevere

Avoid

I will

I don't want to

I can

I can't

Deceive

Imitate

Reject

Be attracted

Not to pulse with

To pulse with

Move away from

Move toward

AWAY FROM   **TOWARD**

Fig. 12. Learning and Behavior as Repetitive Wave Motion

Please read from the bottom up as if you were reading a neutral re-petitive process that begins with attraction and repulsion and, through repetition over time, converts itself into a route and then routines. Once routines are repeated, they become habits and then addictions, values, rituals, religions, professions, and finally institutions.[6]

Day and night we move subtly and sometimes not so subtly toward and away from people, places, ideas, colors, feelings, things, and events. We know this as instinct, although we often refer to this basic sensorial process as the unconscious. We do not yet know how this takes place within the brain, but our behavior reveals a continuous repetitive rhythm. When we move toward something again and again, pulse with it, are attracted to it, imitate it again and again, then we can. If we can again and again, we will, we persevere, and we are then able to enact it or reenact the action. When we do this enough, it becomes our route, our routine, a habit, something we deeply value.

By adding conscious thoughts, art, and music to a routine, we have ritual. From these routines and rituals come our values and conscience. If we construct a routine in space, it becomes an organization or institution. On a larger scale and over time, these routines, rituals, values, and institutions emerge as our routes, our culture, or the nation. Looking back through our personal and family or institutional histories, we can detect the routes that we have traced over time.

In the same way that we move *toward*, we also move *away from*. When we repeat that process of withdrawal or distancing again and again, we are no longer pulsating with; we reject, we become distant and deceive ourselves, we say we are no longer able, we do not want to do the action, and we avoid. We continue to avoid until we displace, meaning that we are not even aware of our own avoidance. We may develop deceitful habits, hiding from ourselves and others. As we move away from persons, things, ideas, or groups, we may very well go on to develop antisocial routines that may then become criminal routines.

I believe this subtle and neutral movement of the basic brain explains why antisocial routines, habits, rituals, and values become as deeply entrenched as any socially rewarding values. We also develop antisocial organizations and professions such as gangs and organized crime to continue this behavior. Observe the high rate of recidivism when we try to change criminal behavior. Neither reward nor punishment has had much success in changing antisocial behavior. Even programs that are well thought out by the neocortex and carried out with the greatest desire, heart, and willingness of the limbic brain do not succeed. I believe we will obtain results with criminal behavior only when we learn to take into consideration this basic brain of pattern and conditioning.

Wave Motion in Other Forms of Life

The basic toward-and-away motion is found not only in human behavior, but in many other areas of nature. We see it in the waves of the sea and in the more solidified waves of rock formations. The river also moves toward and away from its banks. In nature the wave of water flows towards and away from, in constant motion against the parameters of the riverbanks of earth, which also continue to form themselves in interaction with the water. The reptile clearly moves toward and away, its skin close to the earth. The fish follows the same motion, pulsing toward and away through the water. Birds fly through the air using the same wave motion, this time in up and down movement. Thus we see life in water, on land, and in the air all involved in this basic repetitive wave motion.

It would indeed be surprising if human life were not also involved in this constant wave motion. The wave configuration of toward and away from is solidified in the physical human structure of the spinal column. This basic wave structure protects the spinal cord and carries vibrations into the brainstem. Inspired by this characteristic wave motion, I began to study the active, conscious use of the wave as a type of intelligence and formulated the idea of basic intelligence.

This basic wave energy has a "sweetness" that I have difficulty describing. I think it comes from a brain chemical different from those that affect the emotional brain and different also from the meditative bliss of the right hemisphere of the neocortex. I *know* that its vibrational frequency is different. It is pleasurable, but it is not pleasure. The energy of this brain has quietness, tranquility, as if it could go on forever. It has calmness, ease of movement, gracefulness of motion—not form or grace, just ease—as if in any order, the motion will be right.

Its energy is peace. It is alignment. It is as if one is being carried. As much as I love the feelings of passion and excitement and the bliss of meditation, this energy has an addictive quality. There is an elixir, a quietness, a rightness. I get it while in motion, while attending to ordinary things, such as washing the dishes, tending the garden, or rearranging furniture. What I notice is that my body is confined within a certain space. I move easily doing one thing or another without the distraction of thought or feeling. I do not know if my mind is wandering. All I really am sure of is that I am attending to the action and usually within a defined space and defined time. I want to experience this more. I want this energy in all the areas of my life: work, home, play, health, relationships.

As I have described it thus far, this brain's energy is of being gently carried. I have, however, also experienced other energies I attribute to this brain that are more intense. They have the same quality of alignment, such as being in sync while dancing, that sensation of completely going with and being held. At the same time, it is as if my energy is not with the activity I am doing. I feel compulsiveness and a sense of being driven in which I think myself not in control. The moment I feel or think I am out of control, I am in the feeling brain or the thinking brain and not in this brain of action.

Staying in the basic brain, I sense I am not relating my body proportionally to the action I am doing, and the sensations I experience are various: chaos, discomfort, fear, anxiety, and sometimes panic. I feel overwhelmed. I have the sense of doing an action when I don't want to and feel controlled by it. There is the same sense with all compulsion. We say we are driven rather than saying we are being carried. I believe this is because this brain is in control, but our focus or concentration is somewhere else, not in this brain system and not riding the rhythm of the energy. The essence of control in this brain is entering the rhythm, focusing in this rhythm, and through that focus being able to slow the speeds in relation to what we are doing.

CHAPTER XIV

Characteristics of Reptile Behavior

I*n 1979 when I was Director of the Mead*

School an article on reptilian behavior by Paul MacLean affected me deeply. As

founder of the school, I had designed various environments to observe continually

the early learning of children. Interested in the theories of Piaget, Jung, and

Carl Rogers, I was hardly expecting the intrusion of reptiles and brain research.

Yet there it was.

For years I had been working to help children be generous and caring and loving and kind. But often what I saw when observing these younger children was fighting, taking each other's possessions, biting, and struggling for territory. There were no psychological explanations for these behaviors that satisfied me. I had designed the early learning center for ages two through six with the studies of Piaget in mind, but I had come to find the work of Carl Jung much more impressive, especially the four typologies he described. It was evident when a child was a *thinker* and got engaged in mental tasks. It was also easy to distinguish a *sensory-oriented* child and an *emotional-relational* child. It was even more obvious to see the *intuitive* child who always hung back and observed from a distance. However, nothing seemed to ring as true as MacLean's presentation of the reptilian brain with its territorial insecurity, fear, possession, and possessiveness. With the exception of actual mating and breeding, the following list gives an accurate account of major activities of three-to five-year-old children. Reptilian behaviors were subtly and not so subtly present in preschool and kindergarten. Looking further, I found them in my adolescent sons and in my own adult behavior.

You may wish to check your behavior with the following basic behaviors of reptiles. Can you recognize yourself or others at home or in the office?

Special Forms of Basic Behavior

Selection and preparation of homesite ⎫
Establishment of territory ⎬ Domain
Use of home range ⎭
Showing place preferences
Trail making
Marking of territory
Patrolling territory
Ritualistic display in defense of territory, commonly involving
    the use of coloration and adornments
Formalized intraspecific fighting in defense of territory
Triumphal display in successful defense
Assumption of distinctive postures and coloration in signaling
    surrender
Use of defecation posts
Foraging
Hunting
Homing
Hoarding
Formation of social groups
Establishment of social hierarchy by ritualistic display and other
    means
Greeting
Grooming
Courtship, with displays using coloration and adornments
Mating
Breeding and, in isolated instances, attending offspring

Flocking
Migration

Paul MacLean[1]

To those who have difficulty comparing humans to reptiles or animals, MacLean replies: "In neither case is it the intention to equate animals and humans. Rather it is regarded as a reasonable assumption that if particular brain tissue from a variety of species conforms generally in its constituents, construction, and connections, it may have corresponding functions."[2] Please notice that we are not equating humans and reptiles but rather using the information about reptiles to see if it sheds light on our human actions and our basic brain. After dealing with darkness and the unconscious through centuries of mythology, religion, and now modern psychology, we are in search of whatever can help us become conscious in this brain. The reality that one of our three brain structures is similar in formation to the structure of the reptile brain means that we should at least be willing to search for similarities or corresponding functions. After we have discovered and admitted to these associations, what to do? Acceptance, humor, respect, curiosity, and flexibility are all important to enable us to get closer to these other formations of life.

Acceptance is the opposite of denial. It is the willingness to look at what is, without the necessity of defense or explanation. The purpose or value of acceptance as opposed to denial is that it allows us all the data on our actions rather than our hiding them from ourselves or allowing others to discover them bit by bit. Acceptance is easier to describe than to do. Accepting that I am territorial and so is the other and so indeed are my children is not easy. Learning to respect rather than invade the other's territory is the next step. "My husband's desk is his, no matter how sloppy."

A sense of humor in dealing with these natural or primordial behaviors is also vital. It may not be funny if you see your two-year-old son grab back his toy instead of sharing it with his darling friend whom you wish he would love. It may help you to know that this behavior is the basic brain in primordial territorial action. It by no means indicates that a child will grow up as a cool, calculating, selfish adult. When you find your own self being territorial and not wanting to share, you may have even more difficulty taking a light attitude. It takes a while to develop a sense of humor with yourself, but it is vital to self-observation, the key to living with your own reptile brain.

Beyond acceptance and humor I have found curiosity to be extremely helpful. Becoming actively and neocortically engaged in searching for the characteristics of other life and then comparing them with my actions has come to be an interesting hobby. It may also be a vital hobby that will one day play a key role in our being willing to save life on this planet. Answering the question of how all life really relates may enable the environmental movement to take a kinder attitude toward human beings. Rather than castigating us for our bad habits, environmentalists may be able to develop an education sympathetic to *all* forms of life based on our three different brain systems, only one of which is characteristically human.

Having developed this curiosity, I have found it logical and easier to respect the reptilian behavior of those human beings near me as well as other forms of life. To respect their actions and territories I have needed the guiding image of flexibility. Flexibility, which I often call the goddess or mascot of the basic brain, has helped me beyond belief. So great is she that I have developed her into basic intelligence. I am able to respect by moving toward and away, by being flexible when I come across behaviors that I have been conditioned to reject all my life.

Characteristics of Reptilian and Human Behavior

In presenting reptilian behavior, MacLean emphasizes six general forms of behavior: isopraxism (imitation), tropism (innate behavior), deception, routinization, repetition, and reenactment.[3] How do these behaviors correspond to human behavior?

IMITATION

Animals engage in imitative behavior for recognition of one another, self-preservation, and procreation.[4] Human beings also imitate for self-preservation, grouping together in towns and nations. Imitation for recognition as well as self-preservation may explain why, when we become adolescents, we seek to imitate the clothes, speech, hairstyles, values, and actions of a new tribe of friends. The best efforts of school and family cannot stop this primary identification and recognition behavior. Perhaps the formation of gangs is really the effort of adolescence to become secure in a world larger than that of the family. Imitation appears as a human phenomenon in all ages and all cultures. We imitate loved ones in our personal lives. We dress and act in similar ways in our organizations as well as nations.

Imitation has been severely criticized, and yet imitation and its counterpart inhibition, or the refusal to go along with an action, can become useful tools of consciousness, so much so that I have included both in the process of basic intelligence. For example, faced with addiction, only the ability to inhibit certain behavior and imitate other behavior will be strong enough to help someone change. Reason is only slightly helpful. Wanting is more important, but only the physical capacity to inhibit and imitate will be strong enough to redirect physical action toward a new behavior.

As we have sought to emphasize reason and creativity in our schools, we have overlooked imitation as a positive learning experience. Intent on preventing copying and plagiarism, we have failed to see that imitation is also a great way to learn. In children's earliest years we give full rein to their imitative capacities. At unprecedented rates they master the complexities of language through oral imitation and the subtleties of physical coordination through visual imitation. In later years, we reject imitation by describing it as a lack of originality. In this way, we cut ourselves off from this basic learning modality.

As adults, we often fail to see that we need only look out at the world, discover people who are more advanced than we are, and begin to imitate them. Everyone can be our resource. Learning does not have to be limited to textbooks or dependent on a teacher to take the initiative. Resources are always available. It is intelligent to imitate anyone who does something better than ourselves. Schools could restore the power of imitation by organizing and encouraging students to learn in teams. Testing could always remain private to assure individual accomplishment.

INNATE BEHAVIOR

MacLean cites tropism or innate behavior as another major characteristic of reptilian behavior. Innate behavior refers to an unexplained positive or negative response to a stimulus. In animals, colors and sometimes movements elicit a basic positive or negative response. According to MacLean, innate behavior still cannot be explained. He cites the fixed action patterns in fish, referring to Konrad Lorenz's use of the word *imprinting* ". . . as a special form of learning that occurs only in a critical period of the development of an organism." Lorenz describes how a young bird during a critical period "attaches himself to the first creature he meets."[5]

This phenomenon of "attaching oneself in critical moments" is what I believe occurs in our earliest human years during critical periods. What makes something critical or dangerous for the individual is not known. What is evident, however, is how our minds "freeze" or "attach" around certain events in childhood, which then influence our behavior all our life. Often in working with individuals dealing with troubling circumstances in their adult lives, I have seen how their difficulty can be traced back to images that their brain took of their parents or life situations during critical periods. It is as if the mind attached to that image, froze, and continued to hold it. We can call this an imprint, or we can say a pattern was established. What seems clear is that the cause of the behavior is no longer apparent. The adults are no longer aware of why they think or react that way. They believe it is normal, or just the way things are, until with assistance they remember the earlier image. In retrospect they are able to see that they froze or attached around that image.

Mary, for instance, is a fifty-year-old librarian who studied art with the desire but not the courage to be a professional artist. When I invited her to travel mentally into her past, she was able to remember her mother's disapproval of her father's career as an artist. Mary had received this information as an imprint from her mother and registered a reaction against being an artist (basic brain). Though she was able to understand what motivated her mother's disapproval—her mother's need for a secure income for the family—she was not able to overcome a basic resistance to becoming an artist herself. Returning mentally to her childhood memories, she was able to get in touch with her love for her father (limbic system). Supported by that love, she was able to look again at her earlier decision pattern and make a new decision (see the chapter on pattern intelligence). She then set up new parameters that supported her moving into a career as an artist (see the chapter on parameter intelligence). Her success in her new profession reflects her basic intelligence, which helped her change a decision that had been frozen in her mind since childhood.

It is relevant to remember that positive messages can also be registered in our mind in early childhood. Although we might wish to attribute the greatness of our adult life to ourselves or our own efforts, the greatest of all influences may well have been a positive imprint we received from one of our parents in childhood. These imprints that we have been calling innate or unexplained or unconscious in humans are what I believe we can now approach by means of pattern intelligence and change, if we wish to, by means of parameter intelligence.

DECEPTION

MacLean stresses deception as a necessary survival skill for all reptiles. They use deceptive behavior to acquire food as well as other necessities such as home or mate. They also use deception to avoid death.[6] In humans, while we preach against deception in our religion and values classes, we teach deception in every sport. We practice deception in all major affairs, be they diplomatic or military, financial or love. In sophisticated society, we often support deception as cleverness. Here again, we might make great strides by consciously acknowledging the existence of deception and indeed supporting it openly as a life-preservation measure. If the word *deception* is too contaminated by criminality, we might at least acknowledge deception as avoidance.

For example, on a Sunday afternoon, a nation watches television enthralled by the deceptive tactics of a quarterback dodging, weaving, avoiding interception, finally crossing the goal line with a winning touchdown. However, after the game, the husband will probably turn to his wife and children, unaware that skillful avoidance may be necessary to get through dinner or into loving arms for the late show. One wrong throw or criticism from either wife or husband and the other collapses into rational defense, gets hooked by pride, and stumbles in a heap, complaining, "This family is impossible" or "Sundays are always impossible!"

You may indeed need reptilian intelligence, even if you need to call it by another name. I have included avoidance in basic intelligence as the capacity to move toward and away from something or someone. It is basic!

ROUTINIZATION

According to MacLean, animals not only have master routines that they follow but also have a series of subroutines, which can become rigidly structured in terms of patterns and times of occurrence. By means of these routines they stake out territories and engage in the same function repeatedly at the same times.[7]

All of us know someone with set routines or have them ourselves in some area of life. If it is not Archie Bunker's chair, it may be our evening drink or our morning coffee or newspaper. MacLean makes it clear that animals are slaves to their routines and subroutines. Are we also slaves to our routines but just unwilling to admit it? Although as humans we say we value creativity and reason, the easiest way to provoke a human is to interrupt a routine. Interrupting my morning cup of coffee with even the most innocent question provokes either anger or avoidance.

High on the list of major causes of stress are the interruptions of basic routines, such as a change of job or home or spouse. Anyone who has lived through a major change of home or office vows never to do so again. It is clear that we value routine, even if we refuse to honor it. Routines are to this deepest brain what rationality is to the left hemisphere: what it knows best.

In this basic brain we order, arrange, and organize vibrations into routines that we can trust and count on. This phenomenon of ordering vibrations at this level is something so important that I have considered it an intelligence in its own right. Parameter intelligence is the process by which we become conscious of our routines and can see which are the spatial and temporal parameters appropriate to establish routines to guide energy in the basic activities of our life.

Perhaps we might do well to study the ever-so-careful routines of many animals. They cannot count on a neocortex to make excuses about routines. The assiduous attention of a bird making a nest and the cooperation of ants carrying food are just two illustrations. The entire animal world offers elegant examples of parameters and routines. If we could but notice and treat routines with the same respect that animals do and honor them with the same love and consciousness that we give to creativity! Routines and creativity are so different, yet both are necessary and appropriate in different circumstances of human life.

REPETITION

Animals often use repetitious display or signaling. Persistent repetition of display often wins the desired female.[8] In human courtship perhaps the only difference is that the female can demonstrate as much or more persistence than the male.

MacLean also refers to repetitions being used as displacement, that is, at times when the behavior is not appropriate to the situation. The bird preens even though danger is near.[9] It is similar in our lives. The most famous example from history is Marie Antoinette, who continued her rituals oblivious of the impending French Revolution. We all have a tendency toward avoidance, frequently busying ourselves by doing the same thing over and over again rather than engaging directly with energy that would cause us difficulty. Sometimes we are conscious of our avoidance, sometimes not. We need the knowledge of our patterns as well as the practice of self-observation in order to become conscious of such a basic behavior as avoidance.

REENACTMENT

Like repetition, reenactment is a basic phenomenon involved in establishing routines. The reptile is capable of marvelous feats of reenactment. MacLean mentions ten to thirty thousand Ridley turtles that return to old nesting places along the beaches of the Pacific Ocean and the uncounted numbers of female green turtles of Brazil who migrate to an island 1400 miles away in regular reenactments every two to three years.[10] Is it tenacity, or is it imprinted memory that governs the turtle? Do we have imprinted memory? If so, who or what is imprinting us? We now know that the actions of our parents and all the influences that surround us do indeed imprint us by entering through the pores and being processed to our brain structures by means of our afferent-efferent nervous system. Is this sensorial memory that we theorized about in the last chapter located in the basal ganglia, and should we therefore be aware that we have a memory for physical reenactment in this basic brain?

Whatever the physiological discoveries of the future will bring, we at least need not be surprised to discover our human capacity to persevere or to repeat the same habits again and again and again. Do we call these patterns unconscious because we are so unaware of them, so unaccustomed to observing our repetitive behavior, or only unwilling to admit it? Our neocortex criticizes us for acting the same way again and again. We become unwilling to admit our addictions. We may want to change, but somehow, the pattern just happens again.

The Three Rs: Repetition, Reenactment, Routines

The same phenomenon of repetition is involved whether we are emphasizing actions, routines, values, or addictions. Often this propensity for doing the same thing again and again is the source of much discouragement. We are surprised that it is so difficult to change human behavior. After thousands of years of erudition, understanding, law, science, and so many other human achievements, why are there still areas in which we seem not to advance at all—prisons, hunger, crime, poverty, and wars repeated over and over without changing anything? Why do we fail to change these essential aspects of human behavior? I believe it is because we have not taken seriously the phenomenon of repetition.

We act again and again as we did before. We become habituated or addicted, not just to alcohol and drugs, but to our ways of living, our ways of being. We justify or explain our actions by calling them our values, and we do indeed value them. However, beneath this expression of values, we have become conditioned to what makes us secure, and this conditioning seems right to us. It seems right even if its results are painful, like hunger and poverty and prison or more subtle forms of suffering.

All efforts to get us to change are processed through our neocortex or limbic brain. We think wistfully about changing, or we say we want to change. We do indeed try and succeed perhaps once or twice. Then, somehow, without our noticing, we have returned to the same old behavior. The many people who return to prison and the many people who return to dieting or overeating will be able to recognize the relationship of repetition to reenactment.

What we were accustomed to enacts itself again, or how else can we describe what happens? How can we permit ourselves to become conscious? How can we consciously look for the nature and quality of the repetition and addiction in basic areas of our life rather than pretending they do not exist?

I believe we need to take into account that on this deepest brain level we are all addicted to something, someone, or some ways of acting or being. Our addictions are our routines. They exist in all of us because of repetition. Repetition exists in all of us because of our need for security. We make ourselves secure by repeating again and again. What makes us secure continues to make us secure whether we call it routine, reenactment, addiction, or value. I believe we will succeed in changing human behavior only when we recognize the need to become intelligent in this basic brain.

A Fresh Look at Basic Behavior

I am sure you have no difficulty identifying yourself and others with many of these reptilian behaviors. As you probably are aware, most of these behaviors are not held in high regard. The world viewed through the neocortex or through a university degree can hardly appreciate any intelligence in repetition, in reenacting the same behaviors, or in establishing routines. The governing phenomenon of repetition involved in doing things again and again or doing things routinely is considered boring, unsophisticated, and uncreative. Imitation is a sure sign of lack of originality. We do not acknowledge deception except when it is revealed in criminal behavior, and we relegate imprints or innate behavior to the unconscious.

Nevertheless, to master any activity requires repetition. We must continue to act again and again if we wish to succeed. An orderly or peaceful life requires routines, and one complicated area in psychology is still the influence throughout our life of the early imprints on our behavior. The phenomenon of repetition, involved in routines and reenactments, is basic to addiction. I urge us to take a new look at life, this time keeping in perspective the three brain systems that are filtering our perceptions. Of course we must continue to view life through our neocortex and value the nuances of intellect, originality, and creativity. However, now that we know that we also have a basic brain filtering our perceptions and influencing our ability to organize life, we must also take a new look at the importance of imitation, innate behavior, deception or avoidance, and repetition as they appear in our actions, routines, values, and addictions. These characteristics are basic in our search for the intelligence of this brain structure and the valuable contribution that this brain can make to our consciousness, social well-being, and health.

CHAPTER XV

Languages
of the Basic Brain

The spine is your tree of life. Respect it.

Stand up. Keep your back straight. Remember that this is where the wings grow.

Martha Graham

The neocortex communicates through *thought, images, sounds, and intuition. The limbic brain speaks to us through our emotions. How does the basic brain communicate with us? It speaks through our physical body, our behavior, our context, and our dreams. These are the four languages that will permit us to break the code and hear the signals of what we have been calling the unconscious.*

As an infant you learned to speak words; later you learned to read the words that you already knew. You have been speaking through your basic brain all your life:

1. Your deepest brain spoke to you through the spinal cord and brainstem that guided the first formation of YOUR BODY.

2. It registered the stimuli and created the responses that form the

patterns that continue to filter and create YOUR BEHAVIOR.

3. Combined with your behavior, it continues to react and form THE CONTEXT IN WHICH YOU LIVE.

4. At night, when you must stop your neocortical and emotional activity, you enter the delta brain waves associated with the basic brain and release the information stored there, which you know as YOUR DREAMS.

It is now a question of learning to read these languages rather than leaving them dangling in the darkness to create their effects without our consciousness. The reading method that has been tried and proven effective by sages throughout the centuries is called self-observation. If we wish to become fully conscious of our life on this beautiful planet, we must all begin this reading program.

Physical Formation of the Body

The deepest brain speaks to us through the formation of the physical structure we call our body. It therefore becomes important to realize that our physical self is the instrument we are using to live in the world and to express ourselves. To understand life at a cellular level, we need to respect that billions of cells form themselves into the physical structure we are calling our self.

To be able to value the instrument, we must identify with the purity of this formation. If not, we are playing life with a faulty instrument and are hardly likely to win, no matter how hard we try. A musician would not pick up a guitar to play beautiful music and at the same time condemn it as faulty, ugly, or not capable. We would not do that with a musical instrument and must learn not to do it with our life instrument. As the dancer Martha Graham once said, "Our body is our glory, our hazard and our care."[1] At this most subtle level, we need the grace granted to the newborn. We need to consider our bodies as forming part of creation, and consequently pure and sacred. If not, we must spend our life becoming pure through a long process of searching for the Law or the Lord or the God or the events that will make us pure.

Our uncertainty about the purity of human life is costing us dearly. We must hear that we were born in the image of God (Gen. 1:26) and believe, or we must reason with ourselves that human life is part of the creation of all life. If you lost creation on your way to evolution and are still looking for the missing link, I would urge you to perceive life through both your left and right hemispheres. First grasp the oneness of all creation through the perspective of your right hemisphere and then differentiate the development of life or evolution through the perspective of your left.

If we permit ourselves the luxury of doubting ourselves, of feeling guilty or imperfect and therefore guilty, and criticizing our essence instead of loving ourselves, we damage and imprison the essential creation of our body-mind. It is not a small matter of self-esteem, of finally recognizing the good points of our thoughts, feelings, or actions. It is rather a fundamental matter of identifying our physical body with the rest of God's creation. It is a matter of including ourselves in life from the first appearance of our physical form.

Our being against ourselves is the snare of our own mind, more specifically our neocortex. We create within ourselves the existence of darkness that we call the devil. With our minds prepared in this way, we then wander many dark years, enmeshed in our own mental weaving, involved in a journey to discover light and purity. All of this is a perception of life woven by the neocortex and very well described by Dante in his *Divine Comedy*. However, to consider ourselves bad in our essence and lost amid a human world filled with harm, living in a body that is described in the first place as separated from God, is indeed hell.

This perception of the human being as "bad" is an understandable neocortical conclusion because the neocortex's function is to make distinctions, and it is impossible not to see the harmful and negative behavior of humans. Badness or evil is a valid conclusion at the neocortical level. However, if we perceive life only through our neocortical brain of distinctions, we will always be caught in the inevitable duality of good and evil. Dualism or the elaboration of polarities and opposites is one masterful way that the neocortex makes distinctions clear, easy to understand, and popular. Therefore, dualism will continue to exist, and you and I on the neocortical level can never expect to escape from dualism or to lose our critical perception of the world and human nature as good or evil.

However, when we want to understand the nature of the human body, we must look to the two brain systems that govern the human body, namely, the limbic brain governing our organs and endocrine and immune system and the basic brain governing or filtering the world through our nervous system.

Those who do not consider the basic brain a pure instrument will be filtering life at this basic level through what they consider to be an impure instrument, and their life will reflect that impurity. We must look again at physical creation in order to establish the purity of the basic brain and limbic brains. Creation is energy, vibrating into atoms, particles, neutrons, protons, cells, clusters of cells we call patterns, and later patterns we call the structure of the human body-brain-being. Therefore, the first appearance, the very existence of the human being is creation, untouched by any interest or intent to do harm that we might later learn or be imprinted with from our culture. The existence as such of the body-brain-mind instrument is pure as creation.

To have access to this brain we need to accept ourselves first as creation. To love ourselves, our own body as creation is our first task. The sacredness of our body as creation is the key to opening the door to this brain.

Behavior

Our behavior is the second language of the basic brain and can be read only by neutrally observing our body in action. The patterns, rhythms, and routines in which our body is involved are the external signs of action. We must therefore observe our actions to see how our basic brain is continually revealing itself.

What is in me that is conscious of the action? I see myself avoiding my checkbook, then feeling bad, guilty because I have not paid my bills, then withdrawing further, then moving into avoidance by thinking about other things. All this action is happening, except the action of paying my bills. Observing this I recognize a pattern of not paying my bills on time. I think that I am going to change, but the pattern repeats itself. What is happening inside of me? I can try to know. I can analyze, imagine, and feel everything that is going on, but frequently I prefer to defend myself by denying that the action was the way it was. We human beings feel the need to give explanations instead of just accepting our behavior as it is. From the point of view of the basic brain, reading our behavior is the way to know what is going on within us. Therefore, we need to accept our action without resorting to denial. We need to value action as a factor equal to thought, imagination, and feeling if we want to become conscious in this brain.

The Self-in-Context

Consciousness involves observing not only our actions but also the context we have created around ourselves. Why include the context rather than just our actions? The basic brain is exposed to the world by means of the brainstem, the afferent-efferent system, and the openings of the skin. This implies that the context in which we live reveals as much about ourselves as our actions. By context I mean the mini-environments of our life, the territories in which we live—for example, our home, work place, relationships, religion, health, leisure. These are the usual territories where we spend most of our life. They are the areas in which we have been weaving all that surrounds us. Sometimes this weaving is more subtle than the action level and therefore cannot be noted except by observing our context.

We can accept that the contexts in which we live—at conscious and unconscious levels—are what we have been creating. This is what our "I" has been producing. We can study the context of our environment as if it were a textbook. We cannot know the action at this level by what we think, feel, or know that we have done. Rather, we know by stepping back and observing, in a neutral way, what it is that we are doing today.

We no longer need to call this level unconscious. The territories in which we live are the texts to be studied to become conscious. "What you see is what you get." Our home reveals us, our work, our health, our religion, our leisure, our family—everything around us reveals us. We cannot judge a book by its cover, but we can know our basic brain by observing the contexts in which we live.

The fact that we have always been exposed to our environment explains the profound impact of our parents. In our childhood, parents were the principal influences in our environment. Our small bodies were not only continually in the presence of their big bodies, but linked to them because of our need for affection. In this way we were open to receive continuous messages from them, which became our conditioning. This basic brain has filtered the behavior of our parents generation after generation. Therefore, without becoming conscious of our roots, we can never become fully conscious in this brain. Those who like to travel can search for their roots in Europe or Africa, but the real journey toward our roots begins by observing our own present context. Thereby we can discover our heritage and what we personally selected from that heritage.

These contexts thus reveal the imprints of generations, passed on through mother and father in a continuous sequential struggle for life. They reveal values passed to us through our religion, country, schools, and those special teachers who influenced us. They reveal the historic time context and the cultural-national-economic context in which we live. They reveal ourselves as we have lived through the ever larger contexts of family, education, religion, art, and culture. The important issue, however, is that they do reveal us. We can know ourselves at this root level only by accepting the self-in-context.

If we stand outside our context, we cut our roots from their soil. Sometimes we step back and blame others for the quality of the soil context. It is always "the other"—our parents, the times, the economy, the present crisis. By means of a perpetual dualistic battle between "self" and "other," we not only avoid all responsibility but immerse ourselves in continuous conflict and drama. We can overcome this dualism by considering ourselves not as individuals separated from our context, but rather as an I-in-context. The "ability to respond" will then replace blame, denial, and the passivity often masquerading behind the word *responsibility*. Then we will be ready to listen and respond in interaction with all that surrounds us as our inheritance. This is how life presents itself through our I-in-the-context of today.

Dreams

Dreams are information processed through all three brain systems, including the deepest brain. When we sleep we pass from the brain activity called beta waves, in which we are thinking, into a more relaxed rhythm called alpha waves, characteristic of the right hemisphere, and into an even more relaxed state identified with theta waves, more characteristic of the limbic brain, before entering the sleep state itself and the slowest brain waves of the basic brain called delta waves. Dream research shows that information releases itself when the brain waves are in delta. Dream researchers are able to observe that a person is dreaming when they notice rapid eye movement (REM) in the dreamer, signalling that the information has passed into the visual field, thereby producing eye activity. We awake with images, messages, and emotions from an experience that we call dream.

When we enter the delta range, we are relaxed enough to release information about ourselves that we had not felt or thought about, let alone imagined or incorporated into the reality of action, when we were awake. The information from impulses that had reached the brainstem but as yet had not been integrated into conscious patterns, routines, or values and may not yet have been released into our body behavior is finally released into our neocortical awareness by means of the images, words, and emotions we know as dreams.

The field of psychology was born from dream analysis and from our profound desire to know what is going on in this deeper range. I believe that the rivalry between Freud and Jung can be interpreted as their respective emphases on different brain systems. Freud was deeply involved in understanding the limbic system, while Jung's insistence on cultural backgrounds and articulation of a collective unconscious are more suggestive of the basic brain. We now know that we are constantly exposed to what Jung named the collective unconscious, including both our personal environment and the rest of the universe.

In order to become conscious at this deepest life level, we will need to see that the basic brain has its own distinctive intelligence. Some of that intelligence becomes available to us only when we let go of our other two brain systems and permit ourselves to go on automatic into the deepest delta vibrations of sleep. Dreams contain information that is being processed and becoming available to be integrated or set aside by our limbic and neocortical brains. Dreams serve as communication between our conscious and unconscious self or our two deeper brains. In brain terminology, dreams are communication from our basic brain passing through our limbic brain and arriving in our neocortex. Can we listen intelligently to hear what our dreams are trying to tell, to interpret impulses that are arising from our depths and presenting themselves as a language waiting to be read by us?

For centuries people have found many ways to read dreams. All cultures have highly valued the interpretation of dreams, but in general the art of dream analysis has been reserved to a few: priests and wise men in ancient times, psychiatrists and therapists in modern times. For me, all ways of interpreting dreams are valid. Nevertheless, I would like to offer a way that originated with this work of seeing the three brains as energy and that has served me and others in my twelve years of giving workshops.

It is important to realize that the interpretation a specialist can give a dream may never be as clear or as relevant as your own analysis. The dream is your language. You received the communication from your basic brain, and you can learn to read it just as you once learned to read books. You begin by understanding that you are the book and that everything in your dream is yours. Seeing all life as energy, you can look at your dreams as the "night news" from your unconscious (limbic and reptilian brains), finally showing up in picture or word form through your neocortex. In this approach you can hold each phrase or image of a dream to be as rich as the story itself and thereby avoid overall prejudgment or analysis. Ask yourself, "What is the energy in me that chooses to show up as the image of each person, animal, plant, place, and so on in my dream?"

For example, if in the dream your aunt appears in a house with your brother and your son swimming in a lake nearby, ask yourself: What is the energy within me that has shown up as my aunt, the house, my brother, my son, swimming, and the lake? Using this question with each image— nouns and verbs—in your dream, search to understand the message that may be stored in your basic brain. In other words, search to understand what your most subtle being wants to tell you.

You can muse about your dream using these general guidelines on your way to work, resting at lunch, or at any time throughout the day. The following exercise, however, is more structured and requires more time. I do recommend it highly for those dreams that you know intuitively hold important messages for you and deserve more of your time and consideration.

EXERCISE

DREAM TRANSLATION

1. *What are the images in your dream telling you? In order to understand better, write your dream in a notebook, leaving a space between each line in order to fill it in later with your translation into energy.*

2. *On top of each image, note its major characteristics. Be simple and practical. If it helps, imagine that you are explaining to an extraterrestrial who just arrived from Mars and has no experience with what an aunt or house is, and so on down your list. For example, the characteristics of your aunt that matter to you are that she is very sweet and very Catholic. Describe in a few words the essential characteristics of each image.*

3. *Add the words "within me" at significant moments in order to remember that everything that happens in your dreams belongs to you and comes from within you.*

4. *Read your dream in the language of energy. For example, if your aunt was sweet and very Catholic, read to yourself "the energy of sweetness and Catholicism within me . . ." (and continue through each image and action of the dream). The energy replaces the name of the person, thing, action, or place presented in your dream.*

5. *Reflect on the energy within you that wants to communicate with you by means of these specific images.*

Rachel used this exercise to interpret one of her dreams:

The Dream. I'm inside a sailboat with all my best friends, one of whom is Ruth, who is actively redesigning the interior of the boat so that it can be sailed from within while we are under way on the open sea.

The Characteristics of the Imagery. "Sailboat" is a delicate shape crafted to move smoothly by the wind through the water. "Interior of boat" is the cabin below. The design of its small space is crucial to comfort and survival. For me to be "inside a sailboat" is unusual; I feel helpless not being up on deck where I can see out, think, and control the craft while under way.

"My best friends" are those who love me, who help me, who want me to be my best. "Ruth" is the energy in me who is the coach for my inner life. In the outer world I associate her with skillful design on many levels, all of which affect the inner life. For her to figure out how to sail a boat from below decks seems the ultimate of design feats.

"The open sea" is the most awesome of all images of energy to me. Being "under way" is to meet the waves in such a way as to move with them and not be smashed by them.

Dream Translation in Energy Language. I am inside the energy of the delicate shape of myself with all those energies within me who love me, who help me, who want me to do my best. Of these, the energy of the skilled designer of my inner life is arranging the space below my thinking life, so that my delicate shape can be "sailed" smoothly through the waves of the most awesome energy within me I can imagine without being smashed. I feel nervous and helpless not being able to use my conscious eyes to see where I am going, but also I feel confident in being helped by the energy of the skilled designer within me, who knows how to sail the energy of my delicate shape from below.

Self-Observation

Our four languages—the body, our behaviors, our self-in-context, and our dreams—each provide a text to help us become conscious. To have access to these texts, we must train ourselves in self-observation. Self-observation is a process of detachment characteristic of the right hemisphere. Beautifully practiced, it enables us to avoid denial and blame. It lets us include all the data. To be able to observe ourselves, we need to keep in mind the points in the following exercise.

EXERCISE
SELF-OBSERVATION

1. *Avoid judgment and emotional attachment.*
2. *Become curious about studying the structures, habits, patterns, and smallest movements of this interesting life creature that just happens to be yourself. You do not belong to yourself. You are an expression of*

life living in an instrument you are calling yourself.

3. *Observe in a neutral way, only for the purpose of knowing, without intent to act.*

4. *Become a fair witness to all that appears.*

5. *Watch for how your billions of cells will express themselves today. Be as curious and as fascinated as if you were observing the stars in the sky.*

Remember that indeed "There are more cells in one human body than there are stars in the galaxy."[2] Just as you sometimes look up at the sky in awe, now begin to look back at yourself, at those billions of cells. Some are shining in all their brilliance. Some are blinking; others are blocked. Others you need to find with a telescope. Above all, enjoy. As you discover more and more about yourself, remember to be gentle and appreciative. Most importantly, your sense of humor needs to accompany you in any full practice of self-observation.

When we are willing to observe our own life process in continuum without attachment or ownership, we will be accessing information at this deepest cellular level and opening ourselves into a greater consciousness of life itself. Self-observation is a practice, a habit, an art that we can develop. We can practice it walking or working or playing. Also, we can note our observations in a diary, as we might if we were making an interesting trip. Life is a trip. According to Thomas Berry, we have taken forty million years of development to arrive here today, to be here now.[3] If we enter into the practice of observation, recording, and dialogue with ourselves, the trip can be much safer and healthier—and as beautiful as we want to make it.

Self-observation is of course a recognizable feature of many of the Eastern systems of knowledge and meditation. In the Western world it has formed a part of religious training but is usually reserved for the priest, nun, monk, rabbi, or other professional of interior growth. It needs to become a standard process in all teachings if we really want to become conscious and responsible for our own behavior.

We need to be continuously observing our body, our dreams, our contexts, and our actions, rather than putting them on automatic and then criticizing ourselves later. We can respect moral guidelines, have a heart full of love, and establish parameters for our actions. All of these help, but nothing can substitute for the continuous self-observation of our own life.

Fig. 13. Basic Wave (Luis Camejo)>

CHAPTER XVI

Living with Life

BASIC INTELLIGENCE

Oh you who speak so well
I think you know not tortuous silence.
Fluid lightning coiled around the tail
This serpent sleeps not;
Though eyes are closed she knows what stirs.
In tension to respond
Friend or food are one.
She is awake, creature of vibrations;
She receives, senses;
Senses all and says nothing.

She is the path of evolution back to paradise
The serpent stirs and hisses;
Warning those who tread without caring;
Camouflaged and coiled on the dark carpet of the
*   primitive,*
Round roots of life she lives.
Axis mundi on the forest floor she lifts her head high.
The spine flexible and still nourished by the universe.
She is the energetic agent of change;
Holy sceptre of the world
She spirals in the temple of Man.

Martye Kent

Basic intelligence is to be conscious of, to

identify with, to use, or to participate in the basic wave motion of life, which is always going on. It is basic intelligence to enter into the rhythm, to follow the rhythm, to expand with it, and to contract with it. When we separate or leave the rhythm, it is essential to guide ourselves back into it again. It is basic intelligence to guide ourselves by moving toward and away from circumstances, as is most appropriate in our life. Basic intelligence is to be able to guide ourselves on behalf of life.

The basic wave of life is entrained in different forms of energy until it becomes obvious to our perception as rhythm. Sometimes the rhythm is entrained in space, giving us the basic routines of life, such as those that occur in work and at home. Sometimes rhythm is entrained through time, and then we have, for example, the rhythm of eating at certain predetermined hours, hungry or not. Also, as time continues generation after generation, rhythms enter into the collective experience that forms our values. Sometimes rhythm is entrained chemically, and we have our chemical addictions such as alcohol or drugs, coffee or food. Sometimes rhythm is entrained in repetitive action, and through our interaction with others we form our professions and our work in the world. Sometimes rhythm is entrained in recognizing greatness—great teachers, beautiful spaces, music, creation, words, and special practices—until we arrive at the thinner vibrations of artistic and religious expression.

Staying in the Action

The wave motion of life is present as basic rhythm in all action. We hear rhythm in music and love it. We engage our bodies in the rhythms of dance and sports. Can we engage in the rhythms of the more ordinary areas of our life, such as work and home? We are more likely to be carrying these as burdens on our shoulders where they weigh us down as fixed objects, heavy with responsibility. Is it also possible to enter the rhythms of home and work in order to enjoy them? By becoming conscious of this phenomenon of basic rhythm, we can enter directly into any rhythm and consciously extend it into an organic way of moving with life.

Some people live rhythmically. They guide themselves by moving into whatever rhythms are happening in their lives at the moment. For example, some are especially able to respond to the never ending pressure of people constantly entering their office. The best executives are able to expand and contract with each person's problems. While in that process of expansion-contraction, they are exhilarated. Once they release themselves from that rhythm, they may feel exhausted—that is, until they enter a new rhythm, such as being at home, or until they return themselves to the same rhythm the next day in the office. Sometimes we feel relieved to be back in our rhythm, entrained once again.

It is basic to respect rhythm as it presents itself. To do this we have to understand that there are rhythms in all actions. It is our choice to follow the rhythm of the action instead of interrupting it at erratic intervals with thoughts and feelings. Usually we believe that the solution to the action is to think more deeply or to imagine alternatives. Sometimes this is a way to the solution, but at other times it is only sidetracking. Then it is preferable to deepen more directly into the action, trying to catch the rhythms involved and staying with them. For example, instead of doubting and asking continually whether a task is worthwhile, whether it is better to stop or continue, you can simply continue, attending in a neutral way to what is in front of you. Live the rhythms as they present themselves instead of deviating from them by means of doubt, feelings, or alternative images.

Certain areas of life always require attention: work, home, health, leisure, relationships. I used to subject these areas not only to continuous doubts and questions, but also to my feelings. If I got angry at work, I would want to leave for the day or quit permanently. I also fantasized that I could make work disappear and spent hours thinking of ways to change it. All this neocortical activity instead of just staying in the rhythm, attending to what needed to be done, moving toward what pleased me and away from what didn't! It would have been better to follow the path of least resistance, riding the waves involved in work through their intensity, through their expansions and contractions. I know I would have finished each task sooner and with less fuss.

The deepest brain requires from us the acceptance of existence. This is neither mental nor emotional acceptance, but physical acceptance, which we accomplish by attending to, doing, being active, interacting, riding into, and holding with and through the phenomenon of action or the actions of others. What is most important is our behavior, our doing.

Now, although I still think, wish, dream, and get angry, I can also gently return my body to work and enter into neutral energy until I become attracted to and engaged in some aspect of the work. This begins the interaction. The impersonal concepts of "returning my body to" a definite action or place and of "guiding myself toward" are keys to helping me stay in the action. I need to be gentle. It is neither force nor willpower nor discipline that helps me stay in or return to the action. Rather, it is as if I am lifting up a child and carrying it to where it belongs, respectful of her ideas, wishes, tantrums, and anger. Often, I have to coax myself, seduce myself, or reward myself. I am not holding myself to something or making myself do it. I am returning myself to the place of work, to the time, and then spatially placing myself in close proximity to the task, sensorially open to engagement, to being hooked or attracted to. I make gestures to start, act "as if," and on most days, my energy becomes entrained with the rhythms of work.

The image of the serpent helps me when dealing with a project over a long period of time—such as this book! Sometimes it is as if I must be my own snake charmer, playing gentle music to encourage myself to slide out of the basket, to move my body, to sense and ripple my way, slithering into and out of, sensing where to move. This is not an act of will. It is rather a sensorial awareness, and the deeper I go into sensing the movement, the sweeter or more natural the experience of energy.

When I tell myself I have to do something rather than guide myself into the rhythm of it in this sensorial manner, it feels different and the results are different—never as exact, never as effective. It really is as if only part of my being is involved. My neocortex goes, but I leave my body home. No wonder we say of many intellects, "They are only half there," or call others "halfhearted" workers. The clue to this brain that works for me is gently guiding or seducing myself.

Rhythm and Relationships

Rhythm helps me to relate. For example, beginning a new work or entering into a new office or any new environment instead of trying to understand and ask with my rational intelligence about all the details, I can enter with my basic intelligence and begin to identify myself with this new place and with the rhythms that are happening around me. It is a matter of becoming "one with" as quickly as possible.

It is also gratifying to be able to identify with the rhythms of another culture, which is especially necessary if we wish to participate in ceremonies of other religions or fully enter into the culture of other nations. To feel free to identify with people or their actions by means of our basic intelligence, we need to free ourselves from our rational intelligence that prefers to doubt and also from our limbic brain that may reject other people or feel awkward in their presence. We need this basic intelligence in order to be able to follow the rhythms of whatever is going on, moving toward them and identifying with them.

In the same way, we can identify with the rhythms of another person. Each human being is made up of repetitive rhythms. At a thicker level of vibration we call these rhythms values, professions, habits, or personality. To respect other people, we need to discover at least their most obvious rhythms in order to be able to identify with them. I move in tandem with them, observing, imitating, learning, and searching to appreciate something about them. Sometimes I express my appreciation verbally, but this is not always the key. What registers is my ability to identify myself with them, to keep their rhythm, and to travel with them or accompany them in a most respectful manner. If we all knew how to relate with our basic intelligence, quieting our emotional and neocortical brains, it would be much easier to connect with one another. To relate by means of identifying with the rhythm of the other ought to become an option both known and practiced in this world that is becoming smaller and smaller each day.

Rhythms also form themselves on a more subtle level, which probably can only be described as the very integrity of the person. Healers can notice rhythms at this level, and so can lovers. It is here where both healers and lovers can expand the life of the person or most severely reduce it. We must be wise in selecting our healers, therapists, and lovers, and we must be wise in withdrawing from them if the results are not positive.

At this level we also need to find the way to protect life when we trust ourselves to the phenomenon of love. More exactly, we must know that the emerging patterns or rhythms of another person will sooner or later intrude upon our love without asking permission.

At this level of the deepest brain, love involves us in accepting the integrity of the other. To be more precise, to love, at this level, is to accept the different patterns and rhythms of the other even though they may be different from our own. At these moments, instead of entering into and expanding with the rhythms of the other, we can recede or move away from in order to allow the other his or her own space. We can shift our focus to something we really appreciate about the other.

Knowing that expanding and contracting are two aspects of the same wave, we can be aware that our contractions are part of the love process. We can recede, wait, observe, respect, accompany, and return again to the process of catching the other's rhythm and entering into contact.

To catch the rhythm
To expand with the rhythm
To contract with the rhythm
To fade into low waves
and again
catch the rhythm
expand with—
or contract with the rhythm.
Expanding, contracting, organically,
in the measure that function, time, space
and need require it.

This is and could be everlasting peace:
expanding, contracting,
catching life as life presents itself.
Acceptance and motion in one everlasting event.

This sounds like paradise, and it might be. At least it is one of the ingredients: to be able to focus into the rhythms of life as life presents itself through people or places, time or function. To be able to enter into the rhythmic process of life is basic intelligence.

Visible and Invisible Rhythm

From the moment we awake in the morning and even while we are sleeping, we are moving toward and away from people, places, ideas, colors, sounds, projects, and circumstances. Literally everything we meet is visible and invisible energy, involving us in a continuous sorting process of attraction and withdrawal. Whether we are conscious of what is occurring in our body or not, we are always responding to the stimuli around us. The interaction of stimulus and response never ceases until death.

Sometimes we can identify ourselves as thinking what we shall choose (the neocortical level). Sometimes we feel ourselves responding emotionally (the limbic level). However, at this basic level, we often can only say we are unaware: "I just did it"; "I don't know why"; "It seemed right"; "There was no reason"; "That's the way it was supposed to be"; "It was instinct, pure instinct." An array of verbal responses tries to describe this primary, basic, stimulus-response level. What we are sure of is that this selection process is constantly going on, whether we are aware of it or not. We know that no action, no reaction, and no physical movement can be carried out without the participation of this basic brain. Damage to the brainstem leaves us in coma and unable to act or react.

What probably guides our selection process is our sense of security or survival, however we understand that to be, image that to be, feel that to be, or have been conditioned to, through our interaction with our environment.

It is, however, not quite so clear at what subtle level this physical action component is operating. It is here in this deepest brain that we must try to take into account energy that might be easily identified as sensorial or instinctive. At an even more subtle level we have the phenomenon reported as the kundalini experience in which energy rises, creating impulse and sensations along the spinal column, entering and moving up into the brainstem and into the visual cortex, producing white light and other visual stimuli. According to the experiences of Gopi Krishna, as reported by Gene Kieffer, the kundalini phenomenon is capable of producing far-reaching changes in our mental capacity.[1] Both the sensorial and instinctive level as well as the more subtle, thinner energy experience of kundalini are invisible rhythms that indeed affect us without our apparent awareness.

Just as basic rhythm exists at a subtle level in spiritual experience, so too it exists at a dense physical level as the reaction response that guides us in a moment of danger. Therefore, sensation or energy in this brain needs to be understood as existing on a range of vibration from thickest to thinnest and at diverse speeds of vibration from the most rapid to the most slow.

We are accustomed to this varied range of energy vibrations passing through our neocortex when we are thinking, imaging, or intuiting. At times we think slowly; at other times thoughts occur at near electric speeds. With our eyes open we have images of external events, which occur at slower speeds and can be retained in our memory. With our eyes closed we may experience a variety of speeds: those images we can easily remember and those that pass across the screen of our mind at very rapid speeds. Once we are aware of thoughts and images vibrating at various speeds and intensities, we can more easily imagine that this same range of diverse speeds exists within our basic brain as well as surrounding us and continuously impacting our actions and reactions at diverse rates of speed and intensity.

From Anxiety to Illness

Knowing that vibrations extend from thicker to thinnest within and around this basic brain may help us observe and perhaps understand the various illnesses of the nervous system that extend from the common everyday variety of nervousness and anxiety to the more serious illnesses like Parkinson's, Alzheimer's, or muscular dystrophy. Whether we are trying to cure ourselves of anxiety or are involved in healing a more serious illness, we need to take into account the electrical charges that enter our basic brain from our interaction with our environment. It is vital to change from considering ourselves as separate individuals to conceptualizing ourselves as an I-in-context (discussed in the last chapter). We will then have a new grasp of the importance of these external impulses continually bombarding us, entering through our skin to the spinal cord and the afferent-efferent nervous system before arriving at our brainstem, where they may be blocked or available, either to affect our limbic brain with its connections to our internal autonomic, endocrine, and immune systems, or to affect our neocortex with its connection to our motor and muscular system.

If our impulses are blocked or excessively intense at some point in their travels through our three brain systems, can they cause chaotic and irregular contractions and constrictions, which then injure the cells and seriously disturb our functioning? Seeing the basic brain as an energy system of vibrations rather than a system of physical parts may give us a new perspective. Understanding that our basic brain is continually exposed and in interaction on subtle invisible levels may give us new insight into the importance of self care.

Regarding nervous system illnesses, we also need to be conscious of our past environment and the imprints that we have been receiving all our lives. We need to update our ideas about what is included in a family history. Parents need to be able to share the dark and difficult influences if we are ever to become conscious of early imprints that might be causing us serious harm at this basic brain level. Family pride needs to be replaced by full disclosure if we wish to become healthy at the subtle levels of our nervous system. Both to alleviate stress and to create an environment in which the subtle expansion-contraction of our nervous system can be nurtured rather than constricted or ignored, we need to focus on the conditions and history of our life. The gift of this brain is the call to observe ourselves as an I-in-context.

The secret is to open our consciousness to include the entire range of energy, from the slowest to the most subtle. We can observe ourselves in a neutral way without prejudice or guilt, neutral observers of our daily behavior. The practice of basic intelligence is to invite ourselves to move toward conditions that nourish us and away from any that might harm us, whatever the intensity or speed of the energy vibrations.

Changing Behavior

How to change human behavior? This theme has been treated by all the religions, philosophies, great dramas and novels, and more recently, by psychologies and the science of human behavior. All have had difficulty. Each has contributed wisdom, knowledge, and a new perspective on the human condition, yet basic changes in the human condition itself have so far eluded our best efforts. In spite of all the contributions and some undeniable progress, as humans we are still faced with undeniable chaos, poverty, crime, war, and individual suffering of anguishing proportions. Each professional group offers its solution, but no solution has yet been sufficient.

Remember that action or behavior can be stimulated by either visible or invisible vibrations. We may be unaware of what provokes or stimulates us. Perhaps the stimulus comes from our present or past environment, perhaps from a dream or information stored deep in the brain, not yet available as dream or thought or feeling, or perhaps from a pattern learned from our parents or a value inherited from generations past and never examined by the mind that holds it. There are so many possibilities. The stimulus impacting our behavior may not be evident; it may be too subtle for us to see or observe, let alone to move away from.

At the level of our brainstem, at any and every moment, we are subject to an indeterminate amount of information or impulses seeking to be converted to information. Perhaps this bombardment explains the difficulty we have had in developing a science of human behavior. If we are in constant flux, constantly exposed to new information entering at least as far as our brainstem, then how will we be able to fix or quantify data long enough to predict results or performance? The existence of this deepest brain center, linked by means of the afferent nervous system to our skin, which is covered with openings to the world, makes it literally impossible to enclose human data within a test tube or even inside a laboratory within a controlled and predictable environment.

Recent brain research may give us a deeper appreciation of how difficult it is for a human being to change. There are three brain systems involved, and each one is in continuous motion or vibration. Therefore, focusing on any definite change and succeeding in achieving it is very difficult.

Change must be rooted in knowing how to manage our own dynamics. For this reason, the new paradigm that everything is movement is of tremendous importance. Every time we wish to change some aspect of our behavior, we may indeed need to accumulate facts and information, but reaching a conclusion will not produce the change. The implication of the new paradigm is that we can change our behavior only by managing the dynamics involved. We change by changing, not by *knowing* about change. It is similar to desiring in the emotional brain. We want only by living the process of wanting. Perhaps, finally, we can convince ourselves of the need for a focus on the dynamics of the human organism instead of on a definitive, descriptive, fixed approach to information and conclusion.

I feel compelled to repeat the most important points that support a dynamic rather than fixed approach to change. Knowing that the human structure is composed of billions of cells, knowing that all cellular structures are really energy in constant vibration, and finally, knowing that each structure is constantly exposed through this deepest brain and the skin to information from other structures, we can give up expecting a fixed formula for change and turn our attention to dynamic processes. We can turn our attention to constant vigilance, care, and awareness of continuously new interpretations of our individual life in its everyday context. For example, you may learn all about dieting or do the exercise "Energy Profile" (which follows this section) to gather information relevant to your eating behavior. However, then you must live the process of dieting, which is dynamically different each day as well as in the different hours of the day.

This is not about changing our mind. It is about keeping our mind constantly attuned. We need to live our life as a dynamic entity rather than as a fixed personality. Implicit in this knowledge is that we need to be continuously involved in taking care of ourselves. You and I need self care because you are the one and I am the one who is permanently in control and the only one capable of managing the dynamic process in a subtle enough way. Neither health nor quality of life can be attained without our continuous and conscious participation. Others can help at the thicker, more obvious levels of energy, but the thinner range depends on our own capacity to enter into the more subtle vibrations.

It is also possible to understand that pain in the body is a signal at a thick level that something within us is requiring attention at a more subtle level. We can become aware before our health gets worse and requires the help of a specialist. I do not mean to exclude the need for specialists. I do mean that from the point of view of this basic brain always exposed to the world, there is no health without the active and conscious participation of the individual.

ENERGY PROFILE: INSTRUMENT FOR CHANGE

I describe now a process that has been helpful at the thicker level of vibration—the obvious visible range where we can perceive our everyday actions and collect information about our behavior. I call it an energy profile because it involves tracing the profile of our visible energy as we have moved toward or away from in different areas of our life, recently or over time.

The profile enables us to learn about our basic instincts, our sensorial actions, or our deepest self by observing and noting our behavior as it has shown up over time, in a particular situation, or in an area that might concern us frequently, such as health, home, learning, religion, work, rest, or relationships. Our behavior reveals not only our most obvious energy but also subtle patterns that have developed through our experiences. Doing an energy profile is the first step in considering any change in life.

Profiles can be as detailed or as general as we wish. They can be of our entire life until this moment or of one day in particular. They can be of one love relationship or of all our love relationships. They can be in relation to one member of our family or to all of our family. They can be about our food, our health, our work, or anything we consider to be a problem or that we wish to understand, improve, or change.

A profile clearly shows us the design of the behavior that has been going on from the past to the present. It can help us recognize that similar behaviors will continue to occur if we do not consciously choose to intervene. (See Chapter 14 on human and reptilian behavior for a discussion of repetition, reenactment, and routines.)

EXERCISE

ENERGY PROFILE

PART ONE: CREATING YOUR PROFILE

At the end of the day make yourself very comfortable. With paper and pencil in hand, put yourself in a relaxed state, ready to observe your activities of the day (or any period of time) from a neutral point of view, that is, without involving either your critical sense or your emotions.

1. *Be ready to observe with interest and curiosity. Begin with the morning, observing your body in the comfort of its bed. Continue observing the behavior of your body entering the bathroom. Did you put on a robe or get dressed immediately? Then observe yourself going down to breakfast, recall what you ate, and observe your actions throughout the day: What did you move toward? What did you move away from?*
2. *Trace a line in the form of a wave on a blank piece of paper, as shown in Figure 14. On the right side of the line note whatever you moved toward, and on the left side note whatever you moved away from.*

3. You have traced the route of a series of your behaviors in time and space. Your energy profile of today reveals the behavior that resulted from some combination of your three brains living a particular experience. The profile illustrates where you have focused your energy and what behaviors you have repeatedly moved toward and away from.

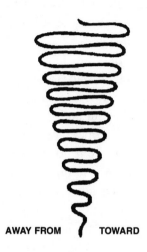

AWAY FROM | **TOWARD**

Fig. 14. Energy Profile

PART TWO: READING YOUR PROFILE

Acceptance. Begin reading your energy profile by completely accepting all the data you included in your profile. Before you allow your neocortex or limbic brain to discard, discount, discredit, or deny any information, first accept the text as if it were a sacred document. At this basic level, you are what you are, and an acceptance of yourself is extremely important before you try to change anything. It is crucial for you to accept all information about yourself as neutrally as possible.

When we consider this kind of information, we may feel tempted to call the basic brain unconscious. We have proven time and again that we do not wish to acknowledge all the available information about ourselves. We prefer denial. I believe this is because we have not been trained in the importance and practice of acceptance. Instead of acknowledging all the data, we screen some of it in what we call self-defense. This defense is based on denial and has produced the phenomenon that we now call clinical denial. We spend our lives observing and analyzing others, but we have great difficulty analyzing something about ourselves that society does not consider appropriate. We are even able to deny our own children or our loved ones, or at least disassociate ourselves from them, when they act against society in ways that embarrass us. We prefer to call this brain unconscious because our need to survive can then protect us from our own critical neocortex and our own limbic brain. Acceptance of all data is the key to knowledge of the self, just as it is the key to knowledge and invention in science and philosophy.

Honoring What You Do Best. Read the right side of your profile that you have marked "toward." On this side you have noted what you do with most frequency. If you have known how to do it well, you can trust that you will continue to do it well. Your body knows how to do this behavior. These are the actions that help you. Here you ought to protect yourself from criticism and doubt. What your body has repeatedly done successfully, you can trust it will continue to do so. Be careful not to meddle or try to improve. Know that you can honor what you do best.

Caution. You may also have noted on this side a behavior that you repeat but now want to change. This is part of the information that you wanted and need to deal with dynamically and carefully. If you do not consciously change, you can be sure that these same behaviors will continue to reenact themselves without your consciousness.

Stress. Read the left side of the profile, marked "away from." Here you have listed what you prefer to move away from. These are the behaviors that you do but that cause you stress. If you do them more than three times a week against your will, or rather against your body, you can be sure they are causing you tension and you should try to change them.

The energy profile is a tool that permits us to reflect on all the information that is brought together as our behavior. Self-observation is a continuously dynamic process. The energy profile is a static process. Combining the two will help us become conscious by owning our behaviors and approaching them neutrally before we try to change them through the processes of pattern and parameter intelligences described in the next chapters.

Present Moment

Basic intelligence is not accessed just to inform us of our past; it is an active intelligence to be used in the present. In order to use this intelligence actively, we need to be willing to treat action as its own phenomenon, that is, not necessarily linked with thinking or feeling. At a subtle level, stimuli occur that make us act, react, and continue to repeat past actions. We need to be able to respond to stimuli without considering that feeling or thinking is what is causing our action.

I am struggling to give this basic vibration its independence from the cause-effect thinking that makes action dependent on thinking or feeling—on the process of deciding before the process of doing. Sometimes that is an important sequence. However, often it is necessary to act in order to receive information feedback that will then enable us to make appropriate decisions.

I am seeking to understand action at a level of experience where we can honor and observe the vibrations of stimulus and response. For us to enter or engage in life at the cellular level within ourselves, vibration on a stimulus and response level needs to be free, independent, and understood as just action. Grasping that action is its own phenomenon is extremely important in order to be able effectively to imitate and inhibit, the two dynamics of basic intelligence.

IMITATION AND INHIBITION

Conscious action is a process of inhibiting what is harmful to our life and of imitating what is helpful to our life. In order to train ourselves in basic intelligence, we must be able to imitate and inhibit. First, at a conceptual neocortical level, we must believe in imitation and inhibition. Although imitation was disapproved of in our education, we can remember how much it enriched us in early childhood. We learned to speak and walk through imitation. Now as adults, we can begin to see each person as a resource: everyone can teach us something. We have only to be selective and imitate what will be most nourishing or protective for our life. We can move toward and imitate the best of our environment in order to develop ourselves and in turn become a useful resource for others.

Second, we need to stop defining inhibition as a word with negative psychological implications of unconscious repression. We also must free it from the implications of "losing the benefit of something." *To inhibit* needs to be understood as a verb of action. It is a signal to stop, and it is vitally necessary before we can change directions or begin the process of moving away from anything that may cause us harm.

We can also see inhibition as a temporary process to separate ourselves from actions or vibrations that we still do not know how to process as advantageous. Although for a certain period we might prefer to withdraw from some areas that are not presently helpful, some day we may be more capable and able to return to those same vibrations, the same people or the same actions. For example, we can inhibit our expression of anger because it is not the right moment or not the appropriate place to express it or because we have not yet learned how to express it safely, but when we do learn and also have a clearer idea of what bothered us, we may be able and may wish to express our difficulty the next day. Inhibition can be useful in guiding our actions in an appropriate way.

CONSCIOUSNESS OR CRISIS

Basic intelligence is about living in the present. The dancer Martha Graham captured the consciousness of the present when she said, "All that is important is the one moment in movement. Make the moment vital and worth living. Do not let it slip away unnoticed and unused . . . Not 'what I will do,' not 'what I have done'—but 'what I am doing.' Whatever you do must be as if it's being done now for the first time."[2]

Unfortunately, we do not usually follow this advice. Even more unfortunately, we do not usually act consciously until we have fallen into some crisis, some threat to our identity or existence. Then we realize or are able in some powerful way to "know" how to redirect our choices at this deep sensorial level. By means of crisis, we are able to put aside our automatic behavior, our patterns, routines, addictions, and, in drastic life-threatening cases, even our values.

With a deep surge of energy we choose life in ways we never "understand": we stop smoking, we give up heavy meals, we exercise, or we have a rebirth in which we claim experiences of enlightenment and even miracles. We experience energy and begin the process of guiding ourselves into new habits. Through crisis we are propelled into actions on subtle and not so subtle levels. Often, without prompting, we move ourselves toward what is helpful and away from what is harmful.

My hope is that one day we can develop this power to engage in life-enhancing choices even when life is not threatened, even before crisis. Basic intelligence exists so that we have a process with which we are able to inhibit and imitate before crisis occurs. Basic intelligence exists to alert us to visible and invisible rhythms and invites us to live these rhythms consciously in the present.

Sometimes we think our habits are harmful or feel very uncomfortable about them, but we do not act on this. We hide in statistical formulas rather than using our own dynamic self-observation. We defer to the analysis of others but ignore what is clearly indicated in our own energy profile. Addicted to rational cause-and-effect explanations, we either wait for disasters or search for more and more causes. We become stuck in analysis instead of moving into common-sense actions that might help us avoid the crisis.

Just as rational intelligence can alert us to the necessity of analysis, basic intelligence can alert us to the continuous necessity of action for change. Basic intelligence is vibrating ourselves in resonance and dissonance with energy, in whatever form it takes, in order to form, reform, deform, conform, or transform ourselves in a continual electrical process of life.

Freedom of Being

For us to use basic intelligence at the thinnest vibrational range, we must be "free to be." Basic intelligence is the freedom to be—free not in order to hear, to see, to receive, or to integrate, but free in order "to be," free to move this organism-mind-body-structure. Is this free will? No, this is freedom without will. This is freedom to be conscious of resonance or dissonance at any level of vibration. Living as deeply as possible, we can guide our structure on any wavelength.

At a cellular level, basic intelligence means to have access to our own life, to be in charge of it, to live with our billions of cells. This requires a detachment, a passivity, a distancing from ourselves as well as an acceptance of ourselves. It requires neutrality. It also requires understanding that life is living itself in the configuration of a body that we are calling ours. We use basic intelligence to observe the trace that life leaves in the action we call ours, but that could very well be the influence of each one and everyone, of generations passed and situations lived before we lived or were conscious. Basic intelligence is there to provide the freedom to act in relation to the integrity of life itself.

In the freedom to be, the practice of self-observation is key because it permits us to collect data from all the sources: from ourselves and our body, from our environment, our behavior, and our dreams. The freedom to be as conscious as possible in any range of vibrations also lets us guide ourselves subtly in favor of our life.

I believe that those who have experienced miraculous healing have had access to this freedom and capacity to guide their cells, although perhaps they were not conscious of it. Nevertheless, in some way or other, whether by faith, belief, or love, they were able to receive the energy contact at this cellular level. Basic intelligence is a spiritual phenomenon when it occurs at these subtle wavelengths. Access to subtle and invisible waves is not comprehensible without referring to the infinite. How can we try to explain the experiences that some people tell about who have been considered "clinically dead" and then return to life? How can we understand these subtle waves or what we are beginning to know as out-of-body experiences? It is difficult to trace a sequential process here, since what is involved is a matter of quantum leaps. We can, however, observe that the first brain continues functioning. In out-of-body experiences, the person's consciousness moves into subtle or thinner wavelengths, which permit the individual to observe the functioning of his or her body and what is happening around it.

Although these events cannot be described by the rational sequential process, we can get a picture of what occurs by realizing that each of the three brain structures is vibrating from thicker to thinner dimensions, depending on where we are focusing. *Mystic* is the name given to someone who reaches the thinner dimensions of the neocortex and *healer* or *shaman* the name given to someone orchestrating the thinner dimensions of the limbic and basic brains. We know that mystics begin their spiritual journeys in the neocortex with instant insights, prayer, or meditation, and we know that meditation tranquilizes the thickest waves of the neocortex. Mystics continue through the wavelengths of spatial intelligence and into the intuitive range, where they receive even more subtle wavelengths. Different emotional wavelengths also present themselves, as well as wavelengths that we still do not know how to describe but that do, indeed, bring about physical and emotional changes in the person. Healers and shamans are able to involve themselves in the thinner vibrations of all three brain structures.

One can notice changes in facial expression and personality in anyone who lives consciously experiencing the inner life. Such physical changes indicate that the profound process of this basic brain is involved. I have not wanted to call this brain the reptile brain because that term does not adequately communicate the levels of subtle and inner energy we find here.

At this level and in this brain, we need to be free to live in relation either to the infinite or to the instinctive, either to consciousness or to the so-called unconscious, with either sensation or the basics of nature, in whatever range of energy is occurring. Freedom to be is necessary to our being able to orchestrate a complete range of energy that extends from the thickest to the thinnest, from stimulus-response to quantum leaps.

Children act out their basic intelligence with more freedom than do adults. We would do well to learn to read their behavior in search of their basic intelligence. Arnold was a four-year-old boy who went to the same story area every day at school to listen to stories on the cassette player. This behavior continued day after day and Arnold never wanted to leave the story area, so the teacher became concerned. When we called home to investigate, we learned that the little boy was the second child to be adopted into the family and that his older brother had recently been sent back to the adoption agency. Clearly he was afraid of being sent back too. At school he exhibited this fear by moving toward the same territory every day. What he was doing in school was making sure that he had a territory, a rock. It was a very intelligent reaction for the situation that the boy was living. It was his basic intelligence acting. Fortunately, we were prepared to observe his behavior and try to understand what was behind it rather than force him to change. When the mother understood what was going on in the boy's mind, she was able to assure him that he would always have a home with her. His behavior then changed both at home and at school.

My favorite adult story about basic intelligence is about a woman's ability to move away from her own feelings and toward her mother's needs at a critical time when her mother's life was in danger. Joan had never had a good relationship with her mother, but she was the only surviving relative and was therefore called to the hospital when her mother suffered a heart attack. Joan felt empathy but couldn't imagine how she could deal with taking care of her mother for any length of time.

As Joan tells it, she asked for a dream that would give her guidance. That same night she dreamed: "My father was in heaven talking with another man who asked him how he got there. My father explained that he had gotten so mad at his son for getting bad grades he had a heart attack from his anger and died."

Joan pondered the dream and came to believe it was a warning against her becoming emotional with her mother. If her mother were to avoid dying, Joan would have to be very careful not to bring up emotions, not to allow her own longstanding anger and sadness with her mother to interfere. Yet there she was, responsible for her mother but still filled with resentment. How could she act normally and not reveal any traces of this resentment? Joan believed deeply in feelings and knew they could not be easily camouflaged. Fortunately, however, she had also studied the triune brain in several courses and knew there was a neutral level of energy below emotions. How to gain access? She remembered that basic intelligence was moving toward and away on behalf of life and decided to practice this with her mother, moving away from her emotions and toward her necessity to help her mother. It sounds simple, but Joan faced further challenges. Her mother lived primarily by seeing and voicing what was wrong with the world. She had lost her husband many years earlier, and her modus operandi for keeping herself alive was struggle and opposition. Joan had frequently been caught up in trying to calm her mother and make her see the beauty of the world. This time, as she reflected on her dream and on basic intelligence, a deeper understanding of the basic brain energy emerged in the following phrases:

> *Life needs to be recognized (basic brain)*
> *Longs to be loved (limbic brain) and*
> *Seeks to express itself. (neocortex)*
> *Life is!*

For the next month during her mother's convalescence, Joan clung to the words "Life needs to be recognized." These words enabled her to go along with and even to understand the need for all of her mother's words and actions that had previously caught her up in emotional turmoil. She now saw that her mother's struggle and opposition to most everything she encountered was not negative for her mother; it was the pattern she used to keep herself alive. Focusing on "Life needs to be recognized," Joan survived and so did her mother—for many more years. Basic intelligence is indeed about the liberty to move toward and away on behalf of life—no preconceived notions, no prejudice, not even socially acceptable ones, just moving toward whatever keeps life alive.

Basic intelligence is basic to all consciousness. It is the process that guides us within the always present moment in a continuous resonance-dissonance with others and with our environment. It enables us to enter into a selective process of being and becoming within the everyday environments of our life. When we are aware that everything that surrounds us is alive and impacting us with its vibrations, we will grasp the value of basic intelligence as a way of coping with this deeply pulsing level of life. We become both conscious and intelligent by moving ourselves toward and away from, through all diverse levels of existence.

17

Living Your Heritage

PATTERN INTELLIGENCE

The reptilian behavior of the Triune Brain is that most mysterious, difficult and intractable part of our being. Moreover to understand it is to forgive ourselves, to accept ourselves and to love ourselves (and then to forgive, accept and love whomever we come in contact with). To understand is basic. To understand that the way in which we behave and react in the present is rooted in how we and our parents and their parents behaved and reacted in the past. To understand which are the patterns that are valuable and which ones are causing me problems, and to understand how to replace deeply-rooted patterns that we don't want to let go of, with new patterns that we wish to include.

Denise D. Ney

We human beings are billions of individual cells arranged in different patterns that organize themselves into physical structures, such as hands, feet, heart, or brain systems. Cells connect or arrange themselves in diverse configurations or structures. Each structure has patterns that identify its form. Patterns shape the structures of our existence.

We cannot describe or identify the vibrations that occur at the basic brain level as easily as we can those of emotions, thoughts, or images.

Sensations refer to what happens at this deeper level, and yet we usually associate them with the obvious senses of smell, hearing, sight, taste, and touch. Touch and instinct are relevant at this deepest level, but neither "sensing" nor "touch" nor "instinct" is sufficient to describe the vibrations associated with this brain. If we do not even have a word to describe vibrations at this level adequately, how can we begin to become conscious at this level?

We can begin with vibration itself. We know that damage to the brainstem does not stop vibrations from entering the first brain. The most basic experience of life continues. Therefore, we can presume that what we call "experience" is about some organization of vibrations at this level. Our experience is composed of the responses we give to the stimuli that surround us, or we can say that the result of the interaction stimulus-response is our experience at this basic brain level. What we are calling pattern is what is formed as the memory of this interactive stimulus-response experience. To put it another way, the experience is recapitulated in the pattern.

A pattern, then, is the first basic organization that we are able to recognize at this deep level. Just as *emotion* is the word that identifies the energy in the limbic system and the words *thoughts, images,* and *intuition* identify the energy in the neocortex, the word that characterizes the organization of energy in the first brain is *pattern*.

Emotions fluctuate, thoughts end, and images can be framed. How can we observe patterns? What do patterns do? Perhaps patterns exist in order to stabilize energy and provide a basic order or a first organization of energy. Could it be because of this function of stabilizing energy that we are so resistant to change?

Patterns are organized energy. Perhaps they exist for the simple act of existence itself. Patterns are the first registration of experience. They record our experience. We learn to walk, and it is recorded. We are afraid of the dark, and it is recorded. Patterns, then, are registered in memory. Memory exists to record past knowledge so it is not lost, and also so new learning can be built upon old learning.

Pattern is the way experience first happens. Memory is the registration of pattern so that it continues to be available. We have to have pattern and memory in order to accumulate knowledge. Without memory, everything would have to be relearned every instant and there would be no possibility of knowledge as we know it, no evolution or "human progress."

We have patterns of behavior as well as emotional, mental, artistic, and spiritual patterns. These patterns summarize how our vibrations interacted in response to early emotional, mental, artistic, or spiritual stimuli. It is important here to recognize all the diverse stimuli that impacted us and produced other kinds of patterns, such as sexual patterns, criminal patterns, and avoidance patterns. This is why it is valuable to know our family history—all of the stimuli that produced our responses, forming patterns that then serve to filter all incoming information throughout the rest of our lives.

A leaf cannot grow other than around and in relation to the vein on the leaf. Humans grow in relation to DNA, which establishes our physical patterns and genes that continue to influence those patterns. Humans also grow in relation to patterns, which we ourselves develop in interaction with our environment. The patterns we establish then continue to filter further growth. Only by becoming conscious of the patterns dictating our behavior can we intervene in them and begin the process of interacting differently with our environment in order to form new patterns. This conscious recognition of our patterns as well as the intervention with old patterns and formation of new is what I am calling pattern intelligence.

It is logical to assume that this organization of experience into patterns continues in the human, as in all nature, until it is interfered with in some way. When we prune a tree, the branch grows again, and when we lose a finger, we experience a shadow effect as if that finger still existed. We diet and inhibit our eating patterns, but when we give up our interventions or our inhibiting, the old pattern of eating returns. In spite of the money spent on dieting programs, it has been proven that most dieters return to their former weight. Only by intervening with old patterns and constructing new patterns of eating, as well as by developing a support system for their new way of eating, can dieters begin to recondition themselves and produce an effective change in their weight. The energy from an already existing pattern has to be rechanneled to produce any change of behavior.

Are patterns erased? Are they incorporated into larger patterns? Or are they only recessed in our memory, available to be accessed again when stimulated?

According to my personal experience, the original pattern continues to exist in memory even though a new pattern is guiding new behavior. This is an important point, because although we may have succeeded in building a new pattern and are enjoying our new behavior, I believe the old pattern still exists and can be stimulated unexpectedly by different circumstances, especially those similar to the environment in which the original pattern was formed.

A regression to old behavior can make us think we have not succeeded in changing anything. We may become discouraged, and if we have a strong right hemisphere we may truly get lost in "I never can succeed in anything," "I'm never going to change," or "Everything is impossible." What we need to do is accept, be kind with ourselves, and then be extremely firm in focusing on our new pattern and extremely careful to make use of our support system. We have already done the work. We only need to remember that the old still exists. We do not intend to tolerate its intrusion: we can take care to affirm and repeat our new behavior.

We must not lose sight of either the real new accomplishment or the possibility that the old pattern can be stimulated once again. Memory is experience stored in code, available for decoding upon stimulation. When I am conscious, I stimulate my brain with my ability to focus and everything goes well. However, stimulation may also occur unexpectedly, without my conscious awareness or desire. A familiar example of this is what may happen when you go to family reunions or visit the old family house. At the beginning you enjoy yourself and you feel fine, but after a while, an inexplicable urge to leave arises within you. Something may have stimulated old patterns, until then recessed in your memory. You sense a nervousness or feel uncomfortable, or perhaps the pattern or patterns were not stimulated clearly enough to produce a conscious response, only enough to produce discomfort.

For this reason alone, it is worth the trouble to become conscious of our patterns. Then we will not have to be surprised when we feel ourselves becoming uncomfortable for no obvious reason. Neither will we find it necessary to blame those who are present with us in our environment. Those who are there with us at that moment will not be able to understand or to help. Only we can understand, then or later, that an old pattern has been stimulated and that we have to do our best to live the situation without blaming or harming others or else move away from the circumstance and toward whatever makes us feel comfortable.

The metaphor that has served me best when I feel myself in the grips of an old pattern is "to grab the steering wheel as if I had driven off the main highway and found myself driving in a ditch along the road." I do not have to lose control. I have to hold onto the steering wheel firmly and get my vehicle back on the main road again.

Discovering Patterns

To become conscious of your behavior or change your behavior, you must first discover the pattern or patterns involved. When you did the energy profile presented in basic intelligence, you may have discovered behaviors that were continually stressing you as well as other behaviors you wished to change.

Whatever the reason, the next step in changing your behavior is discovering the pattern involved. You may wish or need to interrupt a habit or an addiction. You may wish to learn from others and begin by trying to observe the pattern behind their accomplishments. When you wish to learn a new activity directly without imitating someone who already knows how to do it, observe the various functions involved and begin to look for the pattern of reactions that are needed for you to learn this activity.

Of course patterns also underlie your own great successes. If you wish to perpetuate or repeat your successes, it is also wise to become conscious of the patterns involved. You can then reinforce patterns you like by creating parameters of time, so you have a chance to do them more often. You can be more conscious and proud of them and guide your life or earn your living by them. Whatever your interest in your behavior—whether for learning, for interrupting addictions, for changing unwanted behavior, or for increasing successful behaviors—discovering the pattern is essential.

Throughout our lifetime our patterns have become interwoven with all variations of thoughts, images, intuitions, feelings, and actions. The three brains are arrayed in multiple and complicated splendor, interweaving, filtering, covering and connecting with the original stimulus-response pattern haphazardly, by cause-and-effect, by glimpses, by whim, or by mood, necessity, or obligation. Although it is impossible to know exactly how a pattern was woven, certain threads have become obvious at the thicker level of our behavior. They show up again and again when we begin to observe our behavior in search of the pattern.

To be able to discover the pattern we are looking for, we must first identify those obvious threads or links that make up the chain of the pattern. When we are studying our behavior to find the links, sometimes we will find a feeling, sometimes a thought. We should record whatever we find without alteration or censorship.

There are two important ways to discover our patterns:

1. observing our behavior in the present
2. discovering the patterns of our ancestors and looking for how they might have imprinted our behavior

IN THE PRESENT

First, observe your behavior in the present. To discover a pattern, begin a process of self-observation in which you look for how to study your behavior in the situation that is troubling you. To study your behavior means to search and find the many different reactions that occur within you when you are involved in a particular situation. The sum of your different reactions is your pattern. Although your reactions are not always the same, notice how similar they are. By observing your behavior several times, you will find the reactions you repeat again and again.

When the following circumstances present themselves, how do you react? These examples include some of my reactions. What are yours? Practice this with your own situations as well.

When I don't have any money in my wallet, I . . .
    get scared,
    wonder when I can go to the bank,
    wonder where I can get some,
    criticize myself for not planning better.

When I am hungry, I . . .
    go get something to eat,

then think I should have waited,
then complain I ate too much.

When it is time to write, I . . .
go get something to eat,
call a friend,
walk around my desk,
tell myself I ought to sit down,
finally sit down to write.

When I am going to teach, I . . .
get ready,
open myself to connect with people,
use the microphone,
walk around while teaching,
get excited.

When I am going to cook, I . . .
get frustrated easily,
tell myself I'll do it on weekends,
make only what I like,
do not much enjoy doing it.

When I am going to get dressed, I . . .
don't like to,
never do it well,
decide I should do it better.

Please notice from these examples that different kinds of behaviors are involved in our patterns: those that might please us and those that do not. Some are thoughts, some feelings, some actions, some criticisms, and some reminders of obligations. Act as if you were an archaeologist on a serious dig or a Sherlock Holmes working for yourself. Include everything, and then select those reactions that seem to occur again and again. Those reactions taken together form your pattern.

EXERCISE

DISCOVERING YOUR PATTERNS

1. Choose a behavior that you wish to make more conscious.

2. Relax yourself and begin to visualize the situations in which this behavior appears.

3. As if you were seeing a film, notice your reactions: First this happens . . . and then . . . and then . . . .

4. Look at similar situations and observe your reactions in them.

5. From the situation above, select the reactions that are most often involved in the behavior. The total of your reactions is the pattern involved in this behavior.

INHERITED PATTERNS

Much of our present behavior originated in the past and most probably in the years from infancy until adolescence, years in which parents were the dominant factor in our environment. During those years our need for love and affection from our parents or parental substitutes made us extremely vulnerable to imprints from them. They were also the years before we arrived at adolescence, a time when our pituitary gland changes the chemistry and the energy of our limbic brain and leads us to search for love from others.

In general, the behavior we learned in childhood is that which we have neither changed nor accepted in all of our brain systems. Although our inherited imprints are stored in our basic brain, we may not feel good about them in our limbic brain and be decidedly against them in our neocortex. However, we do not succeed in changing our behavior because we have not accessed the pattern that is filtering and thereby forming our behavior. Although it may be easier to locate these patterns from our early years with the help of a therapist, we can also succeed in locating inherited patterns by doing the following exercise.

EXERCISE

SEARCHING FOR INHERITED PATTERNS

1. *Look for the circumstances in your childhood corresponding to the behavior in the present that no longer serves you. For example, if you wish to stop smoking, look to see if your parents were smokers or how they were involved in any related oral habit like eating. It is not a matter of blaming your parents. The decision is registered in your basic brain as if it were a photograph taken in your childhood and frozen until the present. To change your behavior, you must return again to the past in order to find the data and be able to make a new decision in the present. If you do not access your older brain and if your decision is only at the level of the neocortex and based only on its data, your old decision remains in force and will serve as resistance to any new behavior.*

2. *Remember and revisualize your parents—first mother, then father— acting out the behavior that no longer pleases you. See them, for example, in the act of smoking or eating. Ask yourself, How did my mother do that? How did my father do it? Did anybody else do it? A favorite teacher? A hero from my childhood?*

3. *Go deeper into these visualizations, feeling yourself present when they were deeply involved in doing this behavior (smoking or eating). Look at your young self in their presence. Observe their behavior in as neutral a way as you can, then try to understand. What you saw was . . . and the explanation for their behavior was . . . . Was it useful to them? If so, how? In what way did it serve them? Was it painful in any respect? How did doing it affect their lives? What messages did your brain probably receive from being near them in this behavior?*

4. *What did you probably decide? Try to remember what you might have decided or integrated as a child in reaction to that situation. You may not know exactly, but search for your possible decision using the following sentences: "What I probably decided in these circumstances was . . ."; "Probably my organism reacted in such-and-such a way . . ."; "I must have thought, felt, or imagined that . . . ." You will have to guess, but you will also be able to feel which of your answers is the most relevant.*

5. *Based on what you probably decided, complete the following sentence: "Given the circumstances in my early years, I would probably have decided that* _____ *." Express your discovery in as few words as possible.*

When you look at what you learned from this exploratory exercise, you will have at least one clear piece of your pattern of behavior, possibly even a total pattern, that is still active and still affecting your present behavior. If those patterns are helpful, celebrate them. If not, you may wish to make a new decision. As part of the task of changing your behavior, it is important not only to know what you have already registered in your basic brain in reaction to your parents, but also to struggle to change the decision that you made then.

Today, your behavior no longer has anything to do with your parents. It has to do only with that decision you have carried frozen in your brain for so many years. The following exercise has helped many people make a new decision within themselves instead of continuing to blame their parents for difficulties they have suffered.

EXERCISE

LOOSENING THE ROOTS

Place here the answer from the previous exercise, stated as briefly as possible.

1. *What I probably decided was* _____ .
2. *Now, what I want to decide is* _____ .
   Take time to explore many answers. Turn them over in your mind until you are able to feel the right one for the behavior you wish to achieve.
3. *What is required at this moment is an inner energy battle. See the face of the parent who is most related to your old conduct. See your own face. Establish an active internal dialogue, face to face, body to body, mind to mind. In this dialogue, the issue is to be able to convince this parent of the importance of your new decision. To do this, you must permit the other to become real, to talk back and forth with you so the dialogue takes on the dimensions of a real encounter, a battle of internal energies.*

The difference between now and the past is that the old encounter took place when you were young and probably not even conscious of making a decision. Moreover, your little body had no power when confronting a larger one, and you were probably afraid, perhaps even in fear of physical harm or danger to your life. Now, although your past remains registered in your memory, you are creating a dialogue between adults in which you have control of the situation.

4. *Continue working on the dialogue until you succeed in convincing the other of your new decision, until you feel that this decision belongs to you and that you are able to defend it. Do not give up and walk away, weakening or confusing yourself. What you are doing is reprogramming your own brain, so that if a stimulus to the old way of acting should arrive, you will know how to fight against it.*

This loosening of roots is basic to any change. It is as if we are bringing our roots into the present instead of leaving them buried, stuck in the old and resistant to anything new. In time we will be able to honor our parents and our family, because no parent (or anyone else for that matter) is able to know what we have registered in our brain. Our parents were probably not even conscious of what was going on in us, nor could they have been. Only we are able to be conscious inside ourselves. To bring the patterns that involve family conditioning into the present, to celebrate them or bring them up-to-date, will truly free us and give us a real chance to change what needs changing in our everyday behavior today.

Deactivating Old Patterns

Patterns are not active at all times. For example, the patterns that permit us to drive a car automatically turn off when we are sleeping. Only by focusing on driving will we unleash the memory patterns of driving. Therefore there must exist a way of deactivating or defocusing on patterns. In this case, we clearly changed our focus from driving a car to sleeping. We deactivated an old pattern by shifting and then focusing on a new pattern.

Can anyone or anything help convince us to deactivate our already organized patterns? Our patterns organize our reality. They guide our established way of connecting with life. These are the ways we rely on.

They are familiar to us; they are security as we know it. Who or what will we allow to enter our life to interfere with them?

When hypnotists and healers interfere with patterns, do they "see" the link in the pattern that needs to be interfered with, changed, or replaced? Is it our faith in them or in God that permits them to deactivate a pattern?

We know that bacteria and viruses can interfere with our patterns at the physical level of our body, but we do not know how. Discovering the nature of that interference is the work of medical research. However, it may also be our work, for at this deep level our mental, emotional, or spiritual concentration may be required in order to permit new formations to take place. When an individual is healed, what we are calling "faith" may be a matter of individual concentration, deep longing, and spiritual loving. The individual is the one who must open the door to invite the energy passing through the healer to enter and form new patterns. It is we who must open ourselves to the representative of healing, whether that be a spiritual healer, a doctor, a lover, or a friend.

Before we are interested or willing to deactivate an old pattern, we need to find a way to open ourselves consciously to new interventions. First we must ask, Do I really want to open myself? Do I really want a new pattern or a new behavior? Do I prefer to remain with the same pattern until I become ill or a crisis emerges?

This is not a cynical or superfluous question. According to statistics, most of us wait for a crisis. Studies of cultures and civilizations indicate that as groups we also wait for crisis. Cultures reach great heights, continue in their ways, and then decline or are confronted with a crisis such as war that produces death. The very structures or patterns that enable cultures to reach their golden age at some point rigidify, cease to serve them, and help cause their fall. I believe that at both a collective and individual level, we refuse to change because we really do not want to and also because we do not know how to merge with new life.

Developing New Patterns

Three processes have served me and have helped others change the patterns that govern behavior:

1. pattern intervention
2. alternative pattern building
3. merger

FIRST PROCESS: PATTERN INTERVENTION

To practice pattern intervention, begin by selecting one of your habits and discover the pattern involved by using the exercise earlier in this chapter on "Discovering Your Patterns." List the links in the chain of reaction. For example, my pattern of "frustration in the kitchen" involves the following reactions:

Fixing something quickly
No time
Not putting things back
Many things on counter
Too much to do or other activity
Something looking wrong
Frustration

Next decide where you wish to intervene. Where in the chain of stimulus-response do you need or choose to intervene? In my example I choose to intervene at the first step, which is just to fix something quickly.

Now, imagine two or three possibilities you can substitute in place of that step. Continuing with my example in the kitchen, I imagine the following possibilities:

1. I am fixing something for myself only because I want to, and I have lots of time.
2. Fixing food is a creative activity and a sacred affair, and I can give time to it.
3. I like to eat food, and I will make time to prepare it.

Decide which of these you are going to substitute for your old reaction. I am going to choose "Fixing food is a creative activity and a sacred affair, and I can give time to it," to replace "Fixing something quickly."

In order to be able to interfere in the pattern, you have to be able to recognize your old reaction "fixing something quickly." Therefore, memorize your old reaction in an exaggerated image, or else write it out and hang it in a physical place with the following instruction: STOP. To know how to stop or inhibit yourself is essential for any change of behavior. Practice the word *stop* or the word *inhibit* when you are walking, daydreaming, riding a bus or subway, or especially thinking. Just stop in the middle of a thought before you get to the period. We are so entrained in rational, sequential thinking, which always leads us on to the next, that we are programmed to continue on with whatever we may be thinking or doing. To learn to stop yourself is essential.

After stopping the thought or action, remember and practice the new reaction. Now when I go to the kitchen, I remember that my activity there is something creative and sacred rather than an obligation. I always give myself more time. If I begin to rush, I stop and then continue more slowly, thinking about food being a sacred affair.

What will sustain or support this new behavior? What will support the substitution of "food is a creative and sacred affair that I can give more time to"? This new decision is a new link in the pattern and has to be supported until it functions well.

The substitution is not as mechanical as it may seem. It takes time and repetition. It takes failure, so you can learn the difference. Above all, it takes remembering the danger signal and stopping the old behavior. After stopping, it is a question of guiding yourself into the new behavior repeatedly, until you become accustomed. It will seem awkward and definitely not feel comfortable until you become reconditioned. In the process of changing your behavior, you cannot rely on your feelings until well after you are accustomed to acting differently. When your new action is rhythmical or aligned, then it will feel good. You also cannot permit the doubting and questioning of your rational process to erode your efforts. You need to continue to support the new link that you are inserting by means of new parameters.

Decide on new parameters of time and space in order to support the new behavior. In my example, I am giving myself new time parameters until I really am acting as if the preparation of the meal were sacred. Building a support system to sustain any new behavior is a conscious art, explained in the next chapter on parameter intelligence.

My example illustrates that every pattern is composed of a chain of reactions. A stimulus elicits a response, which in turn stimulates another response. This cluster forms a pattern. To intervene in any of our patterns, we need to:

1. find the links in the chain
2. intervene in the chain
3. replace the link with another link
4. support the new link

Pattern intervention is like surgical intervention. We discover what is not useful or harmful or needs to be replaced. Once a new piece has been inserted, we must provide a support, as we would support an arm with a splint and a sling when a bone has been reset. If we wish to use pattern intervention to change what has already grown together, we need the process of observation, intervention, inhibition, substitution, and reinforcement. The process is similar whether what we wish to change deals with beliefs, emotions, or actions.

SECOND PROCESS: ALTERNATIVE PATTERN BUILDING

Rather than intervene in our behavior, many of us simply choose to develop additional patterns. We move away from what bothers us and begin again. Much of our learning we did in this way. We did not analyze our behavior: we simply moved into new places and new experiences, and the feedback we received produced a change in our behavior.

Alternative pattern building requires new and real experience that will provide us new feedback. Deciding to change without offering ourselves new experience is not sufficient. New experience offers you new feedback, and it is in reaction to that new feedback that we may form new patterns.

Building alternative patterns is a viable and often used approach. Without thinking about it consciously, we look for a new physical location, a new love, a new friend, a new job, new hobbies, or new forms of entertainment so that new experiences will provide new learnings, new feedback, and new behavior. The evolution of our behavior comes from moving ourselves toward new experiences, receiving new feedback, and being willing to integrate new feedback into new patterns of behavior.

The process involves a difficulty, however, that most of us have also experienced. In spite of our having learned and carried out new behaviors, the old patterns seem to remain and can be triggered under various conditions. They may be stimulated when we are least expecting it or least aware. The same stimulus involved in the old pattern appears again in a new environment. Or, when we are less alert, such as when we are sick, angry, tired, uncaring, or in a hurry, the older but still present pattern again surfaces.

This occurs less frequently if we have practiced the first process of pattern intervention described above. From having worked so hard to change our behavior and support new behavior, we will have become so conscious that we will be more likely to realize when we are stimulating the old pattern and be able to recover the new one.

In certain difficult situations such as chemical addiction, one must use pattern intervention instead of this process of alternative pattern building.

THIRD PROCESS: MERGER

The third process is to open ourselves to merging our pattern with a larger field. This can be either an overt or a most subtle process. It involves deciding to belong to, becoming a member of, becoming one with, committing, associating with, or joining—whatever relates to belonging with. Merger is an extremely important process for learning new behavior. It provides the experience of belonging that gives us the parameters and the safety to alter the way we first learned in favor of new possibilities. Merger is the experience that most religions try to provide. It is also the experience of clubs in teenage years. Merger has taken place through the art, music, and great literature of our civilization. It also takes place in great teacher-student relationships and great love relationships. Merger is the process of participating with something or someone who has a different and often larger experience, which opens us to new frontiers.

Unfortunately, merger has also taken place in cults and brainwashing experiences, in which the capacity and the identity of the individual are distorted, producing startling but negative results. Throughout history we have numerous examples of individuals willing to abandon their own identity in favor of the group identity. This process enslaves behavior rather than allowing it to change through belonging and adaptation. As I have practiced it, merger does not involve losing my independence. By merger, I am implying the possibility of voluntarily joining with and at the same time being able to maintain my own integrity.

Certainly it has been difficult for me to open myself to larger patterns. What has helped me succeed in doing so has been to see life through the basic brain system. While my neocortex was thinking and dreaming about life and my limbic brain was living its various moods, which sometimes made me feel wonderful about life and sometimes outraged by life, I realized that my deepest brain was just living here day by day. Like it or not, approve of life or not, my deepest brain just kept on living. I already belonged to life, no matter how much my other two brains protested or opinionated.

Simplistic as it may sound, it was a major breakthrough for me to realize that existence goes on with me or without me. At that moment I stopped waiting for. I realized that existence "exists," and if I want to join, I can, but there is no special invitation that a Goddess of Existence is going to send me. Life goes on with or without me. It is up to me to become aware of existence in continuum and then to feel and decide where I want to become involved. I have to invite myself. Believing and feeling myself a member of existence enabled me to open the door, to join more easily, and to feel myself a member wherever I wished to.

We do not always join overtly, asking the requirements and joining with groups formally. We can simply associate with, feel ourselves a part of, accompany, and know within ourselves that we belong. It is a matter of participation—with or without ritual and invitation. It is a matter of already belonging to life, drawing near and acting with, whenever we need to or want to or whenever it seems appropriate.

I have found informal merging to be extremely important whenever I wish to participate in religious ceremonies. I invite myself to belong and to participate in the ongoing ceremony as if I belonged. I am not a spectator; neither am I feeling myself in love with the religion. It helps me to make a distinction between the loving of my limbic brain and the belonging of my basic brain. I can consciously invite myself to participate and to belong. I grasp that I am not a practicing Buddhist nor a practicing Jew, but neither do I have to be a foreigner. I can love my own religion as well as participate in the spirituality of others. During the ceremony I can merge with. I keep my religious patterns as well as open myself to the existence of other religious patterns. This opening provides me with new learning and extended patterning. As a result of being a participant, I may come to feel a respect or even a love for the Jewish or Buddhist religion.

I have also used merger as a way of identifying and being comfortable in other countries. I have never lost either my love for the United States nor my identity as an American, but I am able to add an identity with Venezuela and Venezuelans when I am living and teaching there. It is a matter of becoming one with, of adding different parts of the earth to my heritage.

Indeed, temporarily merging and participating in other religions and other countries may come to be the most important strategy we have as the boundaries of our world become ever closer. It is no longer a matter of a single identity, but rather a matter of adding identities to our experience. Merger requires knowing that we are already one and then gradually experiencing the truth of our mutual existence. Informal merger is about a transformation in my own mind-set. It is declaring myself to be a member of rather than waiting for a formal membership to be offered.

Merger can also involve joining formally and belonging overtly to a group or with another person. The key ingredient is realizing that we are both independent and interdependent. The importance of our independence is to be able to protect the life we are in charge of. This might mean that we withdraw from the group or the person on behalf of our own life, as discussed in the chapter on basic intelligence. The importance of interdependence is to enable us to let go of our old pattern as we learn to depend on another pattern.

To open ourselves to merger, there are three important stages:

1. ceasing to rely on the old pattern
2. shifting from active to receptive energy
3. integrating the active energy from another person or group

Stage One: Ceasing to Rely on the Old Pattern. We must consciously shift or set aside our support for a pattern that is destructive or not useful to us. First, of course, we must discover the pattern involved in our behavior, as discussed earlier in this chapter. If we are not planning to interrupt this pattern actively through pattern intervention, then we need to become tremendously aware of it. We need to know how it is related to our behavior, and we need to have our reasons for wanting to move away from it and deactivate it. If, for example, at an early age a man developed a pattern of hiding his frustration in order to survive, he now needs to know clearly that the repression of his anger may either cause him illness or flare up and harm a relationship when he least expects it.

We need to realize the potential harm of our old pattern before we will be willing to open ourselves to merge with groups or individuals who can express anger in a healthy manner. To deactivate our old pattern and move toward merger we need to see the damage our pattern is doing and give up our support for this pattern. This is the opposite of denial. This means clearly admitting, at least to ourselves, that we do not like it and are out shopping for a new pattern. For example, in order to stop relying on my pattern of repressing anger, I may have to blurt it out in the privacy of my room. In brief, the first step toward merger is to become conscious of our pattern and to cease relying on it.

Edgar, a lawyer, had discovered that his pattern of always being argumentative and always having to win was causing difficulty in his relationships. He had not specifically done pattern intervention as described earlier, but he had tried to build an alternative pattern of being empathetic with people by taking courses in meditation and self care. In spite of all his efforts to relate better to others, he was still not able to challenge his conditioning of many years. In any discussion he had to win, and when confronted by an authority, the need to win became intense and persistent—he didn't know how to lose or let go. In one particular course, after several days of being accepted for his careful observations and for his efforts to relate, a situation occurred in which the approval of the group ran against his action and his arguments. When this happened a second time, he was determined to win and continued to speak out in an effort to gain support for his point of view. Eventually I cut him off: it was late at night and time to close. This restraint by an authority together with the loss of group support must have registered in his brain as total loss, as an unacceptable rejection of the pattern of winning, which was dictating his survival.

It was sad to see Edgar lose the support of many people whom he was trying to love, only because this old pattern was lurking behind all his new efforts. He walked away believing that he was uncomfortable because the group had rejected him and the authority figure had not allowed him continuous debate until he could win. By blaming his predicament on others, he prevented himself from looking into his own behavior to discover his destructive pattern. Of course this is not easy to do because very frequently our destructive patterns are also our most powerful ones. In Edgar's case, the need to win had served him well in his successful career as a lawyer. Perhaps more profoundly, this dominant pattern had enabled him to survive an outrageously authoritarian father. Somewhere within he must have built his self-esteem around the decision "I also can win."

The story illustrates the need to check even our most successful patterns when we are looking for our destructive ones. Often they originated in childhood as a means of survival, but as we continue through life they may be preventing us from opening our lives to new experiences. We may die with our boots on—die with our original patterns—unless we get interested in continuous living and become willing to challenge consciously our old ways of doing things.

Stage Two: Shifting from Active to Receptive Energy. Before we are likely to shift to receptive energy, we must actively and consciously choose with whom we wish to associate more deeply, know whether or not we feel comfortable with that person or group, and find it easy to move toward them. (Note the participation of all three brain systems.)

Shifting from active to receptive energy is something all of us practice in our everyday life, even though we may not be conscious of what we are doing. For example, when we are speaking to someone, we are in active energy, but when we are truly listening, we have shifted to receptive energy. That is, we are really interested in taking in, grasping, and understanding what the other is saying. The emphasis is on truly listening and being really interested.

In most team sports, the offense are those who are playing in active energy, and the defense, those who are receiving the attack. In the martial arts of Tai Chi and Aikido, this shifting from active to receptive is continuously interwoven rather than being a matter of team play. In the learning process of merger, we become aware of the shift to receptive energy so that we may become profoundly impacted by the new pattern.

Although we may become conscious and shift our energy in an instant, there seems to be a bridge or intermediary process before we will become truly receptive. That bridge is a process of "relying on." It helps to know, feel, and have active experience in reliance on. Family is one example of an interactive structure that ought to have taught us to rely on. Unfortunately, many of us have not had successful or trustful experiences in our families. Religion also offers an invitation to reliance through faith and trust, providing a figure of a loved one and many interactive religious experiences. But many people in our rational, scientific culture also have had difficulty developing the experience of reliance within the context of religion. Some therapists provide a structure through which we can develop the experience of relying on. Practice in relationship offers us invitation to rely on friends. Indeed, genuine participation in any larger context provides a continuous opportunity to gain the experience of relying on. Indeed, life itself could be considered one long list of experiences in learning to rely on. To be able to rely on seems to be a key to opening ourselves to new life.

Once we have actively chosen an association and have entered a process of relying on, then we need to shift to a receptive state. That means we need to let the other person influence us, teach us, show us, and give to us. Our job is to receive. If we do not make this shift, if we stay in active energy, then we are likely to resist at some level, whether that be through neocortical doubt, limbic resentment, or basic brain denial. If we want to merge in order to acquire new learning, new feedback, and new patterns, it is up to us to shift from active to receptive energy.

Stage Three: Integrating the Active Energy of Another. To integrate the energy coming from another, we need to enter fully the process of merger—that is, through some action, subtle or overt, of joining, becoming part of, identifying with, opening ourselves to, relying on, or becoming loyal to. We are then in the presence of the others' patterns and actively able to imitate them and learn from them.

The more we are able to feel or sense ourselves one with, the more natural will be the learning. The process of belonging provides the parameters. When in Rome it is natural to do as the Romans do. Indeed, it is expected, and if we are able to identify with them, there is no doubt we can begin to take on their mannerisms. We may indeed leave not only with their cookbooks but with their pattern of eating pasta guiding us for the rest of our lives.

This process of merging with can be the most seductive way of changing patterns. It provides parameters for safety, new experience for new feedback, and individuals and groups that we have consciously chosen to associate with. Merger is a form of adult education without the school building or official classes. We must choose the person or the groups that have the patterns we need to learn and move close, associate with, belong, practice with, and learn from. When we move away, we will have been enriched by our experience. Deep learning requires association and merger. When we have integrated the patterns of others, we will experience deep appreciation, for in a sense they will have become part of us.

If destructive patterns can hide within our successful ones, how can we discover them? One way is to check the emotional history of our families and review especially the illnesses in order to discover dominant family patterns that may have been involved. The behavioral history of a family may be distinguished or marked with courage, but what does our emotional history tell us? It occurred to me to challenge my own strong pattern of independence only after reflecting deeply on the death of my brothers from cancer. Both were fiercely independent, one leaving a major corporation in order to establish his own business, the other leaving the city to wander around Alaska writing poetry. Both were free, both independent, both outrageously stressed, and both dead from cancer before reaching mid-life. Previous generations had included outstanding entrepreneurs and inventors as well as more cancer. The pattern of independence is a heritage that my brothers followed without questioning. It was their strength and their glory. It is also mine. I went to India and the Middle East before the age of nineteen, created two organizations in my college years, a school for children before I was forty, and an institute for adults before I was fifty. I am still creating—a program of multiple intelligences and four eight-day courses. Most people would be impressed. I am less so. I am exhilarated when I am creating and am glad that I have been able to do so much, but finally I have come to recognize that all of these creations would have died early deaths if it had not been for the work of many others. I have also come to recognize all the things, people, and institutions I have left behind because of my independence. I have come to challenge this pattern of independence and in the last seven years I have consciously worked at developing a pattern of dependence.

The first stage was to see the potential destructiveness of my independence pattern, to recognize how it gradually robbed my brothers of life and how potentially it might do the same to me. As I challenged the pattern, I began to see the need to add a pattern of dependence. It was not about forsaking my independence but about limiting it to my creative work and not letting it interfere with my relations with people. I began to think consciously about the importance of dependence and its value not only in relationships, but also in honoring what others do to keep the Mead School and Mead Institute programs alive.

It was another matter to enter the second stage: to learn the act of relying on. I was awkward and not good at it. It also didn't feel good. I liked and was addicted to the adrenaline rush of doing things myself. I still prefer to run away, as my brothers did. However, I consciously now use meetings and events to experience relying on, to experience the feedback and to feel the feelings.

I have done much of this work in a new culture, practicing the third stage of merger, joining and becoming a member of, while giving courses in Venezuela. It has been a new and exciting experience shifting away from my own active energy to receive the active energy of the Latins. I have declared myself a member of and have slowly developed a new pattern of dependence in many of the small ways of life. Often I lose patience, often I resort to my independence, but in a very profound way I feel a new integration of my being with life itself and the everydayness all around me.

Usually we talk about everyone being interdependent, and so to some, this story may not seem relevant. Cognitively or neocortically, I know that all life is interdependent. However, it has only been by challenging my deepest pattern of independence and by gradually cultivating dependence that I have come to feel interdependence with other life. In any case, I intend my story to invite us to challenge even our most cherished patterns, not to lose them but to add new life.

When we were born we were invited into life. Let us not wait or fish around seductively for additional invitations. Know that we may go beyond our own limits whenever we really wish to by engaging ourselves in a larger experience. We will emerge with a new recording and new memories that will become the basis for our new pattern and serve us as a design for new action.

We can describe ourselves as an accumulation or integration of patterns. From where do all the patterns come that make up the human? At least we can become conscious of those that come from our heritage, our early experiences, our conscious interactions throughout life, our intervention in patterns we do not like and reinforcement of patterns we do, our alternative pattern building, and our conscious mergers. Let us become intelligent about the patterns that shape us, become as curious about our own patterns as we have been about the leaves on a tree or the clouds in the sky. We are all forms of life.

Pattern intelligence is about recognizing our patterns either formed by ourselves or inherited from our past. It is about reinforcing and expanding our successful patterns and about being able to change those that are not helpful. Pattern intelligence is about reaching deep into the creation of life, respecting the structures that have developed, and adding our conscious participation in the creation of new life within ourselves.

Sustaining What You Love

PARAMETER INTELLIGENCE

I*magine energy constantly entering the body. Imagine the hundred million impulses per second entering through each vertebra of our spinal column. Even though we turn off our thoughts when we fall asleep, areas of our brain are always awake. In the basic brain, we are a cellular system always at work, always exposed to energy. How can we manage this continuous influx of energy?*

In physical nature, riverbanks serve as natural parameters to guide the flow of water. In human nature, lungs provide parameters to contain the oxygen in our bodies, veins to guide the flow of blood. Each parameter serves as a boundary or limit, as a frontier that guides energy in a definite way and by specific means.

To describe this intelligence, I chose the word *parameter* instead of the word *limit* to avoid the connotation of repression. I prefer *parameter* as it is a neutral word that emphasizes our creative ability to establish our own frontiers, to guide our energy in the same way that an artist puts lines and colors on paper to guide our eyes toward seeing what he or she wants us to see.

One way or another we need to deal with the constant influx of energy entering our deepest brain. Nature has already provided us with a reticular activating system that serves to channel off energy into our limbic and neocortical brains. However, what do we do with the energy continually entering our brainstem from our outside environment? We guide incoming energy by the parameters we have consciously established or unconsciously inherited. Social parameters are the many ways we have all created to channel and limit our energy.

What Are Parameters?

Parameters are already channeling our energy, whether we are conscious of them, resistant to them, cooperating with them, or engaged in changing them. Parameters are our way of intervening in life and consciously creating and organizing it. We inherit or create parameters of time, of space, and of innumerable life functions. We have inherited many of the parameters that are affecting our life from the past; therefore, they may be difficult to recognize.

For instance, values are parameters established around the beliefs that have been honored generation after generation in our family and culture. Our values provide us with a constant reference point. The profession we choose and the friends we choose share our values. We did not have to stop and check what each friend believed, but when we reflect we notice the similarities. Values are the boundaries for our beliefs. They influence or channel our actions without our needing continuously to make new decisions.

When we do not act according to our values, the same parameters remain and we experience what we call pangs of conscience or guilt or a sense of shame. For example, if you value the action of going to visit your parents on Sundays and one Sunday you do not go, you will feel a tension or guilt about not having followed the parameters of your value system.

Religions are also parameters. They serve to limit the energy not only into a belief system, but into formal ways of devotion and "proper" ways of action. Religion also offers parameters to guide our energy into more subtle vibrations, such as revelations, images, and glimpses of the infinite. Religious parameters preserve the original teachings of major figures such as Jesus or the Buddha and enable them to be shared with the public in a formal way through religious ceremony.

Routines are parameters. For instance, by your routine of sitting in the same chair, your body and especially your spinal column can count on similar conditions every time you sit there. You have formed a spatial routine by repeatedly going to the same chair, in which you feel relaxed. When you find the chair occupied, you may feel frustrated. Someone has intervened in your space and is preventing your repetitive action of sitting there.

Parameters are involved in all routines. For example, if you always like having a cup of coffee after dinner, you are delimiting your action within chemical parameters as well as time parameters. Playing tennis every weekend involves you in physical and time parameters.

By means of parameters we enter into a number of limitations, which we then count on to produce certain effects of stability and security in our life. Upon losing those effects, we experience an imbalance, which in turn may provoke any emotion from sadness, if we are accustomed to losing, to frustration if we are accustomed to fighting. Such an imbalance can also cause stress, tension, and even fear.

Addictions are, of course, routines to which we have become habituated. The word *habituate* simply emphasizes the intensity or repetitiveness of our habit or routine. Generally we use the word *addiction* instead of *routine* when it is a matter of chemical parameters. When people interrupt a chemical routine or addiction, their bodies will also react with imbalance and disturbing emotion. All they want is to get back to their parameters, meaning their chemicals, to get out of their state of insecurity, tension, and chaotic vibrations.

When we understand that all food is chemical, we will realize why it is so difficult to make changes in our diet. Eating is an addictive process in which many patterns are interwoven, and parameters of eating repeat themselves all day long and day after day. When we interrupt an addiction, it may be either sadness or frustration that subtly drives us back to eating even more after dieting. Or it may be the imbalance, anxiety, and disequilibrium of chaotic vibrations that we are trying to calm by again putting food in our mouths.

Professions are parameters of work that let us guide a great deal of energy during the day. I am convinced that to deprive ourselves suddenly of work parameters when we retire explains why so much illness, especially heart attacks, occurs after retirement. The energy continues to enter through the basic brain but is not channeled as before. To leave a routine of forty or fifty years without replacing it with other parameters leaves energy free and loose in a state of chaos, which in turn can affect the body adversely.

Stories and books are parameters. Myths are the parameters of story, wisdom told again and again and contained in metaphor. The same myth provides different wisdom for different ages. We look at the same story within the same parameters, but we make new associations and receive new meaning. Books serve as parameters containing stories and certain kinds of knowledge to which we wish to return.

Rituals are parameters. The rituals that we have established we have repeated over centuries. We build exquisite places to honor these routines, sometimes cathedrals, sometimes temples or mosques, sometimes tiny shrines by the roadside; sometimes the earth itself is our holy place. We love to return to our sacred places. We sense deep rest there, grounding as well as elevation, fullness, richness, soul satisfaction. It is difficult to find sufficient adjectives to describe ourselves when we are engaged in ritual that we know is ours. It is right.

In all areas of the world, people have created rituals that communicate their comprehension of life. Every culture has developed its religion as its interpretation of life. The ritual is the performance of that understanding of life. The ritual has served as a meeting place, a common ground on which we reach levels of understanding, feeling, and action in all three brain systems. Music, art, words, and reason are invoked. Love and moods are involved. Action, rhythm, and repetition are always present, and through these many languages of the three brain systems we grasp the intelligence of life.

Creative Control of Life

By setting up parameters we seek to control the influx of energy. We seek to know what to expect. Parameters feel orderly and seem natural because we have habituated ourselves. Our habituation to parameters provides our stability and our safety. Parameters serve to guide energy so we are not constantly having to feel it, think about it, or imagine what to do with it. They enable us to go "on automatic." We can examine our entire life in terms of the parameters or limits we have set up for ourselves, within which we function. You can also choose to create a new life by establishing new parameters within which to function.

TEMPORAL PARAMETERS

We can set parameters to limit life within the spectrum of time. "There is a season for everything . . . a time to be born, a time to die . . . a time to sow . . . a time to reap" (Eccles. 3:1–2). We recognize the ancient wisdom of Ecclesiastes: it resonates in our bones, our depths. I understand Ecclesiastes as wisdom calling us to act. For an inventive, creative act, I can set aside times in my life to plant, to invent, to play, and to work. To establish parameters is a creative act. I believe it is a fundamental key to this deepest energy. We need to set parameters at the very least for the following:

a time to work
a time to rest
a time to play
a time to relate
a time for my health
a time for my home
a time for reflection and learning
a time for inspiration

The well-known excuse "I don't have time" comes from not accepting the time we have. It comes from not wanting to accept that there are social parameters of twenty-four hours a day, seven days a week. Instead of accepting this social order, we impose our personal power with the comment, "I will just make more time." We act with the desire of our limbic brain instead of with the acceptance and understanding of our basic brain. The result is stress.

It took me many years to realize that to eat well, I must cook, and to cook, I must dedicate time each day. The key point was to stop deceiving myself with the idea that I would be able to prepare rapidly something that I would be willing to eat. Having granted myself time, my improvisation and creativity now have a chance to function, and I feel a peace and security preparing meals. I am convinced that we all can have more peace in our lives if we consciously establish time parameters for each of the basic areas of life. Of course, everything cannot be done each day, but rather within a range of time, such as a week, month, or year. Never is also an important choice.

SPATIAL PARAMETERS

Just as we can set parameters in time, so too can we set them in space. The most primitive action of a reptile or an animal, that of marking its territory, is evident in human life. The animal repeatedly leaves its scent and excrement in the same place to mark its territory; we leave graffiti on trees and subway cars. The reptile senses its way to a rock, a corner; a human moves again and again to a favorite chair. If someone steps near the reptile's rock, into its territory, it will strike; if someone takes my favorite chair, sooner or later I will strike. Territoriality is our attempt to fix parameters, to limit space, to define security.

Limits can help me enter more deeply into the experience. If I limit my garden, I have more time for planting, more intensity, more effectiveness in a small space than in a larger one. The same is true of my home or my office. To continue building large homes and public spaces when there are no longer people or money to maintain them is a habit from the past that needs to be reconsidered in relation to present conditions. Of course the greatness of generations past is keyed into the memory of our basic brain, and we continue to act, following old patterns. We need, however, to reflect on what it costs today to maintain such buildings and whether, with small families, we still need them. Perhaps we need to move toward the new pattern epitomized by E. E. Schumacher's slogan, "small is beautiful."

The parameters of space help us feel or sense ourselves as more secure. Our skin, our nervous system, and our senses are accustomed, habituated, addicted. We feel secure as we return again and again to the same space. Our body lives on the ground, in a spatial territory. Knowing our parameters and returning to them can stabilize our energy. Our body returns home just as homing pigeons return home.

Sometimes we return to the office in the same manner, habituated but without the guidance of thought or feelings. Some days we can be thankful that there is a habituated automatic mechanism to get us there. Rather than criticizing ourselves as unfeeling or unmindful, we can be grateful for our capacity to operate on automatic.

Returning again and again to the same hobby can give our body and our nervous system deep rest. Hobbies are repetitive forms of enjoyment: we wear the same sports clothes and carry the same tennis racket or fishing pole. This happens whether the hobby is a sport like tennis or scuba diving or simply a game like checkers. Although creativity is not excluded, neither is it dominant, and often not even necessary. Rest comes from just returning again and again to the same pastime.

Establishing spatial parameters in the home or office can also give us a certain relaxation. Often we forget the importance of establishing spatial parameters in our homes. For example, filled with love and good faith, newlyweds may not see the need to divide space within their new apartment. It even seems selfish or divisive, because everything belongs to both according to the neocortex and limbic brains. However, the first disagreement soon breaks out and frequently has something to do with boundaries. An unconscious territorial battle eventually explodes, and the warmth of the relationship diminishes unless the feelings are expressed and territoriality acknowledged.

We often forget that children also have territorial needs, and we enter their space continually, imposing our rules of order and cleanliness. However, if someone cleans or rearranges our own desks, we act as if an enemy invasion has taken place. We could give children a greater sense of security by giving them the territory of their bedroom or at least an area around their bed. It would only cost us negotiating with them for someone occasionally to come in and clean. Teaching them to negotiate might provide a better experience than teaching them how to sabotage rules and hate cleanliness. To arrange space is an innate characteristic. It is a trait that animals possess as well as the basic brain of every human being—child as well as adult.

Security

The parameters we set up in our spaces at home and at work can provide not only a deep rest but also a sense of security unmatched by any other phenomenon. Referred to as the security blanket in childhood, this need to cling to territory is primal. As we recognize its importance to our individual security, we may also develop greater awareness of its impact on group behavior, tribal behavior, and national behavior. I believe our social behaviors are just an extension of our individual efforts to find a secure place for our nervous system within the constant motion of life.

As the histories of war show, we can talk about, think, or imagine that we are going to give up territory; we can even want to give it up or to share it. However, the energy of this brain eventually insists on returning us to the territory or else adversely affects our equilibrium.

We feel insecure, sense ourselves insecure, or decide we are insecure when we cannot return again and again to the same place. In terms of the basic brain, we are creatures of habit, addicted to space, to time, to chemicals, drugs, and food, even to similar ways of dress, similar ideas, and similar actions. When we take this collectively, we call it habit, hobby, value, profession, or addiction, depending on our opinion of its value or acceptance in society. Whatever name we use, I am persuaded that the repetition gives us security and that we will always seek security through some form of repetition.

When we accept that energy at this deepest level must find its way into some parameters, we will become alert and conscious of our choices. We will know that we are all addicted to something, and we will search consciously for the routines we wish to addict ourselves to: professions, gardens, sports, work, home, love, alcohol, chemicals, nations, culture, world.

Caution! You need to be especially alert to whatever goes into the three openings of the limbic brain: the nose, mouth, and genitals. When these limbic openings are combined with the repetitive rhythm of the deepest brain, the resulting addiction is indeed hard to rechannel, so it is vital to choose habits that nurture and protect rather than harm your life.

Addiction and compulsion are security for this brain. No amount of talk from our neocortex or love from our limbic brain will sway the basic brain from its repetition. Only by knowing and accepting the existence of repetitive rhythms and being willing to channel them ever so gently into new action will we govern this brain system. As individuals and nations, we need to know our addictions. We need to choose them wisely: they are basic to our health, our security, and our development.

Changing Your Behavior

The numerous programs on dieting in the market work for only a short time because they provide only short-term behavioral solutions to eating. As soon as the person becomes satisfied with the results of the new weight, the underlying pattern of eating that was present from birth, developed through early childhood, exaggerated in adolescence, and sustained in adulthood returns to the command post. The dieting program provides new parameters for a short period of time, but what people need is to learn how to interfere with their former patterns of eating as well as how to set up and sustain new parameters of eating. It has to be an action program and has little to do with thought or feeling.

My own experience with dieting is relevant here. Before menopause I had no idea I would not be able to keep on eating as I had done all my life. Neither did I know that I would have to become again the athletic person I had left behind in college. I thought dieting was for fat people, and because I was thin, I never bothered to associate with the diet and exercise world. Seven years later I am well aware that menopause changed the chemistry circulating in my limbic brain which should have been an indication to change my parameters of eating. As I became aware of what was happening, I chose a dieting approach sustained by weekly hospital checkups. I did indeed lose the weight I wanted to, but like so many others, I gained it back within two years. At that time I did not realize how deeply I needed to change my eating and food preparation patterns. After learning about food, I placed my trust in new eating habits. It took me two more years of stubborn resistance before I was willing to admit that my habit of not exercising was also involved. By this time I certainly had heard enough about exercise, but since I had never liked it in gym class, I thought I could keep on escaping. More particularly, I did not want to look at my patterns of resistance to exercise and preferred to stay within my busy and satisfying parameters of work. I had to go back and find my resistance pattern to exercise as well as find my positive success pattern of playing sports. I had then to reframe exercise into sports, picking up once again the athlete that I had left behind in college.

The combined new parameters for eating and sports enable me now to keep my weight within bounds. Although I still dream of losing more pounds, I no longer deceive myself into thinking it is a simple matter. It is about sustaining these new parameters every day and planning special times of the year where I can consciously give myself the necessary parameters for dieting. Every older person has lived something similar to this experience. I tell my story to show that it takes more than thought and desire to change. It takes intervention in age-old patterns and life-long habits that subtly affect the chemistry of our own brain system. It takes establishing new parameters to protect our changes.

When we are not satisfied with our actions, our addictions, our values, or any of the repetitive rhythms of our life, what can we do? Parameter intelligence includes not only consciously setting parameters but changing those that are no longer working for us.

EXERCISE

CHANGE OF A BEHAVIOR

1. *Know that the old behaviors will remain or that you will return to them unless you engage in the physical action of constructing new parameters. Unless you set up new riverbanks for the energy to flow into, it will continue to flow where it has always flowed. The expression "Go with the flow" cannot be applied here. At this deepest level, "Go with the flow" means nothing will change, since patterns and repetitive rhythms are registered in your memory, and memory serves as a magnet to attract and return you to its old habits.*

2. *You need to engage in constructing a positive support system for new energy. Saying no and using prohibition and discipline are not sufficient. Only by adding a yes to new parameters to guide your energy can you hope to sustain a change of behavior.*

3. *Determine what new behavior you want to give birth to.*

4. *Think and decide the reasons for that change. Imagine and find one image about how the behavior will look when it is firmly entrenched as a part of you.*

5. *Find in pattern intelligence how to change the pattern involved in your old behavior. Discover the pattern involved and practice one of the three forms of changing the pattern. When you have the desired pattern for your new behavior, go on to the next step.*

6. *Plan the parameters or boundaries that will provide the new channel or support system by exploring the following:*
   —What will help sustain this new behavior? What do you think or imagine will help?
   —Whom do you want to help you? Who do you think or imagine will help? Note that often this is where a professional can be especially important. Friends or family are accustomed or conditioned to your old behavior. Consciously or unconsciously, they may not want

it changed. Also note you may have to be specific with a professional—they may be more interested in another area of your development unless you are clear or express commitment or specifically ask for their help in this matter.

—*When will you start? Be warned: you yourself will probably try to sabotage the starting point because you are accustomed or addicted to your own way of being until the change is firmly rooted on new ground. Even when we do start, we often are uncomfortable with the new, and we find it easy to sabotage ourselves so we can return to our old routines.*

—*Where will you be building these parameters? In your home? Your office? Your bedroom, study, or kitchen? Choose how to protect yourself. Start on the terrain where you are safest, that is, where you have most protection, familiarity, or neutrality.*

—*What evidence will you accept as evidence you have succeeded? Be exact. Vagueness now can prevent you from being satisfied with your accomplishment later. Set small goals, or, if the change is a really big one, set small goals over a long period. Note that it takes nine months to make a life; it may take longer to change one.*

7. *Check your planned parameters with your limbic brain system. Is this what you really want? If no, forget it; do not waste your energy. Or start again differently. If yes, go on to the next step.*

8. *Action! Make sure your support system exists in time and space. Call whomever you want to help you. Move to get whatever you need to help you into place. Prepare the environment and gradually and sensorially move into it.*

9. *Be aware of the greatness of guiding old, repetitive rhythm into new routes. Almost always we run into what I call "the crisis in the middle of the river." A horse can easily jump into a river, but when it arrives where the current is strongest, it wants to turn back and head for known territory. It is at this moment that many people lose all they have invested in the change. By being conscious that this may occur, you can stop, give yourself a great deal of love and rest, but not entertain the thought of turning back. Take the reins of life strongly in your hands. Then proceed with calm assurance, giving yourself love, and continue until you arrive. You become accustomed little by little and day by day.*

If by chance or some circumstance you do regress to an old behavior, do not get lost in criticism, guilt, or resentment with yourself, with another, or with the world. Return to steps three and four described above in order to reaffirm yourself in your desire, your image, and your reasons for wanting the change. Then continue forward again. You have not lost anything. You have not returned to "square one"— this is not a game of Monopoly. This is an experience of regression in your life; it is not a loss. On the contrary, it is a gain because now you are more conscious of the territory that you have to cross. The only loss would be to abandon your capacity to succeed in making changes in your life.

10. *Congratulate yourself. Be conscious of the greatness and importance of being able to guide old, repetitive rhythms toward new roads, new riverbanks. This is transformation in its most difficult form. To take yourself from a behavior that no longer serves you across an area of tension and insecurity to a new behavior that you have consciously created is a most courageous process. This is really to create new life, and it merits our most profound respect and attention.*

With our capacity to establish parameters in time and space, to change boundaries and to set new boundaries, we are incubating life, sustaining life, and creating new life. With this capacity we can build toward whatever we are most wanting to be or most thinking and imagining is possible in this life. With this capacity we can sustain what we most love in life.

From Routine to Ritual in Our Everyday Life

I believe that the continuous practice of parameter intelligence will enable us to have peace in our daily life. Practicing parameter intelligence, we can establish routines that respond to the necessities of our daily life. Routines well managed and practiced become rituals. For example, for some the routine of health may become elaborate and can be practiced with the same attention and care that goes into a religious ritual. Others practice the routine of work, organizing papers and projects as if they were involved in a church ritual.

All that has been said about rhythms and routines applies to ritual. Ritual is an advanced routine, practiced with care, attention, faith, and beauty. It is a way of elaborating repetitive rhythms ever more exquisitely, until they become ritual.

We have learned in our temples and cathedrals the implications of sacredness: of order, attention, music, art, consensus and agreement, joining and belonging—of being in rhythm within ourselves and with others. It is these qualities that we long for in our everyday life. We can no longer wait until Saturday and Sunday. The ground of our being calls for this quality of attention that now we find only in our consecrated holy places.

We need to enrich our daily life. Work has all too often become obsession or obligation instead of an interaction with existence. We try to order relationships by reason or by our latest analytical theory—rather than seeing them as the ground of being between one life and another life. We see health as something we must protect rather than being the ritual of caring for life itself. The areas of everyday life beg and invite us to give them the same quality of sacredness and the same attention we give now to our religious images.

Earth Zodiac

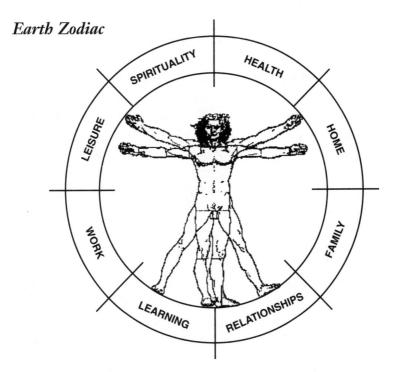

Fig. 15. Earth Zodiac (Elaine de Beauport and Luis Camejo)

The earth zodiac indicates the areas of life through which and in which we are always living and developing. Each area can become a temple, and our activities can become the rituals we live. Admittedly, this is a high calling. However, it is urgent that we call ourselves to improving life on this earth. We have the prophet of every religion as well as the prophets of modern science urging us to do so. We now have the possibility of seeing all life as energy extending from the visible finite that surrounds us to the invisible infinite that also surrounds us.

I have chosen an age-old symbol from our ancestors who looked to the heavens for guidance. Webster describes the zodiac we are familiar with from astrology as "an imaginary belt in the heavens extending for about eight degrees on either side of the apparent path of the sun and including the paths of the moon and the principal planets; it is divided into twelve equal parts, or signs, each named for a different constellation."[1]

The earth zodiac presented above describes an imaginary belt on earth extending as an apparent path on which each human moves throughout his or her lifetime. It is divided into eight equal parts, each one with a sign of the different energy fields in which the human engages. We can read the earth zodiac either sequentially or spatially. We can see ourselves arriving into existence in the area called health. Health is about our existence. We are then brought into a physical space called home, designed for our nurturing and protection. There we meet our family and sooner or later open ourselves to other relationships. We begin to learn and work. The need for leisure becomes apparent, and the field of spirituality continually reminds us of our inner life, of spirit or energy that is forever present in finite and infinite dimensions. These paths of life are presented in circle or zodiac form rather than linear form so we will realize that these fields of life all exist simultaneously. They are continuously available. Life is about the dance that we are continually weaving in these different areas.

The carefulness and attention that now exists in our cathedrals and temples can exist in the everyday affairs of our life. If we consciously select which areas of life we care most about or on what terrains of life we spend most time, we can begin a process of honoring our life. Each of us can convert at least one of these areas into sacred ground.

We usually think of women as being able to create the great rituals of home. Paul, however, is an extraordinary man who has made his art the creation of various homes for his children, his friends, and himself. He is not an architect but a master of what creates beauty in the home. Architects come to study how he has done it. His kitchen, for example, honors all the functions of preparing food. The refrigerator is framed with stones and wood, and the area above the stove is decorated with antique utensils framed like the ancient shields we used to keep above a fireplace. Even the garbage disposal is covered over by a beautiful piece of wood. Every function has been respected and carefully constructed within a stone base, inviting the person not only to a routine but to a ritual performance. Other areas of the house equally honor the daily necessities of living without any touch of luxury or excess. In simplicity, everything in his home invites one as if into a temple.

As we seek to develop our routines into rituals, we should first select the areas where we wish to concentrate. It takes time, knowledge, practice, love, sophistication, beauty, and action to transform routine into ritual. Take your time; go slowly. In the great work of honoring creation in these thicker dimensions of earth, all efforts are welcome. Let us use all past and present knowledge. With tenderness and love we can begin to honor life, one by one. The following exercise may be helpful.

EXERCISE

HONORING LIFE

I would urge you to select your playing fields. The earth zodiac offers you a choice. Make your decision: Where do you wish to concentrate your attention? Select one area for practice.

1. *First, decide what functions are involved. For example, in the area of work you might find these functions: giving and receiving, earning money, having an ability, producing or improving something, receiving recognition, relating to people, relating to information.*

2. *Do an energy profile exercise. Observe what you actually have moved toward and what you actually have moved away from during your life—not what you should have done, which you might have listed as a function, but what you have actually experienced.*

3. *Then accept and honor both what you move toward and what you move away from. Honor yourself for knowing and respecting both as natural.*

4. *What you move towards: trust these as already-established routines. You may wish to go on and develop some part of them to the level of ritual.*

5. *If you wish to change what you move away from, then*
   —get Help with the task, or
   —get Out of it by delegation or resignation, or
   —give yourself more Time.
   Get help, get out, or get time. This can easily be remembered as Get HOT.

6. *If that is not sufficient and you want to change more profoundly, then engage yourself in pattern intelligence and go on to set new parameters, as described above.*

Being clear about which fields are really important to you and working with them consciously, you will be able to concentrate more deeply and put to better use the time you have available. Also, you will know what you are cultivating and what you feel proud of in your life.

Focus all your attention on planting and growing. Be willing to listen to intruders like worry, fear, or guilt, to hear what they want to tell you and then to ask them to leave. This is your life. What you plant is what you get. If you plant worry, you will get worry. Observe what is growing well: the routines that are providing the fruit. Observe what is not growing and the nature of the weeds that are preventing growth. Be willing to remove them; this is your life.

Make sure that you, the gardener, are also proud of yourself. Do not be a critical or dissatisfied parent to yourself. Be careful of perfectionism, too. It stresses, produces fear, and invites withdrawal. Improvement is a concept more in tune with the gradual care and long term that are necessary to produce long-lasting results and beauty. Observe neutrally and realize that at this level of action, which incorporates all levels of the unconscious, it is truly great if you are able to attend with care and grow some small area of life that nurtures you. If you are able to nurture anyone near you, that is cause for celebration.

Remember that you are the ground of being that needs to be cared for if the larger ground, the context in which you live, is to produce fruit that is of value to you and the earth. Do not indulge in weakening the gardener. Search to appreciate yourself and to know why you esteem yourself, care for yourself, make yourself secure, and nourish yourself, until you are able to love yourself as creation. Then the gardener will be planting with love, and love will appear throughout your context. Remember that at this level you are an I-in-context, inseparable from what shows up in your life.

Be willing to act as if your life were a temple, one that you could go to every day to experience the comprehension and depth of life, the finite and the infinite. As you catch the rhythms and live your routines in the basic fields of life, you may indeed enhance your actions with so much beauty that your routines will become your rituals. That is the full promise of parameter intelligence.

Difficulties of Parameter Intelligence

Perhaps the greatest difficulty is our tendency to believe that parameters last forever. We become entrained by, entranced by, and addicted to them. The addiction then becomes our reality, the reality our "eternal" truth. We lose our own awareness of motion and the need for changing parameters. We become fixed in our reality, a reality that we once constructed, seduced ourselves into, and now defend against "outside" forces. We can easily become a victim of ourselves and our parameters. They become the first line of defense and our first line of resistance. We can forget that to be secure we must live in motion and be able to engage in the rhythm of what is happening. That rhythm is always changing. (The chapter on basic intelligence examines how to live the changing rhythms of life.) We can contain the rhythm temporarily through parameters, and in that way they can serve to stabilize and even enhance our energy. However, if we lose energy in any field of our life, we need to change them. Habits help, but habits also harm.

Grace is an example of someone unable to change her mental, emotional, or behavioral habits even when her life was in danger. She was a brilliant woman with a far-reaching right hemisphere and a specific left hemisphere. She was the type who could exhaust herself, first by seeing the greatness of the world and then by making herself miserable by going to the left hemisphere to pierce, criticize, and doubt everything. Rather than acting on her doubt, she would then shift back to right hemisphere generalities, and in this way she systematically exhausted herself.

Grace had been alcoholic for many years and spoke admiringly and rationally about the time she had spent in Alcoholics Anonymous. She was unable, however, to follow the parameters of the Twelve Steps. Her brilliant neocortex, never at rest, was unwilling to follow an organizational explanation of God. She went back to relying on the parameters of her own neocortex, searching for her own explanation and understanding of God. Because she was unable to be flexible and identify fully with the parameters of AA, she lost the tremendous benefits of their system of behavioral, emotional, and affectional support. Early physical abuse had left her the message, "Don't trust anyone; depend on yourself." Even though she came to see me and felt close to me, she had to question everything. She had seen many specialists as she sought to cure herself of cancer. What she was unable to do was rely on any of their advice. She is an excellent example of not being able to change early messages and the parameters that developed from them, namely "rely on yourself." Parameter intelligence includes the necessity of flexibility and willingness to change parameters.

Routines, habits, addictions, values, rituals, and institutions can be intelligent automated systems when they are first created but then become unintelligent with the change of time or circumstances. This is most evident today in our reliance on old government institutions to improve new cities, on ancient values to hold families together, or on ancient religious parameters to guide us through a world exposed to and governed by science and technology. Old values never die—nor do they fade away. They just become ineffective. Usually we wait for crisis to change. We could, instead, be constantly alert to the revision of values, routines, and habits, actively bringing them from the past into the present. We need to continually update the patterns and parameters of our lives.

There are many reasons we do not do so. There is a value in being able to go on automatic. It is efficient. Besides, we enjoy and become entranced by our parameters. We act and interact intelligently in the world with them. For example, the parameter or routine of being an educator serves me well and feels good. I am secure in it, and I know how to defend myself as an educator. My reason for being, my standard operating procedure, my good feeling and good results are all interwoven in the routine of being an educator. When did it not serve me? When I was in the mother role, explaining and giving advice, acting as an educator instead of as a mother was actually detrimental. Or in another moment, like now: it may be necessary to establish parameters that will guide me as a writer instead of keeping myself as an educator. Indeed, not only the readability of this book but even my future life may depend on my being able to change.

Why do we at this deepest level inhibit outside impulses rather than integrate them? What makes the difference between inhibition of new impulse or invitation and excitation to new impulse? How can we recognize new opportunity as something friendly that can excite us rather than as something scary that we will defend ourselves against? Can we invite ourselves into new parameters that in turn will enfold us and serve as a new system of defense? It may first become necessary to see how easily we also become woven in the thinner vibrations of roles.

Roles are what we adopt as a consequence of living within parameters. We say we live different roles: the role of educator or businessman, of mother, father, child. What role are you in as you enter your office, as you enter your home, a party, a business meeting, or a family meeting? We have acquired subtle and not so subtle vibrations from living within those different parameters of work and home. We have acquired certain ways of acting within each framework, and we move into each role just as an actor moves into different roles in different plays.

These roles are like robes we put on or become accustomed to, become conditioned to, or have inherited. Sometimes they are put upon us when we are unaware or pretending to be unconscious. These roles-robes are similar to habits, values, routines, and addictions. The longer we wear our roles-robes, the more accustomed we grow and the more they seem like our very being, natural to us. We are identified with them, which has its beauty and its danger. What is the danger? It is falling asleep, being in trance, and not recognizing the need for change. *Trance* is a word usually reserved for psychology but valuable to us all at this basic brain level. It is "a state of altered consciousness, somewhat resembling sleep, during which voluntary movement is lost, as in hypnosis."[2] The danger is of losing voluntary movement, of becoming so accustomed to our parameters and roles that we believe they are life. They are only the small portion of life in which we have involved ourselves.

How can we conceptualize this in a way we can remember? I have chosen to identify the word *roles* with robes because it has helped me to remember. I can take off my robes; I can take off my roles. I can change my robes, put on heavier ones if it is cold outside to protect me from those thicker vibrations. I can change into lighter clothes. I can wear my roles lightly. It is this metaphor of wearing my robes-roles lightly that has most helped me to dance the dynamics of every day rather than become rooted in them as realities that I controll. I change my clothes; I change my robes-roles. I put them on and I take them off. This lightness also enables me to be more open to changing the parameters in which these roles were created. Lightness is the bridge over which I must pass from the old paradigm of "defense through control" to the new paradigm of "defense through dynamics."

Danger

Sudden loss of parameters occurs in at least three major life situations. All three are known to be major causes of stress and illness, and they all involve changes in our routines and interruptions of well-established boundaries.

Loss of a Loved One through Death or Divorce. For better and for worse we become deeply entrained, deeply addicted to our loved ones. Energy once absorbed and engaged in activities with them is now set loose, in chaos, scurrying for new boundaries.

Retirement, or the End of a Job. Energy that was once occupied within well-established boundaries for eight to ten hours a day now runs loose. Although we may feel jubilant, free at last, or glad to be released from obligation, it is also true that now we must invent new ways to burn or guide or use that energy. I am convinced that one of the reasons for illness and heart attacks when people retire is lack of awareness of how to guide the energy running loose within our nervous systems. We need to shift to basic intelligence to guide our life until there is time to set new parameters.

Ralph was seventy-two years old and had been a dedicated administrator of a company for thirty-five years. His main pride in life was his fantastic appetite, his ability to eat anything, and his continuous health. All his life he was on time, faithfully opening the office every day and closing it at night. When the company moved to another city, his boss kept the office open even though there was little to do. That was when Ralph began to complain of circulatory problems and of being frequently tired. The fatal moment came when the director finally had to close the office and direct his attention to a large contract in the new location. Unable to change his habit of work, Ralph lost interest in life, spent long periods of time in bed, and within two months died of a heart attack.

Often we imagine freedom from work as the promised land. However, to arrive in paradise, we may again need to set parameters, this time perhaps around more pleasurable activities or at least ones that guide and sustain our freedom and creativity.

Change of a Home. All the space that our nervous system is accustomed to without reflection is no longer available. It takes time to condition ourselves to a new space. Knowing this, we need not be surprised by our nervousness or by a vague sense of loss when we move.

Usually we do not identify these events as loss, unless they make us sad. With the exception of losing a loved one, we are usually happy and looking forward to the change—at least, in our neocortex or limbic system. Meanwhile, our deepest brain is waiting for a new routine, a new way to contain the influx of energy continually entering. During these great periods of transition when our customary routines are no longer available, we need to remember to live our basic intelligence—to move toward and away from, in tandem with, in rhythm with, in sensorial or instinctual resonance with. Above all, when there is loss, danger, or instability, we need to move from an old system of survival and self-defense by control to a new system of survival by dynamic defense.

New System: Dynamic Defense

The new defense is not about dancing with wolves but about dancing with our own tendency to fall asleep, seduced by what felt good in the past. The opening of ourselves to new information is basic. It is also basic to be able to observe the actions of our life with some degree of neutrality and impartiality, almost as if we were observing another human being. We need to be a fair witness to what is occurring in our life rather than be in continuous identity with ourselves, resisting all newness as if it were intrusion or attack.

What is the new dynamic defense?

1. Comprehending, feeling, and acting life as a dynamic rather than static process. Information is continually available, continually bombarding you. You live in a web of information. We say we live in a changing world, but every human has always lived in a changing world. The new news is about seeing yourself as a dynamic entity living in that ever-changing world. You must modify your belief system from one based on fixing your life in permanent stability to living your life as dynamic process. In popular language, that means you cannot stop the world; you can only dance with it.

2. Remembering to evaluate the effects of existing parameters. Are they useful? Do they bear fruit? If yes, do not tamper; if no, look again.

3. Flexibility is essential. This is the capacity to stay loose, to try, to give up, to try again, to expand, to recede, always moving toward and away, and keeping always your skilled capacity to shift, to look again, and to focus elsewhere. I have a floppy doll named Felicia Flexibilidades in Spanish and just Flexibility in English. Whatever her name, everything about her moves. I consider her to be the mascot and guiding light of the basic brain.

4. Changing parameters and creating new parameters. You need always to be alert to the presence or absence of energy in your life. When you are losing energy, that is the moment to change parameters and create new ones. To be able to do this, you need to grasp the idea of universal energy—that is, that the entire universe is made of energy. You personally or your response to your environment is doing something to block that energy. That is the moment to believe in energy and *do anything* to access more energy rather than giving up on life or on yourself. Move quickly to what you most enjoy and set up new parameters to sustain that enjoyment in your life. Energy is like a thermometer. Read your body temperature and when it is sinking low, do something, change something, create something new.

5. Wearing robes lightly. Whatever you create in order to live, whether it be new or old, parameters or values or belief systems, habits or roles, wear it lightly. Don't let any reality get too heavy. As dynamic energy, the issue is staying in motion.

6. Acting your basic intelligence. Keep on moving toward and away from anyone or anything on behalf of life.

CHAPTER XIX

Behavioral Intelligence and the Openings

*B*ehavioral intelligence is our capacity to

act. Many people have a high behavioral quotient of intelligence: they are able to act, to establish parameters that guide their action, to change patterns that are not helpful to action, and to move toward and away in continuous action. Those who act are insistent and persistent; they get things done. They are little offended by obstacles. They value action and are as recognizable as those who value emotions or those who value ideas. Using behavioral intelligence is about being able to act appropriately in our environment, which not only requires the three behavioral intelligences, but also requires being able to respond to information continuously impacting us through the openings of our body.

All the openings provide information that we may or may not be able to integrate into actions and behaviors that we find satisfying. Very often these openings provide information that overloads our nervous system, causing us insecurity, discomfort and a disequilibrium with ourselves. We say we feel anxious, nervous, uneasy, or uncomfortable with "things" as they are. "I don't know what's the matter with me"; "I'm really worried about . . . or scared that . . ."; "I can't get a handle on things." All of these expressions indicate that in some way we cannot control events the way we are accustomed to. We feel anxious, even scared. Taken together these can be described as an anxiety process. We are on overload. Simply stated, we cannot manage comfortably the amount or kind of information impacting our body through our senses. We are too open or sensitive to the information, and some form of anxiety is our attempt to close off as a way of dealing with overload.

It is certain that the anxiety phenomenon registers in us at an emotional level. However, from experience with myself and others and the study of the deepest brain, I believe the anxiety process can be brought under control only when we are willing to relate it directly to our own action and basic brain. In some way our actions and behavior are producing this anxiety, and therefore our response needs to be at a behavioral level. Emotions alert us to this feeling of anxiety, but dealing with anxiety requires our behavioral intelligence.

Charting the Anxiety Process

At the core of the anxiety phenomenon is some variation of worry, fear, or guilt. Books have been written about each one. My intention here is only to indicate their relation to our actions or lack of them so that we may be aware of how behavioral intelligence can help us intervene at an early stage of the anxiety process.

Worry. Worry is a mixture of vibrations from each of the brain systems. We are concerned about something and say we are worried—for instance, "that my son will not arrive home on time." There is a generalizing from the right hemisphere—"that he may have been in a car crash"—and the specificity and reasoning, albeit late, of the left hemisphere—"I told him that if he took more than two drinks, he wouldn't be able to drive safely." If the worry persists, there is the repetitive phenomenon of the basic brain.

Indeed, we may become addicted to our worries. Stop for a moment and consider what is worrying you right now. Then consider how many years you have been worrying about the same thing. Worry is a socially accepted addiction: it is verbal, it sounds logical, and thus it resonates with our logical culture. It always expresses some concern or caring. From the generalities of the right hemisphere to the details of the left, worry is a continuous ping-pong between the hemispheres. It is vibration in each of the brain systems but unwillingness to close in any of them. It is:

- a sequential reasoning process in the left hemisphere but unwillingness to come to conclusion
- an ever increasing imaging process in the right hemisphere but unwillingness to close around or frame any smaller image
- a caring and concern in the limbic brain, but not a deep enough feeling to lead to the action of checking on what is really happening
- a repetition of nervous vibrations in the basic brain, but unwillingness to take action

Without closure in any brain system, information continues to impact and overload us. Anxiety continues.

Although we may be thinking, when we are worrying we are not thinking effectively. We need to bring closure in each of our brain systems. For instance, you are thinking and imaging about a physical event or action that you suppose is going to happen, but you are not verifying whether your thoughts or images are related to your external reality; nor are you moving your body to act. Shift to basic intelligence. Move yourself to action. Where is your son, and what is happening? Check on your reality by picking up the telephone or getting into your car to find out, or get into your left hemisphere, check the details, use your rational process, come to a conclusion, and then act. Once you have reached a conclusion, inhibit your right hemisphere from intervening with more images. Breathe deeply in your abdomen to relax and move to entrain the rest of your energy by involving yourself in another routine.

We must consciously shift to busy ourselves in a different activity, preferably an agreeable habit, so that we do not return to our head and begin the process of worry all over again. If we are long-time worriers, we will not believe these things are possible. If we are willing to take action to avoid the habit of worry, we will experience the difference.

Worry can be a positive signal calling us to action. If it becomes a habit, it robs us of our power of action, easily tumbling us into nervous reactions. It is the beginning of the anxiety process. If you are anxious or frequently anxious, check your list of worries and verify to see what action you are avoiding and what action you need to take to close out the continuous bombardment of the same information.

Fear. Fear is a major phenomenon that most of us will not admit to. We are taught in our early years not to be afraid, or if we are afraid, never to admit it. Instead, we usually say we are nervous or anxious or "just" stressed. Whatever variation of fear we will admit to, it is important to have some way of recognizing it in our body. It feels uptight, jagged, chaotic, uneasy, nervous, unstable, not like our self. Our vibrations and body are not only contracted, but constricted. We are unable to expand and relax. Often fear is accompanied by repetitive behavior like pacing, biting nails, tapping a pencil, or doing the same thing over and over again. All of this tells us that we are anxious, nervous, afraid. We are on overload and cannot manage the incoming information.

Fear is an important signal to STOP and wait. It tells us not to cross the street. If we are already in the middle of the street or a project, if we have already started spending money, or if we have agreed to marry and feel nervous, anxious, or afraid, fear tells us to STOP and return to the beginning, to go back to our rock or the territory where we feel secure. Then we can consider why we started the project: Do I need such an expensive house? What made me decide to marry? What new information is impacting me?

One of the great causes of fear is not knowing what to do or how to do it. It is as if the territory underneath us is shaking, is not secure. Our basic brain of action is confused and warning us to get back on the sidewalk until we learn to cross this territory. Either we never learned how to cross it safely, or we learned poorly and had bad results. Fear is projecting a previous bad experience onto the present or the future.

Our experience is calling us to STOP and LEARN. Fear is an intelligent signal. We need to listen to the signal, and find out what we need to learn in order to act successfully or at least safely. Security, as we now know it, comes from living our life within certain parameters where we have learned to act safely. When we step outside those parameters or when events or people intrude in our parameters, it is intelligent to feel insecure. It is also intelligent to stop, to give ourselves time to recover, and to learn how to become secure: to greet the stranger, take in the new event, or learn how to deal with the unfamiliar so that we can establish new parameters for safe action.

Right hemisphere imagery is another source of fear. As beautiful as some images may be, a good right hemisphere can continue to travel into more and more expansive images until we are caught far from our body. If we stop the imagery process on a harmful image, we may indeed feel disassociated and register shock, anxiety, and fear. The frontal lobes of both the left and right hemispheres are like horses galloping at top speed and need to be brought under control. We need to take the reins and bring them back to a reality closer to our body and the present moment. We need especially to reign in the right hemisphere, whose natural ability is to go galloping far afield bringing back information that we do not know how to handle. Stop until your basic intelligence can guide you toward something that you do know how to handle.

Fear is camouflaged behind such names as anxiety, insecurity, nervousness, uneasiness or stress. All belong to the great family of fear— brothers, sisters, first cousins, but all with the same family name. We need to become acquainted with this family: they are all telling us something about the environment in which we are putting our body—the behavior we are demanding of ourselves or the actions we are engaged in. Let us learn to recognize the different members of this family and how they speak to us. Do I feel myself nervous, or just find myself unable to act as I usually do? Can I admit I am anxious? Can I stop? We must learn to deal with the incoming information before it steals our energy and intensifies our anxiety.

Guilt. Perhaps there is no greater energy thief than guilt. It is not fashionable to admit to feeling guilty. In fact, it has become so unfashionable among sophisticated people that many no longer can recognize the feeling of guilt. Guilt is a feeling and a phenomenon which indicates that we have not taken the action prescribed by our culture, our religion, our family, or our conscience. We say we should instead of doing it. "I should have gone to see my mother last Sunday; instead I went to to the movies." I say I feel guilty, which at least communicates that I have a conscience. I care, or I know what is considered the right thing to do.

Where there is guilt there is always a value involved, such as the value of honoring or taking care of our parents. Values are the collective wisdom of previous cultures passed on from generation to generation. Values indicate the action that was lived and valued in previous generations, valued because at some time in history it meant survival for the community. For example, at one point in history it was a matter of survival to take excellent care of the mother so that new life might be added and the tribe strengthened. Values are patterns of action originating in the past and repeated again and again throughout history.

Values are transmitted to us usually through a particular person that we loved or admired. Often we can recall the person and the event through which this value imprinted itself on our minds. Values come to us through our family, religion, school, or country, less frequently through professions or heroes. The point is that values do not originate in the present. I do not wake up on Sunday morning and think or feel, "Oh, what a great idea to go see my mother!" I wake up and there is some pressing vibration that forms itself into, "I should go see my mother today."

When we say we should, do not take the action, and then feel guilty, guilt becomes a further excuse for not acting. The feeling of guilt—the malaise, uneasiness, or sensation of burden—increases our anxiety and weakens our action. If we act, we act out of obligation, with less enthusiasm and less clarity. We act less frequently. We keep saying we feel guilty, but the gap between word and action grows wider with every repetition.

We have tried to teach action by teaching values. We have used words hoping that these words will guarantee action. The neocortical brain of words can suggest, but it cannot guarantee action. We are stunned by the number of "children criminals" who show no evidence of remorse or conscience. If we wish to bring the values of our ancestors into our generation in order to guide us and transmit them to our children, what can we do? We must focus on our actions as well as our words. We can first make a list of all the situations that make us feel guilty, check the value involved in each one, and then begin to reflect on what action I would be willing to take during my lifetime on behalf of that value. Will I really visit my mother every Sunday, phone her every other week, or send a fax? What action is really possible? Really genuine? Let us not widen the credibility gap by continuing to speak about values that we refuse to act on. What is needed is to update the values from the past that make us feel guilty because we are not acting and make them our own values by deciding on the action we will really take rather than only talk about. To know what action we will really take will relieve us of the anxiety and the tension we feel. This is not only important to free ourselves from guilt, but it is important for our society. If our action is authentic, that value will live. It will not be the same in our generation as it was in generations past, but the value will be transmitted through our behavior. Values must be updated and integrated into behavior in each generation or else they will be weakened in each generation.

Old values do not die; they just become shoulds! We say we should, we doubt, we avoid, we say yes but do no. We ask forgiveness or make excuses. In the end we say we feel guilty, which at least makes us feel acceptable in our own eyes and usually to those around us. Let us admit to guilt, become aware of when we feel guilty, observe our actions, hear our shoulds, update our values, and use pattern intelligence to inhibit old actions that do not serve. Then, with basic and parameter intelligence, we can guide ourselves to new action.

Hopefully you can now distinguish the anxiety process from other emotional processes. Worry, fear, and guilt can indeed be felt, but to be healed they call us to take some form of physical action, some improvement in our behavior. We need our basic intelligence to free us to move either toward or away from. Our pattern intelligence reveals our values and patterns that are limiting our actions or making us feel guilty about the ones we are not taking. Our parameter intelligence invites us to new action.

The Skin: Open to the World

How have we fallen into habits of worry, fear, and guilt? Why does the anxiety process exist? It exists because we are sensitive vibrating systems, continually exposed to the life of this earth. We are continually exposed to information. Whether it be the collective unconscious that enters while we sleep or the specific unconscious that is continually registering around our body, the key point is that we human beings are a dynamic system whose spinal column is continually responsive at skin level to all the vibrations from other life around us. The pores of our skin are a system interfacing between our environment and our internal self. As previously discussed, information enters through the openings of our skin and is drawn into our afferent-efferent nervous system, up our spinal column and into our basic brain system, without any conscious invitation from our neocortex.

Our basic brain weds us to our environment—for better and for worse. Our skin exposes us to information; our spinal column channels the information to our basic brain. We must have some signal to indicate that we are not "managing" or "friendly" to that information. We have many signals or many ways of blocking this incoming information. The anxiety response is a first basic healthy warning system. Check the following chart to become aware of the impact of your environment on your sensory system.

AWARENESS CHART

Body Signals	Parameter	Pattern	Basic
Anxiety	What are the	What patterns	What would
Back stress	major routines	or values are	enable you to
Skin irritations	of your day	involved in	move away
Fatigue	and night?	keeping you in	from those
Boredom	How do you	your routines?	parameters
Lupus	spend your	To what values	of stress?
Epstein-Barr	time? In what	were you	Toward new
Nerve failure	space are you	conditioned	values and new
Disequilibrium	working? What	in childhood?	routines?
Awkwardness	are your ties	How are they	
Accidents	to your home?	related to	
	To your work?	keeping you	
	To your family	in routines	
	or the other	of stress?	
	basic areas of		
	your life?		

The questions in the chart invite us to become aware of what may be impacting our health or well-being through our skin or spinal column. Our skin is our whole-body register. It is not a thermometer registering internal heat in relation to stress and illness; it is rather an external thermometer registering our healthy, adequate, or inadequate response to life or the environmental conditions in which we have placed ourselves. We have tended to seek an understanding of the illness and its cure, all of which is good. However, it would be even better to become aware of the first signals that our skin is communicating to us before they are transformed into illness.

The chart above is an invitation to relate the well-being of our skin, back, and nerves to those routines that we take for granted but which may be stressing our health. Our response to the stimuli from our parents or other influential members of our environment formed our values and our patterns that then dictated our behavior. From these subtle beginnings, we have formed the action or routines of our life: routines of health, home, family, relationships, learning, work, play, and spirituality.

We have unconscious routines. We may be living within parameters that we did not decide upon consciously. We were not studying those values or patterns of behavior with our eyes reading textbooks, with our ears hearing professors, or with our neocortical brain making rational choices about those values and patterns of behavior. We were probably hearing our parents' voices, seeing and feeling our parents' behavior. The totality of that experience was present in the environment and being communicated unconsciously through all the pores of our body. Just as we learned to walk and talk by imitation rather than by explanation, so too we imitated values and patterns of behavior that continue to influence our parameters, choice of routines, and actions.

Stress on our skin, back, or nerves may therefore be a result of continuously restricting ourselves, closing off the pores of our body and the nerves of our spinal column under years of pressure and imitation of behavior formed in the early years of our life. If the routines of life are causing us stress, from minor signals of anxiety to full-blown nervous system weakness and illness, it is important to challenge the values or patterns involved in keeping us in those routines. Again I do not wish to deny the need for medical assistance for these illnesses. I only wish to draw attention to the signals of the skin, back, and nerves so that we might apply our behavioral intelligences before the signals reach the serious proportions of illness. Our own behavioral intelligence may serve either to protect us before illness or enable us to make changes in our actions, behaviors, and environment in conjunction with the medical advice that is offered.

Behavioral intelligences are not only for our awareness but also for our action. Our skin is a sensing system. The pores sense the vibrations around us. We call it instinct, and many people have a well-developed instinctive intelligence. They walk in a room and can sense what is going on. Given a situation, we say they instinctively know how to handle it. They have behavioral intelligence, action intelligence. Is it that their skin is more alert, more close to the earth, to all that is going on? The reptile's skin protects it, warns it when danger is near, and enables it to prepare to strike even when the "enemy" is at a distance. We may not wish to consider ourselves reptiles, but we might wish to consider instinctive intelligence, or the possibility that our skin has an intelligence system that we call sensing or instinct that can guide us intelligently in situations of immediacy. We do not need to strike; we can use our basic intelligence to move away.

Parameter intelligence invites us to find the many ways of surrounding our skin that will nourish and protect it. In the womb, skin is surrounded and nourished by the amniotic fluids of the placenta. The fact that we were born healthy is due to the surrounding in which we were nourished and protected for nine months. Most of us continue to love water and bathe ourselves with great pleasure. We love warmth and cannot live without it. We know how we love to be hugged or held by human arms. We know how great it feels to put on old clothes. No matter how much those close to us protest the age or ugliness of the old clothes, our body finds them again and again. "I thought you threw that out" gets the answer "Never!" Our skin has learned to like them. In our favorite chair, we're home and the world is right. And how good it is to sleep in our own bed. What surrounds us makes us feel secure and comforts us. All these are parameters that we have been accustomed to. Indeed, they rest us; again and again we return to them. This is parameter intelligence at its best.

When we are nervous, overly fatigued, or experiencing any other serious symptom related to nervousness or unaccountable fatigue, let us return to our rock, the parameters that comfort us. However, if we are suffering, we may need to challenge those parameters. In some way they are not serving us. Our skin is not resting. The pores and nerves are contracting-constricting rather than relaxing and expanding. We may wish to change and experiment with new parameters. A shopping spree for new clothes, a change of house, a change of job, or a vacation may be in order.

However, going directly to pattern intelligence may be cheaper and in the long run give us substantial clues as to what is going wrong. What patterns or values did we inherit about taking care of our body? Was it right to buy beautiful clothes, or should we be saving our money? Are our values or patterns of behavior adversely affecting our work? Is it important only to succeed at work and less important to create a beautiful home? What is going on? In our behaviors we can find the pattern involved. Can we intervene in the pattern, seek alternative patterns? Or is it simpler: can we just move away from those parameters and toward more protective and nourishing ones?

To develop the sensitivity and sensorial intelligence of our skin, we must look to the conscious use of parameter intelligence. Let us seek the patterns involved when something is going wrong and repattern to improve the routines or surrounding that is affecting our skin. Basic intelligence is the fastest and most basic: it is moving away from the territory of harm and toward one of comfort and protection. The skin is the doorway to our nervous system as well as its expression. Let us not underestimate its importance.

The Back: Channeling System from Environment to Brain

The impulses through the openings of the skin are channeled to our spinal column. There they are rapidly fired through a nervous system extending to the brainstem of the basic brain into the limbic and neocortical systems and throughout the rest of the body. Our skin is the entry point, and our spinal column is the major channeling network. I like the image of an antenna. I no longer think of taking care of my back or even of my spinal column; I think of how I will take care of my antenna. It is a delicate image and reminds me that indeed my spine is channeling information into me, much as the antenna of my television is channeling information onto the screen. Becoming conscious at this deepest level is trying to become aware of the incoming information that my antenna is channeling from the world to my brain systems.

Parameter intelligence means giving this antenna or spinal column the routines of movement so that it can relax and be flexible, giving it rhythm that it may be aligned. What we call exercise is movement and rhythm for the spinal column. A cardiovascular workout serves to heat the body and stimulate the heart muscles. However, the repetitive rhythm of walking, swimming, dancing, yoga, tai chi, or other martial arts not only exercises the muscles but also aligns the spinal column. We, or more particularly our spinal column becomes accustomed to or addicted to continuous movement and rhythm.

When your back becomes stressed, ask what rhythm or routine or habit you have interrupted. Look to pattern intelligence. Yes, you may have sprained a muscle by picking up that heavy package, but was some pattern operating within you that made you pick it up in an unaligned way, thereby twisting a muscle? Were you ashamed of doing manual labor? Were you thinking about taking a vacation instead of working? What were you thinking or feeling while you took the action? By taking another look, we can become conscious of any patterns that might have caused constriction rather than expansion.

Basic intelligence is moving in appropriate alignment toward and away from, throughout the day or at least in relation to particular activities. We experience it on those days when all goes well, when we are working easily, or in those great moments of alignment, whether in sports or with friends, walking in nature or making love.

Parameter, pattern, and basic intelligences all help us protect our spinal column and the openings of our skin. As our behavioral intelligence, they enable us to overcome anxiety and interact sensitively with our environment.

The Secret Weapon of Life: To Expand and to Contract

No matter what intelligence we are using, no matter what brain system is involved, there is a reverence we must have for the human instrument. We need to respect the integrity of the instrument: to use it in equilibrium with the world around us; to have both self-esteem and yet be willing to yield to the importance of others. Psychology proposes the importance of the ego; spirituality urges us not to have one. I propose that it is a matter of respecting all life as energy and expanding and contracting in relation to the energies of others around us. Also there is the healing aspect of entering more deeply into the energy affecting us. This is like being willing to enter into my most contracted states or lousy habits or illnesses without criticizing myself, simply knowing it is about being more resonant and more expansive. It is a matter of knowing that I have missed the wave that would expand me into health. It is not me against the world; it is discovering the energy wave that would be helpful and putting myself into it.

In terms of the deeper brain of action, I don't walk around in a state of full consciousness; I walk around moving toward and away from. I try to be aware of when I am too expanded and return back into myself. Equally I try to come out from my contracted, interior being to be more expressive and expansive with others. If you will, this serves me as a guide to the practice of consciousness. I have found the concept and the practice of expansion and contraction to be continuously useful to me.

Life is energy, and riding the wave motion of life
  is what heals life.
  Staying with the energy,
  and expanding and contracting within the energy.

Expansion allows energy to travel
  into previously constricted areas.

  I am conscious of entering
  the wave of constriction and
  riding with it into expansion.

The serpent was used in symbols of ancient religions
The dove, a religious symbol of peace in our time
  Both to convey this
   essential
    wave motion.

Einstein confirms this, describing
  all life as energy.

All life is vibration.
  All vibration is expansion and contraction.

All expansion and contraction take place
  on different wavelengths, different intensities,
   different speeds.

Some we recognize as sound,
  some as light,
   some as diverse physical structures: plant, animal, mineral, human,
  or smaller cohering of life
   into atoms and molecules.

The issue for us
    is to enter
    expanding and contracting the waves of energy
            which appear in our lives under various headings: health . . .
            work . . . pleasure . . . home . . . family . . . friends . . .
            relationships . . . love . . . problems . . . opportunities

The issue is:
            When we are expanded, be willing to contract
            When we are contracted, be willing to expand
                On Behalf of Life

Conclusion

The boundaries of cognition have now been opened to include the many characteristics of being human. The concept of intelligence, so valued in our Western culture, we can now associate with the many gifts that enable us to live life fully. We now identify spirituality, art, and creativity as processes open to all through intuitive, spatial, and associative intelligences.

The heart, indeed, has a brain, and we have dared to delineate the process of loving as affectional intelligence. In mood intelligence, we finally honor the darkness of sadness and anger, side by side with the greatness of love. Desire, which for so long we tried to enclose within the limits of reason, has been freed to serve as the life-fire that warms and guides us through existence as motivational intelligence.

We now know that the everyday conditions of life are not a reflection of fate or destiny but a "call to attention" for the basic brain. We can actively and consciously search for our old patterns and change them by means of our pattern and parameter intelligences. We are free to move toward and away in continuous motion, being clear now that our basic intelligence enables us to honor and live creation in the present moment.

Knowing that our human life is in reality energy, just as all other life is, we feel free at last to play our own instrument as a basic instrument of creation. We become the conductor of our mental orchestra—the neocortex, the limbic, and the basic brain sections—each one capable of vibrating through all the ranges of energy that extend from the finite to the infinite.

Finally, it is important to note that it is the rational process that has helped us overcome the limitations of our own mind and chart the possibilities of these new intelligences. It was the rational, scientific process of brain researchers like Sperry and MacLean, as well as all those who accompanied them, that discovered the mental capacities of the right hemisphere of the neocortex and the physical and chemical differences of the two deeper brain systems. Einstein and all those involved in new physics have enabled us to understand that all matter is energy in various states of coherence and vibration.

Energy is now our common ground. As human matter we vibrate, the control panels we call our brain systems vibrate, and our whole brain-mind-body vibrates. We are energy beings. This is even more descriptive of us and our potential future than saying we are human beings. It is energy and vibration that now unite us, whether through visible or invisible wavelengths. Our three brain systems have always orchestrated the human being. What is new is that we can now know and join together around the unifying perspective of energy and begin consciously to orchestrate each of the brain systems through the multiple processes of intelligence and consciousness we have described. I am sure there are many more pathways to be shaped in the future and many subtleties of these intelligences still to come.

For the moment, we can celebrate that we have freed ourselves from the Newtonian concept of matter and our own mental reliance on only one intelligence. We have opened ourselves to explore matter and reality as energy, as we prepare ourselves to become the conscious orchestrators of our own vibratory systems through multiple intelligences.

We have seen that what was formerly called the unconscious now is called the limbic brain and the basic brain, filtering various wavelengths of energy, including quantum realities. Even if you wish to continue to say you are unconscious, you must know that as long as you are alive you will always be present in one of the three brain systems, vibrating within some range of energy.

If we wish to acknowledge or indeed if we have experienced clues that there is much more to this cosmos than we are fully feeling or able to express, we must also realize that while we are alive, we are living in this cosmos, not only expressing but also receiving and being sustained by all other life vibrations. The least we can do is not limit this cosmos to what we can perceive mentally or emotionally. As live energy systems, we are being sustained by vibrations that have made the earth and the cosmos and that are still engaged in the process. It is for us to join the process consciously.

We are always connected to some aspect of the universe with which we are attuned in some energy range between the finite and infinite—with one of our three brains:

With our neocortex: we can know that we are conscious, that we can think, imagine, receive intuitively, and reflect, which means to integrate feedback mentally.

With our limbic system: we can feel some aspects of the universe. This means we allow ourselves to be affected by something and to receive feedback emotionally.

With our basic brain: we incorporate the universe. We receive feedback at a vibrational level, sensorial and cellular. This means that vibrations literally affect our basic and physical structures. There is a stimulus from our environment and a response from our nervous system, whether or not we can feel that response in our limbic system or are able to reflect on that response in our neocortex.

Therefore, just by being alive, we are always present in some aspect of the energy filtering through our three brain systems. The challenge for human development is to be conscious. I believe that the greatest obstacle to developing our consciousness has been trying to use the same process to access the limbic and basic brains that we have been using to access the neocortex.

As we have seen, the process needed to access each brain system is different. One particularly important difference is that the neocortex can be accessed directly, whereas we need an indirect process in order to become conscious in the two deepest brain systems. Allowing ourselves to be affected by in the limbic brain is an indirect process by which energy is received before we can guide it consciously by means of emotional intelligences. Access to the basic brain is also by an indirect process of self-observation. Becoming aware of our body, our behavior, our I-in-context, and our dreams is what enables us then to guide ourselves consciously by means of behavioral intelligences. Thinking, associating, imagining, and visualizing are all direct processes of the neocortex; only intuiting is an indirect process of receiving in the neocortex. Therefore, in order to become more fully conscious, we must know how to shift from a direct process of active energy to an indirect process of receptive energy.

If we continue to refer to the two deeper brains as the unconscious, we permit ourselves to continue to ignore them, as if we were accepting the darkness of our mind. The purpose of knowledge has always been to overcome ignorance. I believe that we will be able to overcome ignorance only by being able to access these two deeper brains and by becoming as familiar with these various intelligences as we are with rational intelligence. The new thinker will use these and other intelligences in an effort to become more fully conscious.

Toward a Law of Connections

The sequence of connections known as the law of cause and effect has been basic to the rational process. Indeed, in science, this pattern of thinking has resulted in outstanding successes. The process of searching for the cause and determining the effects has been sacred to us for so long that it is difficult to believe it is not the only guiding process for understanding reality. However, after studying the three brain systems for fifteen years, I must conclude that cause and effect cannot help us distinguish the kinds of connections involved in the vibrations of the different brain systems. Moreover, our insistent search for the cause actually blinds us to more important connective processes occurring in all areas of the brain except for the left hemisphere.

In order to be free to identify the capacities of the right hemisphere and the two deeper brain systems, we need a much more encompassing guideline than the law of cause and effect. I propose a law of connections, which would, of course, include the law of cause and effect but would also open us to more appropriate descriptions for the connective processes involved in each of the three brain systems.

The connections of associative, spatial, and intuitive intelligences are vibrations that correspond randomly rather than by sequence and cause. For example, in a Picasso, one aspect of the painting is not *caused* by the other. Rather, the images are juxtaposed in relation to such things as size, color, form, or the many other possibilities occurring within the artist's mind. The connections are random, corresponding to the imagination of Picasso. Our attempt to analyze the reason he created something one way or to seek a cause why he placed the figures in a certain manner is a kind of reductionism that does not benefit either the artist or ourselves. It blocks us from the richness of multiple associations instead of opening us to them.

The connections of the limbic brain are made through relationship, through origin, or through factors we cannot yet describe, but one of which might be chemical. To try to understand emotions by their cause instead of by their internal origin or by their relationship with many factors has caused us a great deal of suffering. For example, trying to get hold of the cause of an emotion has led us to the act and art of blaming each other, our fathers, mothers, society, or whomever will listen to us.

A connection such as cause and effect, which is used in order to be precise, cannot be used with emotional vibrations, which by their nature are more generalized. Sometimes to deepen into the origin of an emotion helps us, but to call the origin the cause can get us involved in guilt, shame, anger, even hatred. When we apply the analysis that helps us in the left hemisphere of the neocortex to this emotional brain, it throws us off the track of any real investigation of emotions based on their unique characteristics and leaves us in blind alleys, thinking we know how to get out.

Music presents a clearer analogy to emotions, giving us clues to the tremendous variety of connections involved in them. Music elaborates different tones and intensities according to scales, which are in effect diverse connective processes. My experience with emotions is that they, too, are diverse connective processes, and we would do well to invent a notation system that enables us to appreciate their richness. If we did, we would be more interested in their variety, tonality, contraction, and amplification than in their cause.

In the basic brain, applying the law of cause and effect prevents us from adopting a neutral perspective for the process of self-observation so necessary in this brain. It also inhibits us from perceiving the integrity and complexity of the experience. When we go into detail in search of the cause, we may find a root but miss the whole tree. The search for a single cause also inhibits our observation of the multiple links involved in the design and origin of our patterns. Clearly, cause and effect do not help us grasp the continuous and subtle movements of basic intelligence. It is more like trying to measure an ocean wave with a ruler. Neither does it help us elaborate the different connections involved in dreams. The question What causes dreams? does not help as much as asking What are the different connections being made by vibrations in the journey from the delta range of the basic brain to the REM stage of the neocortex, where they are officially recognized as dream?

We are searching for causes and missing the processes. We are missing the variety of connections necessary to chart our way through the vastness of our brain-mind-body system. We can celebrate having so successfully identified the cause-and-effect connection, which has served to advance human life in this century. Imagine if we could just as successfully identify nine or more other connective processes and set them to work on our behalf. I suggest that we initiate research into the possibility of formalizing a law of connections.

Social Action

What is the social impact of knowing that we are energy systems orchestrated by three brains and multiple intelligences? My particular interest in working with the three brain systems has been to develop innovative education programs for adults. I believe the triune brain provides a charter to guide us, and the multiple intelligences a beginning. I cannot end this book without making suggestions for social action based on my experience and deep feeling about what we can do.

If we want to live fully the promise of human life, we need to expand the limits of education beyond those of the universities and beyond those of youth. We need to open adult education centers in all areas of our social life: business, religion, hospitals, clinics, prisons, and government offices. As part of formal education, we need to create schools for adults dedicated to life-long learning. Universities will remain great centers of research and preparation for professions. However, we also need to learn how to live with our own human nature: to acquire the skills of communicating with one another, of expressing emotions without doing harm, and of respecting the integrity of each other's actions and cultures. We need a common ground of learning, a basic education for adults as part of a necessary infrastructure for society.

We now know that we are dynamic energy systems in a continual dance of life. We cannot just learn information and walk away satisfied. Life is about experiencing, reflecting, and experiencing again in a continual process of learning. Each stage of life offers new challenges. That means that education at eighteen does not do much for us at forty and even less at sixty. Each area of our personal life also offers different challenges. Each of the eight paths of the earth zodiac contains different secrets, some jewels, some stones, but all there waiting for us. Education for language, math, science, and the liberal arts and education for certain professions are all wonderful but not enough—not enough because they are not directly and continually related to the new educational horizons needed in industry, health, psychology, religion, governmental institutions, and formal educational institutions. Let me suggest how different intelligences may be applicable to those areas of our social life.

INDUSTRY

Industry has already taken the leadership in beginning to develop innovative programs in personal development. Nevertheless, many problems lie beyond the training courses directed toward the requirements of work. Absenteeism, lack of motivation, sickness, stress, and attitudinal problems are areas in which emotional and behavioral intelligences offer real solutions. Development programs based on these intelligences would offer a broader-based training, going beyond the limits strictly defined by personnel and professional requirements.

HEALTH

A new educational center dedicated to continuous health needs to be added to the present hospital structure. How many illnesses could be prevented if there existed more continuous education about health? By health I mean the health of the mind and the body, in which the different specialties of medicine, psychology, and psychoneuroimmunology would be offered in continually available courses by professionally trained educators. This type of educational service would open a new area in which these disciplines would be united for the benefit of everyone. Separated as they are now, they are research specialties and important in their own uniqueness. However, there is an additional preparatory process needed before the fruit of their investigation can be effectively made available to the public. I believe this is an educational process that is at present not being performed by anyone. The public snatches bits of research released haphazardly by newspapers and television. Although it may be better than nothing, this is also creating a considerable confusion and may in the long run lead to a tremendous lack of credibility by the public. Information released about the harmful effects and health value of different foods is a prime example of this lack of preparation and public confusion.

After an adult has his or her first encounter with illness, specific courses should be available in order to avoid the recurrence of the same or similar illness. Such courses could provide much more support and knowledge than can be offered by medical prescriptions or private assistance. For medicine to have a true preventive function, it needs to include much more than what medicine to take or what to do after an operation. Preventive medicine needs to expand to include courses to people who have suffered illnesses in any organ of their bodies, and those courses ought to include the three emotional intelligences—affectional, mood, and motivational—in order to prevent the return of a new illness to any of the organs of the body governed by the limbic system.

I think of my father, who first suffered an ulcer, then a colostomy, then two heart attacks before suffering a stroke. Apparently he died before he hit the ground. The doctor's words were: "It was as if a light went out; he never knew what was happening." It is time for us to know what is happening. Now that we are so much more aware of the connections of all the organs to the limbic brain, interconnected in one system, it is time to share this news with the public. That would mean that when one organ is ill or has been damaged, patients would learn about the entire limbic system in order to become aware of signals in all the organs of their body. Recent brain research now makes such a course a real possibility as well as a necessity.

Patients with illnesses related to the nervous system and AIDS patients ought to receive courses in the basic brain intelligences in order to know how better to care for their nervous system in everyday life. According to a Venezuelan gastroenterologist, Dr. Isidoro Zaidman,[1] and Candace Pert, the outstanding researcher of chemistry and emotions quoted so often in the chapters on emotional intelligence, we now know that natural brain chemicals are capable of influencing the cells of the immune system. Therefore, individuals will need to know that their health with respect to cancer, AIDS, or any other illness related to the immune system, requires learning how to govern their limbic and basic brains consciously in order to access their own natural chemicals. The fact that natural chemicals are being discovered in those two brains should be important for those interested in health since it implies that we may be able to release our own chemotherapy before needing medical chemotherapy.

Hospitals and physicians can help open an educational frontier in continuous health, but we need to remember that maintaining our health has to be in our hands. We have learned to maintain our homes and our cars, leaving health to chance or to crisis, at which time we go looking for medical help. One of Dr. Zaidman's favorite points is that it is important for the physician and the patient to work together as a team, for them to be conscious of what the individual can do and what the physician can do.

My dream is that when patients exit a hospital, there would be among their exit papers information announcing self-care courses. It is well known that human behavior usually does not change until crisis occurs. I believe educational units in hospitals could do a great deal to change our behavior. I see hospitals as second chance hotels, providing a place and a time to change our ancient attitudes about health. When we experience a crisis to our physical bodies, we are likely to be listening again and ready to learn new approaches.

PSYCHOLOGY

I believe firmly that neurology, united with the perspective of new physics, brings new horizons that enable us to see human life in very different ways from those provided by the pathological perspectives of today. It is not that pathology has not served us, but that it has done us damage by not also offering pathways toward improvement and prevention. It has been useful in order to treat the most urgent and difficult cases, just as the medical model has served to treat the most urgent. However, to amplify the capacities of human beings by means of multiple intelligences would offer a preventive educational model as well as new pathways for development.

To be more precise, education needs to join with psychology in order to offer courses in mental, emotional, and behavioral capacities before the individual falls into the serious difficulties that indeed require a psychological specialist. Therapists as well as physicians need to be trained to give these courses in addition to private and group therapy, or psychological clinics need to bring in an educator to offer the necessary courses.

I believe we can offer basic courses in relationships by teaching associative intelligence and teaching how to use it to think appreciatively. Such courses would also include emotional and behavioral intelligences, the latter with emphasis on family patterns. Every couple needs to know that sooner or later the difficult patterns of their beloved, as well as their own, will arise during their marriage and that these patterns will be hard to manage. We drag our heritage from past generations into our new relationships. Although we say we get divorced because of lack of love, it is really sad to confuse the imprints from past generations with lack of love in the present. If one person's pattern conflicts with another person's pattern, it is a question of different heritages, and not a question of love. Pattern intelligence needs to be included in all premarital courses.

A basic education about the human brain ought to be available to everyone so that we may have a base and be able to help ourselves before having to search for external assistance. For this to occur, we need to bring together in new educational courses the discoveries of the last hundred years in psychology as well as neurology.

RELIGION

Religions hold the key to many of the values of our society. Nevertheless, very often those values are not being lived but rather are producing guilt and rejection that in the long run weigh heavily on the energy of each human being and contribute to destructive actions. Instead of condemning people for the human difficulty of trying to live this finite reality, we need religions to open themselves to a wider educational spectrum in which the values of the past and the beauty of the infinite are integrated with the realities and difficulties of the present.

This model of multiple intelligences also serves as a map for programs related to religious doctrine and values. To teach emotional intelligences is to teach how to love. Affectional intelligence opens us to love anything or anyone in our environment, mood intelligence leads us into loving ourselves, and motivational intelligence teaches us to love life. To teach the behavioral intelligences of patterns and parameters as well as basic intelligence is to teach individuals how to bring peace into their own lives. Love and peace, so central in the doctrines of all religions, have to permeate from the brain of thought down into the emotional brain and the action brain of each individual if the religious mission is to be successful.

GOVERNMENT

For democracy to survive, we must seriously study how to include within its framework and its institutions the knowledge that we now have about the limbic and basic brains. For example, the pattern we have of relying on a single leader is our heritage from ancient empires, from churches, kings, and more recently the military. We have to know that this pattern of reliance on a single strong person is still within our brain system and must seriously be taken into account. History repeats itself because the pattern is remembered by the human brain. We must establish new parameters to inhibit this pattern and guide us toward another. Leaving it loose, we can count on its reappearance.

Democratic institutions depend on verbal representations and problem solving in a very neocortical way. However, often passions make us impatient, even desirous of changing or overthrowing "a government of words." Politicians have always offered us verbal neocortical promises. With the arrival of television, however, it is easy to focus the camera on all the promises that are never carried into action: the potholes that have not been repaired, the cost of living that has not come down, the violence that is still not being controlled, and the hunger that increases rather than diminishes. The real point is that there is a great distance between the words of the neocortex and the action of the basic brain. More specifically, democratic institutions must seriously address the fulfillment of promises as a priority. Perhaps in democracies, people should be able to elect their cabinet ministers directly rather than only their president in order to be able to hold directly responsible those who fail to act according to their announced promises.

Conflict resolution has brought us close to successful mediation, but sometimes the success has been short-lived because of the emotion of hatred that remains untouched by verbal agreements. Often it is like superficially curing the wound and leaving the infection to continue its journey through the body. Emotions and passions reflect vital human information about human pain. If they are boiling beneath the surface, regardless of what the neocortex is saying, the conflict is not healed. We need to add a limbic focus to conflict resolution.

Drugs and prisons are two specific areas of responsibility in which multiple intelligences can be of great help to governmental institutions. Any effort to educate or rehabilitate the prison population has to include, at least, mood and motivational intelligence, as well as a complete training in behavioral intelligences.

The repetition of our behaviors is the primary way of making ourselves secure. Security is survival, and survival is a basic law of life. Therefore, with the new knowledge of the basic brain, we have to realize that criminals and all the rest of us are going to repeat behaviors until we are retrained in new behaviors. Only a support system with new parameters will help produce change. Punishment only serves to deepen the resentment in the limbic brain, making the next criminal act more intense and more precisely aimed. Unless old behaviors are retrained, this increase of emotional vengeance only increases crime.

Research into the natural chemicals of the limbic brain ought to warn us that the drug problem is a brain problem. We consume drugs either to excite us or to relax us. We can drop our dependency on artificial drugs by learning to access our natural brain chemicals with the use of affectional and mood intelligence. Emotional intelligences are basic training for drug rehabilitation.

EDUCATION

Although many changes are needed in education, there are six areas that, according to my experience, have priority: a center for developing intelligence; elementary schools; educating adolescents; educational administration; education for adults; education for parents.

A Center for Developing Intelligence. For me, the most urgent priority is to begin courses in multiple intelligences. At present most educational systems hope that the student will learn to think by following and memorizing the content of different subjects over a period from twelve to sixteen years. We do indeed learn a wide variety of content in many subjects, but we never become conscious of the learning processes involved. Only certain courses at the university level teach critical thinking based on the rational process.

One of the many key reforms necessary in basic, secondary, and university education is the creation of a center that teaches how to learn at each of the three levels. The basic or core curriculum is not a question of learning more languages and mathematics mixed with science and literature. Nor is it a matter of a special combination of courses to produce a well-balanced student. Rather, it is a matter of developing a center in which courses are offered about learning, whether they be called "epistemology," "learning to think, feel, and act," or "learning to learn." Such a center for learning to learn could be based on this as well as other models of multiple intelligences that are now available. I want especially to mention Howard Gardner at Harvard University who first broke open the door of single intelligence with his proposal of multiple intelligence; Robert Sternberg at Yale University whose presentation of a triarchic mind emphasized three different intelligences; Rachel Lauer whose Learning to Learn Center at Pace University continues to break new ground in epistemology; and Edward de Bono in England who took us into the right hemisphere with his proposal of lateral thinking even before brain research was available. In Venezuela, I want to mention the work on intelligence done by Luis Alberto Machado, Minister for the Development of Intelligence, in which specialists where included from his country, Israel, Europe, and the United States.

Both administrators and teachers can join in opening such a learning center for the purpose of studying in the center themselves before taking it to the level of the students. I hope that this book can serve as a study guide. Groups of administrators, teachers, and parents studying one intelligence a month could eventually produce far-reaching results.

Elementary School. A second necessary change in education is to add the intelligences of the right hemisphere to the already existing rational intelligence of the left hemisphere. More specifically, associative thinking and visual and spatial thinking are not a luxury but a requirement if we want to prevent what we are presently calling children with learning disabilities or underachievers, as well as prevent the high percentage of students who drop out as soon as they reach the legal age of sixteen. I am

convinced that a great number of those children drop out of school because they have a stronger right hemisphere than left hemisphere. This
makes them unable to succeed in our sequential educational system. If we
want to educate them, we have to open our sequential curricula, at least
in reading and math, in order to include visual and associative ways of
learning.

The purpose of elementary education in a democratic society ought
to be some level of success for all students. This cannot be reached with
either pressure or political propaganda, but only by changing the group
structure that we have inherited from seventeenth-century Germany. By
group structure I am referring to the usual classroom in which students
are under the authority of the same person, teaching the same subject in
the same way to the whole group, and "may the best one win." The best
left hemispheres are winning, but many students with strengths in the
right hemisphere are becoming resentful and angry for having been labeled second-rate students. Their hurt and resentment are then carried
into secondary school, into drugs, into crime, and then on into second-
class citizenship on the streets and in prisons. I am convinced that the
greatest cause of crime, drug use, and violence is the structure of the
elementary school that sows bitterness, jealousy, and resentment among
those who are labeled losers. Our new knowledge of the limbic and basic
brain systems makes it imperative that we discover a new structure that
gives all students a fair chance to succeed in something that will be useful
to their lives. Society cannot afford to teach people that they are stupid
and then release them to vent their anger indiscriminately when either
they or we least expect it.

I invite administrators, teachers, and parents of every school to join
in studying the three brain systems and their implications for education,
with the purpose of proposing new structures for the elementary school.
A group structure with only one teacher cannot succeed in the education
of the three brains. Let us join in an effort to invent and try out a new
structure in which the three brain systems and diverse intelligences will
be respected.

Limbic Brain and Adolescence. Another important change in educa-
tion must be to teach all students that they possess a limbic brain. This
ought to be done before their pituitary gland opens to the chemical changes
that take place in the brain during adolescence. Mood intelligence ought

to be taught before the age of eleven or twelve, when children become capable of finding weapons in order to express their anger violently or capable of finding cocaine to release them from their feelings of sadness and lack of power. It is vital for our society that young people learn to govern their emotions if we want to succeed in changing the consumption of drugs and alcohol, adolescent pregnancies, or violence on our streets and in our families. Adults, of course, need to learn this simultaneously with our youth. However, to leave adolescents exposed to their own limbic brains mixed with the sexual and drug advertising of television seems to me extremely painful for our youth as well as irresponsible on the part of educators.

Educational Administration. Nothing will change in the school system unless it is permitted and supported by administrators as well as by the legislators responsible for educational funding. It is essential that the multiple intelligences influence those in the relevant governmental offices who design the curriculum for elementary and secondary schools. This model of multiple intelligences can also serve as a reference guide in order to evaluate to what extent schools are educating the three brain systems.

Large companies have sought to assure changes by creating departments for research and development within the company. I believe that school systems and the local governments that control funding need to do the same. When new ideas bombard schools from outside the administration, the norm is to defend ourselves. The reptile defends territory. However, if suggestions come from within a department of the administration itself, then administrators can identify with new programs and struggle for change instead of against it.

School for Adults. Adult educational centers are structures that need to be added in order to communicate the need for life-long learning. Television, pop culture magazines, and private therapy for the wealthy are not sufficient to create the infrastructure of learning that needs to be available to all throughout our lifetime. Skills of communication, relationship, and respect for each other are basic to developing a safe and nurturing society.

School for Parents. It is incomprehensible that the parent, the most influential teacher during our entire lifetime, is neither educated nor supported by society. Parents are left to their own devices to discover the art of parenting at each new stage of development of their children. The parental role changes drastically, from being highly protective in infancy to the need to be highly relational in adolescence.

When we remember the billions of cells of the neocortex, sensitive and available for connections from the earliest moments, is there any parent who would not want to know what that means for the early education of a child? Although toilet training and behavior may be important, so too is the potential rich development of the neocortex. And those "terrible twos"—do we really have to buy into the perpetual struggle, deeply imprinting the word *no* and not knowing how to imprint the alternative *yes*? Motivational and mood intelligence become real at age two. It is then when the parent needs to know how to encourage desire and satisfaction as well as teach safety. The imprints continually registering in the child's basic brain indicate a need to know how to create appropriate environments from earliest childhood.

I have mentioned only a few issues related to the preschool years and the brain. However, parents continue as major learning influences throughout a person's life: in school, in marriage, and on into the development of new families.

We can talk all we want about improving families, but I believe improvement begins with creating an education for parents that offers continuous support to the leadership of families in all the stages of human development. The direct education and recognition of parents is another important spoke in a new infrastructure for society.

These calls to social action in industry, health, psychology, religion, government, and education are some points that have concerned me during my years of studying the triune brain. What we really need is the creation of special committees to study the significance of the triune brain for social and institutional life. Every reference in this book to characteristics affecting individuals has its social reference. Just as there is a neocortex, a limbic brain, and a basic brain for every individual, so also is there one for each institution and each nation. The United States has a basic brain, a limbic brain, and a neocortical brain, which if it were observed as such, might enable us to act differently in many situations. I hope that this book can help existing committees to begin to study the implications of the triune brain in national and international affairs.

Individual Action

I know that all the intelligences are helpful to the individual, but I cannot finish this book in peace without suggesting particular intelligences for individuals involved in difficult areas of life.

My heart goes out to the man deeply threatened by cancer who is in a hospital today. He has analyzed his feelings and squared them into a pattern of duty and suffering rather than given himself time to feel them. Nobody has told him that his emotions are carrying information of life and death importance to the rest of his body.

To all who are not capable of feeling their emotions or who are suffering from depression, cancer, or any disease of an organ, I specifically ask you to pay careful attention to your affective intelligence and to make mood intelligence a constant practice.

To all who suffer from depression, I ask you to learn to deal with sadness and anger as well as understand the importance of pattern intelligence.

To all who suffer with alcohol or drug problems, I recommend you study the three limbic openings as well as all of the emotional and behavioral intelligences.

To artists who struggle to enhance your creativity and believe that it is not possible to have order in your lives at the same time, I invite you to study the intelligence of parameters.

To brilliant intellects, I dearly recommend that you cross over into your right hemisphere, using the words "as if true," study your associative intelligence, and start a meditative procedure on a regular schedule as a base to anchor your intuitive intelligence. When you wish to become more deeply involved in your emotions, I suggest starting with the territory of emotions.

To my dear friends of Latin American countries, who inherited from their Spanish ancestors a great love for words and added to that their own combination of sun and salsa that permits them to express more feelings than those of us living in the North, I suggest you might wish to look again at your action brain, specifically studying parameter intelligence. I believe the basic brain is particularly important in building a democratic governmental system.

To parents, it is important to be aware that the limbic brain explodes with the opening of the pituitary gland in adolescence. The better you understand and can orchestrate your own emotional brain, the better you will be able to model this brain to your children and perhaps prevent the intense antagonism now usually associated with adolescence. It is also important to study pattern intelligence to communicate to your children the patterns they have inherited from you and their grandparents. In their early years, you can teach children parameter intelligence, showing them how to establish their own space at home and then allowing them to live their basic intelligence within those parameters. Perhaps the most essential is to teach children from their earliest years that knowing what they want and how they feel about things is as vital to their growth as thinking and imagining. Teach them that all their desires need not be satisfied but that they do need to be honored, encouraged, and supported. As your children grow, helping them to satisfy their own needs is as important a parental job in relation to the limbic brain as teaching values is important in relation to the basic brain.

To each educator, I ask you to open yourself and your courses to these intelligences.

To each reader, I ask you to study these intelligences and practice them wherever appropriate.

The Top Ten

To any reader who may find this book too long, too complicated, or requiring too much time or effort, my gesture of simplicity is to offer you my top ten favorite actions that do indeed guide me in my daily game of life.

Basic. Make up your mind about the value life holds for you. Put your answer in a few words, in a symbol, or in whatever form seems personal to you. Stick up for life as you value it.

Pattern. Do not curse the darkness. After you have lit a candle, find the pattern involved in the difficulty and change it.

Parameters. Protect a rhythm, routine, or ritual that you love by giving it more time and space in your daily or weekly life.

Motivational. Know five things that excite you and use them as matches to light up your life.

Mood. Know how to get something valuable from an experience of sadness or anger.

Affectional. Each day spend ten minutes loving something you appreciate in someone, in your environment, or in yourself.

Rational. Once a week or once a month try to understand something that upsets you in your daily life. Look for a solution and carefully try it.

Associative. Every day associate yourself with someone or something you like or appreciate.

Spatial. Choose a few words, an image, or sounds that can inspire and guide you. Place them in your personal environment to enrich you.

Intuitive. Practice meditation or quietness daily.

I hope this book has helped convince you of the splendor of human creation. It is precisely this creation we must now honor and develop as a resource for our planet. Our new construction is human by human, not stone by stone. I invite you to be part of a human network dedicated to taking care of and celebrating each life for the purpose of improving all life on this planet. Please invite yourself and then organize to sustain one another in this network of finite and infinite dimension.

Summary of the Ten Intelligences

Rational Intelligence

Definition:
To reason, explain, and connect thoughts sequentially and logically

Major Purpose:
To be able to question anything
To be able to construct and invent

Main Characteristics:
Cause and effect: If this happens, then . . .
Use of reasons, exact and logical connections, and a sequential procedure

Vibrational Range:
Normal speech range

How to Begin:
Study data, doubt, and question any whole until you find the parts.
In the second phase, build a new whole from the parts.

Access through Speech:
I think . . . .
I know . . . .
In my opinion . . . .
I believe . . . .
If . . . then or therefore . . . .
The next step is . . . .

Difficulties. Try to Avoid:
Quick and partial application to human beings
Automatic criticism
Persistent doubt
Criticism without creating alternatives and constructing new solutions

Special Uses:
Science and philosophy
Political freedom and democracy
Personal freedom

Associative Intelligence

Definition:
> To link, associate, or relate to whatever you want to associate with

Major Purpose:
> To discover, create, and make meaning

Main Characteristics:
> Free association
> Mind leaping
> Multiple connections
> Juxtaposition

Vibrational Range:
> Normal speech range to higher speeds

How to Begin:
> Inhibit concepts, conclusions, and decisions to open in favor of a continuously expanding process.

Access through Speech:
> It seems possible that . . . .
> It reminds me of . . . .
> What I like is . . . .
> As if . . . .

Difficulties. Try to Avoid:
> Not being able to bring closure, decision, or conclusion
> Losing track of the next step

Special Uses:
> Exquisite mental freedom
> Being able to appreciate something about everyone and everything

Spatial-Visual Intelligence

Definition:
> To see images either internally or externally

Major Purpose:
> To be able to visualize the ideal or the possible before acting

Main Characteristics:
> Spatial rather than lineal
> Completion not necessary
> Present or futuristic
> Real or imaginary

Vibrational Range:
> Three-dimensional
> Medium range

How to Begin:
> Close your eyes and focus at a point between your eyes, or with eyes open, lift label or name and look directly at the object.
> Look at the contours or look at the space between the objects.

Access through Speech:
> It looks like . . . .
> What I see is . . . .
> The image I have of that is . . . .
> It appears that . . . .
> I imagine that . . . .

Difficulties. Try to Avoid:
> Being scared by negative images
> Fear

Special Uses:
> Removing boredom
> Enhancing memory
> Preplanning
> Endless and inexpensive entertainment

Intuitive Intelligence

Definition:
To know from within, from direct perception, without known procedure, without reason

Major Purpose:
To avoid outer dynamics
To "listen" over distance
To have access to higher and faster brain waves

Main Characteristics:
Stillness
Letting go
Attunement
Reception

Vibrational Range:
Internal
Very thin
High speed

How to Begin:
Open yourself to a belief system in multiple realities.
Observe yourself.
Search beyond limitations of self.
Engage in prayer or meditation.

Access through Speech:
I guess . . . .
I wonder . . . .
My hunch is . . . .
Do you suppose that . . . ?
Is it possible that . . . ?

Difficulties. Try to Avoid:
Receiving too much information
Loss of interest in everyday reality
Detachment from earthly matters

Special Uses:
Glimpses of God
Being quiet
Receiving information

Affectional Intelligence, Entering the Emotional Brain

Definition:

To be affected by experience, ideas, objects, images, intuitions, situations, feelings, music, art, people, or any other aspect of life

Major Purpose:

To stay connected to physical life

Main Characteristic:

Warmth

Vibrational Range:

Very slow

How to Begin:

Slow down.

Stop speaking if possible.

Become enveloped by . . . .

Access through Speech:

I love you . . . .

I am affected by . . . .

It really touches me that . . . .

What gets me is . . . .

I feel impressed by . . . .

Access through Image:

Visualize any situation, making it larger on the screen of your mind, and let it affect you.

Access through the Body:

Focus on any area of your body.

Maintain your focus until you feel sensations.

Pay attention to any signal you call pain or pleasure.

Difficulties. Try to Avoid:

Getting lost in painful emotions

Special Uses:

Energizing your body

Deepening empathy, love, and compassion

Mood Intelligence, Living in the Emotional Brain

Definition:
> To enter into and shift from any mood, whether you consider the experience painful or pleasurable

Major Purpose:
> To access the middle deepest regions of your brain
> To help expand and contract the vibrations for the health of your organs
> To acquire information contained in the form of emotions
> To access natural brain chemicals

Main Characteristics:
> Variation
> Tonality
> Dissonance
> Resonance
> Shaking
> Tears and laughter

Vibrational Range:
> From slow, thick ranges
> to chaotic vibration
> to high-speed, thin vibration

How to Begin:
> Reconceptualize emotions.
> Disconnect from rational cause and effect thinking.
> Be free to feel without expression, conclusion, or action.
> Ask how you feel as you focus inside your body.

Access through Speech:
> I feel . . . .
> I'm feeling . . . .

Difficulties. Try to Avoid:
> Action immediately linked to feelings
> Conclusions based on emotions
> Self-criticism

Special Use:
> The "taste" of life

Motivational Intelligence, The Love of Life

Definition:
> To know what moves you and to be able to guide that movement

Major Purpose:
> To sustain your life

Main Characteristics:
> Insistent
> Searching
> Continuous
> Exciting
> Hot

Vibrational Range:
> Deep and intense

How to Begin:
> Allow yourself to feel.
> Allow yourself to want.
> Know what excites you.
> Search for the spark.

Access through Speech:
> I desire . . . .
> I want . . . .
> I would like . . . .
> What moves me is . . . .
> What really gets me is . . . .
> What I love is . . . .
> My real passion is . . . .

Access through the Body:
> Feel the signals of pleasure that excite you.

Difficulties. Try to Avoid:
> Giving up

Special Uses:
> Being able to choose, direct, and guide your life
> Getting what you want

Basic Intelligence

Definition:
To move toward and away from freely and appropriately

Major Purpose:
To give you liberty, health, consciousness

Main Characteristic:
Neutral energy.
Sometimes recognizable only after you have completed the movement toward or away from

Vibrational Range:
Subtle, almost unrecognizable
When conscious, delicate, instinctive, sensorial, and in feedback with or in tandem with

How to Begin:
Begin silently and consciously.
Detach.
Move slowly and softly.
Affirm and guide your movement consciously.
(This may not "feel" good until your energy becomes stabilized in some new ability, action, or behavior.)

Access through Speech:
I need to move toward or I need to move away from.
I am going to try to disconnect from.
I say yes or no, depending on my intention.

Access through Action:
Move toward, imitate, accompany or go with.
Move away from, inhibit, or stop the action.

Difficulties. Try to Avoid:
Permanent decisions or sense of permanency
The concept of a fixed or unchanging world

Special Uses:
Exploring the new
Taking appropriate action

Pattern Intelligence

Definition:
> To know the patterns governing your behavior and be able to change them when necessary

Major Purpose:
> To change your behavior

Main Characteristics:
> Hidden within your behavior
> Found by discovering the links involved in your action
> The way life has added itself up as yourself

Vibrational Range:
> From invisible to obvious

How to Begin:
> Start with anything that is causing you difficulty.
> Find the links in your chain of reaction to the situation.

Access through Speech:
> Neutral internal dialogue between your conscious self and your behavioral self

Difficulties. Try to Avoid:
> Despair
> Giving up
> Attributing the difficulty to fate

Special Uses:
> Helping with harmful addictions or harmful behavior

Parameter Intelligence

Definition:
To know, transform, and continue major repetitive rhythms and routines of your life

To be able to protect the basic areas of life, especially what you love, by entering into the rhythms of the different functions and then establishing parameters in space and time

To be able to transform parameters in tandem with the dynamics of your life

Major Purpose:
To set up a sense of belonging, continuity, order, entrainment, and reliability

Main Characteristic:
Active intervention in your own life

Vibrational Range:
Thick vibrations of physical action

How to Begin:
Study yourself in relation to time, space, and functions in the basic categories of your life.

Observe your habits, addictions, and values by observing your actions and how you spend your time.

Access through Action:
Action of continuity: be able to continue to act in repetition or rhythm.

Be capable of changing parameters in order to open yourself to new rhythm.

Difficulties. Try to Avoid:
Creating or acting as if a routine or parameter would last forever

Special Uses:
Sustaining activities of your daily life

Extending new learning until it becomes reliable

List of Exercises

NOTES

INTRODUCTION

[1] Paul D. MacLean, *The Triune Brain in Evolution* (New York: Plenum Press, 1990), 9.

[2] For a description of other intelligences, see Howard Gardner, *Frames of Mind: The Theory of Multiple Intelligences* (New York: Basic Books, 1993) and Robert J. Sternberg, *The Triarchic Mind: A New Theory of Human Intelligence* (New York: Penguin Books, 1988).

CHAPTER I: NETWORK OF POSSIBILITIES

[1] See Richard M. Restak, M.D., *The Brain* (New York: Bantam Books, 1984), 41; and *The Human Body: The Brain: Mystery of Matter and Mind* (Washington: U.S. News & World Report, 1981), 37.

[2] Restak, *The Brain*, 247.

[3] J. E. Bogen, M.D., "Some Educational Aspects of Hemispheric Specialization," *UCLA Educator* 17, no. 2 (spring 1975).

CHAPTER II: CAREFUL PROCESS OF COMPREHENSION

[1] *Webster's New World Dictionary*, 2nd College ed., s.v. "cause."

CHAPTER III: GIVING MEANING TO YOUR WORLD

[1] Edward de Bono, *Lateral Thinking* (New York: Harper and Row, 1973).

[2] Jean Houston, *The Possible Human* (Los Angeles: J. P. Tarcher, 1982), 33.

[3] Quoted in *The Brain: Mystery of Matter and Mind*, 77.

CHAPTER IV: SYNTHESIZING THE CONNECTIONS

[1] I am using the word *spatial* to refer to the spatial area of the neocortex, rather than according to its traditional use in psychological and educational studies in which space refers to the outer physical surface, as well as to the space between objects, the movement of objects in space, or the calculation or solution of problems in relation to space.

[2] Diane Ackerman, *A Natural History of the Senses* (New York: Vintage Books, 1995), 290.

[3] Gaston Bachelard, *The Poetics of Space* (Boston: Beacon Press, 1969), 201.

[4] For a description of musical intelligence, see Gardner, *Frames of Mind*, chap. 6; Don Campbell, *Introduction to the Musical Brain* (Edwardsville, Ill.: MMB Music, 1984); Alfred Tomatis, *The Conscious Ear* (New York: Station Hill Press, 1991); and Kenneth G. Mills, *The Golden Nail* (Toronto: Sun-Scape Publications, 1993).

CHAPTER V: TRAVELING TO THINNER VIBRATIONS OF QUANTUM REALITIES

[1] For a greater understanding of the intuitive intelligence of children, see Joseph C. Pearce,

The Magical Child (New York: Dutton, 1977).

[2] *Webster's*, s.v. "intuition."

[3] Gary Zukav, *The Dancing Wu Li Masters: An Overview of the New Physics* (New York: William Morrow and Co., 1979), 313–23.

[4] Meister Eckhart, *The Cloud of Unknowing* (Middlesex, England: Penguin Books, 1961).

[5] Sri I. N. Venkataraman, *Bhagavan Sri Ramana* (Madras: Prasad Process, 1981).

[6] *Webster's*, s.v. "prayer."

CHAPTER VI: EXPLORING THE LIMBIC BRAIN

[1] MacLean, *Triune Brain*. See also MacLean, P. D. "Psychosomatic Disease and the 'Visceral Brain.' Recent Developments Bearing on the Papez Theory of Emotion," *Psychosom. Med.* 2 (1949): 338-53.

[2] See Daniel Goleman, *Emotional Intelligence* (New York: Bantam, 1995); Joseph E. LeDoux, "Emotional Memory Systems in the Brain," *Behavioral Brain Research* 58 (1993): 69–79; and *A Compendium of IHM Research Papers and Abstracts*, vols. 2–3 (Boulder Creek, Cal.: Institute of HeartMath).

[3] *Dorland's Pocket Medical Dictionary*, 23rd ed., s.v. "thalamus."

[4] MacLean, *Triune Brain*, 380.

[5] Ibid., 345.

[6] Ibid., 291.

[7] Ibid., 341.

[8] Joseph E. LeDoux, "Emotion and the Amygdala," in *The Amygdala: Neurobiological Aspects of Emotion, Memory, and Mental Dysfunction*, John P. Aggleton, ed. (New York: Wiley-Liss, 1992), 339–51. See also LeDoux, "Emotional Memory Systems," 69–79; Goleman, *Emotional Intelligence;* and LeDoux, *Compendium*, vols. 2–3.

[9] Eric R. Kandel and James H. Schwartz, *Principles of Neural Science*, 2nd ed. (East Norwalk, Conn.: Appleton & Lange, 1985).

[10] A simplified diagram by Luis Camejo from John G. Nicholls, et al., *From Neuron to Brain*, 3rd ed. (Sunderland, Mass.: Sinauer Associates, Inc., 1992), 18.

[11] Robert L. Isaacson, *The Limbic System*, 2nd ed. (New York: Plenum Press, 1982), 10.

[12] *Dorland's*, s.v. "hypothalamus."

[13] MacLean, *Triune Brain*, 41.

[14] Ibid., 503–506.

[15] Ibid., 25.

CHAPTER VII: A NEW LOOK AT EMOTIONS

[1] Candace Pert, interview by Bill Moyers, *Healing and the Mind* (New York: Doubleday, 1993), 186–87.

[2] Stanley Keleman, *Emotional Anatomy* (Berkeley: Center Press, 1985), xi.

CHAPTER X: HIGH WAVES AND LOW WAVES

[1] Candace Pert, interview by Bill Moyers, *Healing and the Mind*, 191. Please also see appreciative thinking in support of positive thinking found in the chapter on associational intelligence and the use of appreciative thinking and selectivity found in the chapter on affectional intelligence.

[2] Ibid., 193.

[3] Tom Cox, *Stress* (London: Macmillan, 1978), 51.

[4] Candace Pert, interview by Bill Moyers, *Healing and the Mind*, 178.

[5] P. Svanborg and M. Asberg, "A New Self-Rating Scale for Depression and Anxiety States Based on the Comprehensive Psychopathological Rating Scale," *Acta Psychiatr. Scand.* 89, no. 1 (Jan. 1994): 21-28.

[6] Redford Williams and V. Williams, *Anger Kills*, Times Books (New York: Random House, 1993).

[7] Candace Pert, interview by Bill Moyers, *Healing and the Mind*, 190.

[8] Judith J. Wurtman, *Managing Your Mind and Mood through Food* (New York: Harper and Row, 1988).

[9] Michio Kushi, *The Cancer Prevention Diet* (New York: St. Martin's Press, 1983).

CHAPTER XI: LIGHTING YOUR OWN FIRE

[1] Rollo May, *Love and Will* (New York: Norton and Co., 1969).

[2] Pierre Teilhard de Chardin, *Toward the Future*, trans. René Hague (New York: Harcourt Brace Jovanovich, 1975), 86-87.

CHAPTER XII: EMOTIONAL INTELLIGENCE AND THE OPENINGS OF YOUR BODY

[1] Herbert Benson, M.D., *The Relaxation Response* (New York: Avon Books, 1975).

CHAPTER XIII: CROSSING THE THRESHOLD OF THE UNCONSCIOUS

[1] MacLean, *Triune Brain*, 23.

[2] Thomas Merton, in talk presented at the Spiritual Conference of the Temple of Understanding (Calcutta, India, 1968).

[3] Simplified diagram from *The Brain: Mystery of Matter and Mind*, 123.

[4] *The Brain: Mystery of Matter and Mind*, 123.

[5] Restak, *The Brain*, 88.

[6] Notice that three of the basic characteristics of MacLean's research—imitation, deception, and reenactment—described in Chapter XIV are included in this learning and behavior diagram.

Chapter XIV: Characteristics of Reptile Behavior

[1] MacLean, *Triune Brain*, 100.

[2] Ibid., 228.

[3] Ibid., 142.

[4] Ibid., 143.

[5] Ibid., 146.

[6] Ibid., 148.

[7] Ibid., 142.

[8] Ibid., 147.

[9] Ibid.

[10] Ibid., 148.

Chapter XV: Languages of the Basic Brain

[1] Quoted in Agnes de Mille, "Martha Graham: The Steps of a Giant," *New York Times*, 7 April 1991, sec. H Dance, p. 22.

[2] Philip Morrison et al., *Powers of Ten: About the Relative Size of Things in the Universe* (New York: Scientific American Books, 1982), 10^{-6} m.

[3] Thomas Berry, *The Dream of the Earth* (San Francisco: Sierra Club Books, 1988).

Chapter XVI: Living with Life

[1] Gene Kieffer, ed., *Kundalini for the New Age: Selected Writings of Gopi Krishna* (New York: Bantam Books, 1988).

[2] De Mille, "Martha Graham," 22.

Chapter XVIII: Sustaining What You Love

[1] *Webster's*, s.v. "zodiac."

[2] *Webster's*, s.v. "trance."

Conclusion: Toward Full Consciousness

[1] Isidoro Zaidman, conversation with author, April 1994.

Bibliography

Ackerman, Diane. *A Natural History of the Senses*. New York: Vintage Books, 1995.

Andreasen, Nancy C. *The Broken Brain: The Biological Revolution in Psychiatry*. New York: HarperCollins, 1985.

Arnheim, Rudolf. *Visual Thinking*. Berkeley: University of California Press, 1969.

Asimov, Isaac. *Fantastic Voyage II: Destination Brain*. New York: Doubleday, 1978.

Assagioli, Roberto. *Psychosynthesis*. New York: Viking Penguin Press, 1971.

Attenborough, David. *Life On Earth*. Boston: Little, Brown & Co., 1979.

Bachelard, Gaston. *The Poetics of Space*. Boston: Beacon Press, 1969.

Bandler, Richard, and John Grinder. *Structure of Magic*. Palo Alto, Cal.: Science and Behavior Books, 1975.

Benson, Herbert, M.D. *The Relaxation Response*. New York: Avon Books, 1976.

Berkus, Rusty. *Life Is a Gift*. Encino, Cal.: Red Rose Press, 1982.

Bernstein, Jeremy. *Quantum Profiles*. Princeton, N.J.: Princeton University Press, 1990.

Berry, Thomas. *The Dream of the Earth*. San Francisco: Sierra Club Books, 1988.

Blair, Lawrence. *Rhythms of Vision*. New York: Schocken Books, 1976.

Bogen, J. E., M.D. "Some Educational Aspects of Hemispheric Specialization." *UCLA Educator* 17, no. 2 (spring 1975).

Bohm, David. *Wholeness and the Implicate Order*. London: Routledge and Kegan Paul, 1980.

Brain-Mind Bulletin. "New Neurobiology Era Parallels Leap in Physics," Oct. 14, 1983, Vol. 8, no. 1.

Briggs, John P., and F. David Peat. *Looking Glass Universe*. New York: Simon and Schuster, 1984.

Bronowski, Jacob. *The Ascent of Man*. Boston: Little, Brown & Co., 1973.

Brown, Barbara B. *Super Mind: The Ultimate Energy*. New York: Bantam Books, 1983.

Bruner, Jerome P. *On Knowing: Essays for the Left Hand*. New York: Atheneum, 1965.

Burrow, Trigant. *Preconscious Foundations of Human Experience*. New York: Basic Books, 1964.

Buzan, Tony. *Use Both Sides of Your Brain*. New York: Dutton Paperback, 1976.

Campbell, Don. *Introduction to the Musical Brain*. Edwardsville, Ill.: MMB Music, 1983.

Campbell, Joseph. *The Hero With a Thousand Faces*. Princeton, N.J.: Princeton University Press, 1949.

Capra, Fritjof. *The Tao of Physics*. New York: Bantam Books, 1977.

Carrington, Patricia. *Freedom in Meditation*. New York: Anchor Press, 1978.

Chall, J., and A. Mirsky. *Education and the Brain*. Chicago: University of Chicago Press, 1978.

Churchland, Paul M. *The Engine of Reason, the Seat of the Soul*. Cambridge: MIT Press, 1995.

Cox, Tom. *Stress*. London: Macmillan, 1978.

Damasio, Antonio. *Descartes' Error: Emotion, Reason and the Human Brain*. New York: Avon Books, 1994.

De Beauport, Elaine. "The Feeling Brain," *Dromenon* 3, no. 1 (1980): 33–35.

_____ . *Las Tres Caras de la Mente*. Caracas, Venezuela: Edit. Galac, 1994.

De Bono, Edward. *De Bono's Thinking Course*. New York: Facts on File, Inc., 1985.

_____ . *Lateral Thinking*. New York: Harper and Row, 1973.

Eckhart, Meister. *The Cloud of Unknowing*. Middlesex, England: Penguin Books, 1961.

Edwards, Betty. *Drawing on the Right Side of the Brain*. Los Angeles: J. P. Tarcher, 1979.

Eiseley, Loren. *The Invisible Pyramid*. New York: Charles Scribner's Sons, 1970.

Ekman, Paul, and Richard Davidson. *The Nature of Emotion: Fundamental Questions*. New York: Oxford University Press, 1994.

Faraday, Ann. *Dream Power*. New York: Berkley Publishing Group, 1986.

Feldenkrais, Moshe. *Awareness Through Movement*. New York: HarperSanFrancisco, 1972.

Ferguson, Marilyn. *The Aquarian Conspiracy*. Los Angeles: J. P. Tarcher, Inc., 1976.

_____ . "Prigogine's Science of Becoming." *Dromenon* 2, no. 5–6 (1980): 28–33.

Gardner, Howard. *Frames of Mind: The Theory of Multiple Intelligences*. New York: Basic Books, 1993.

_____ . *Multiple Intelligences: The Theory in Practice*. New York: Basic Books, 1993.

Gazzaniga, Michael, and Joseph E. LeDoux. *The Integrated Mind*. New York: Plenum Press, 1978.

Gendlin, Eugene. *Focusing*. New York: Bantam Books, 1981.

Glasser, William. *Positive Addiction*. New York: Harper and Row, 1976.

Golas, Thaddeus. *The Lazy Man's Guide to Enlightenment*. New York: Bantam, 1983.

Goldstein, Joseph. *The Experience of Insight*. Boston: Shambhala, 1987.

Goleman, Daniel. *Emotional Intelligence*. New York: Bantam Books, 1995.

Goleman, Daniel, and Richard J. Davidson, eds. *Consciousness: Brain, States of Awareness and Mysticism*. New York: Harper and Row, 1979.

Gray, John. *Men Are from Mars, Women Are from Venus*. New York: HarperCollins, 1993.

Guénon, René. *The Multiple States of Being*. Burdett, N.Y.: Larson Publications, 1984.

Guy, James. *Metasphere, The Altered State of Word*. Seattle: Lampkin Publishing, 1980.

Halpern, Steven. *Tuning the Human Instrument*. Belmont, Cal.: Halpern Sounds, 1978.

Hampden-Turner, Charles T. *Maps of The Mind*. New York: Macmillan, 1982.

Hillman, James. *Re-Visioning Psychology*. New York: Harper Colophon, 1977.

Hollingsworth, L. B. *Adrenaline: The Key to Your Behavior*. Radnor, Penn.: Chilton Book Co., 1973.

Hooper, Judith, and Dick Teresi. *The Three-Pound Universe: Revolutionary Discoveries about the Brain — From the Chemistry of the Mind to the Frontiers of the Soul*. New York: Dell, 1987.

Houston, Jean. *Life Force: The Psycho-Historical Recovery of the Self*. Wheaton, Ill.: Quest Books, 1993.

_____ . *The Possible Human*. Los Angeles: J. P. Tarcher, 1982.

_____ . *Public Like a Frog*. Wheaton, Ill.: Quest Books, 1993.

_____ . *The Search for the Beloved*. Los Angeles: J. P. Tarcher, 1987.

The Human Body: The Brain: Mystery of Matter and Mind. Washington, D.C.: U.S. News & World Report, 1981.

Huxley, Laura A. *You Are Not the Target*. New York: Avon Books, 1963.

Isaacson, Robert L. *The Limbic System*. 2nd ed. New York: Plenum Press, 1982.

James, William. *The Varieties of Religious Experience*. New York: Collier Books, 1961.

Jautsch, Erick. *Design for Evolution*. New York: George Braziller, 1975.

Jenny, H. *Cymatics: Wave Phenomena, Vibrational Effects, Harmonic Oscillations with their Structure Kinetics and Dynamics*. 2 vols. Switzerland: Bas. Presse AG., 1967.

Jung, C. G. *The Archetypes and the Collective Unconscious*. Vol. 9i of *Collected Works*. Bollingen Series XX. Princeton, N.J.: Princeton University Press, 1990.

_____ . *Man and His Symbols*. New York: Doubleday, 1964.

_____ . *Modern Man in Search of a Soul*. New York: Harcourt Brace Jovanovich, 1933.

_____ . *On the Nature of the Psyche*. Princeton, N.J.: Princeton University Press, 1960.

Kandel, Eric R., and James H. Schwartz. *Principles of Neural Science*. 2nd ed. East Norwalk, Conn.: Appleton & Lange, 1985.

Kanigel, Robert. "What's All the Fuss About in Physics?" *Johns Hopkins Magazine* (December 1980): 13–20.

Kazantzakis, Nikos. *The Saviors of God: Spiritual Exercises*. Translated by Kimon Friar. New York: Simon and Schuster, 1960.

Keleman, Stanley. *Emotional Anatomy*. Berkeley: Center Press, 1985.

Keyes, Ken, Jr. *Handbook to Higher Consciousness*. Berkeley: Living Love Center, 1973.

Kieffer, Gene, ed. *Kundalini for the New Age. Selected Writings of Gopi Krishna*. New York: Bantam Books, 1988.

Koestler, Arthur. *Janus, A Swimming Lap*. New York: Random House, 1979.

Kravette, Steve. *Complete Relaxation*. Atglen, Penn.: Whitford Press, 1979.

Krishnamurti, J. *Think on These Things*. New York: Harper and Row, 1964.

Kushi, Michio. *The Cancer Prevention Diet*. New York: St. Martin's Press, 1983.

Langer, Susanne K. *Mind: An Essay on Human Feeling*, 3 vols. Baltimore: Johns Hopkins University Press, 1983.

LeDoux, Joseph E. "Emotional Memory Systems in the Brain." *Behavioral Brain Research* 58 (1993): 69–79.

_____ . "Emotion and the Amygdala," in *The Amygdala: Neurobiological Aspects of Emotion, Memory, and Mental Dysfunction*, John P. Aggleton, ed. New York: Wiley-Liss, 1992, 339–51.

_____ . "Emotion and the Limbic System Concept." *Concepts in Neuroscience* 2, no. 2 (1991): 169–99.

_____ . "Emotion: Clues from the Brain." *Annual Rev. Psychol.* 46 (1995): 209–35.

_____ . "Sensory Systems and Emotion: A Model of Affective Processing." *Integrative Psychiatry* 4 (1986): 237–48.

Leonard, George. *The Silent Pulse*. New York: Viking Penguin, 1992.

LeShan, Lawrence. *How to Meditate*. New York: Bantam Books, 1974.

Lilly, John C. *Programming and Metaprogramming in the Human Biocomputer*. New York: The Julian Press, 1987.

Luce, Gay G. *Your Second Life*. New York: Delacorte Press/Seymour Lawrence, 1979.

MacLean, Paul D. "Brain Evolution Relating to Family, Play, and the Separation Call." *Arch. Gen. Psychiatry* 42 (1985): 405-17.

_____ . "A Mind of Three Minds: Educating the Triune Brain," in *Education and the Brain*,

J. S. Chall and A. F. Mirsky, eds. The 77th Yearbook of the National Society of Education. Chicago: University of Chicago Press, 1978, 308-42.

_____. "On the Evolution of Three Mentalities." *Man-Environment Sys.* 5 (1975): 213-24.

_____. "Psychosomatic Disease and the 'Visceral Brain.' Recent Developments Bearing on the Papez Theory of Emotion." *Psychosom. Med.* 2 (1949): 338-53.

_____. "Some Psychiatric Implications of Physiological Studies on Frontotemporal Portion of Limbic System (Visceral Brain)." *Electroencephalogr. Clin. Neurophysiol.* 4 (1952): 407-18.

_____. "The Triune Brain," in *Encyclopedia of Neuroscience*, G. Adelman, ed. Cambridge: Birkhauser Boston, Inc., 1987, 1235-37.

_____. "The Triune Brain, Emotion and Scientific Bias," in *The Neurosciences Second Study Program*, F. O. Schmitt, ed. New York: The Rockefeller University Press, 1970, 336-49.

_____. *The Triune Brain in Evolution.* New York: Plenum Press, 1990.

_____. "A Triune Concept of the Brain and Behavior," in *The Hicks Memorial Lectures*, T. Boag and D. Campbell, eds. Toronto: University of Toronto Press, 1973, 6-66.

Masters, Robert. *Neurospeak.* Wheaton, Ill.: Quest Books, 1994.

Masters, Robert, and Jean Houston. *Mind Games: The Guide to Inner Space.* New York: Delta Books, 1973.

May, Rollo. *Love and Will.* New York: Norton and Co., 1969.

Metzner, Ralph. *Maps of Consciousness.* New York: Macmillan/Collier, 1971.

Mills, Kenneth C. *The Golden Nail.* Toronto: Sun-Scape Publications, 1993.

_____. *The New Land! Conscious Experience Beyond Horizons.* Toronto: Sun-Scape Publications, 1978.

Morrison, P., et. al. *Powers of Ten.* New York: Scientific Books, 1982.

Moyers, Bill. *Healing and the Mind.* New York: Doubleday, 1993.

Muler, Robert. *New Genesis.* New York: Doubleday, 1984.

Nadel, Laurie, Judy Haims, and Robert Stempson. *Sixth Sense.* New York: Prentice Hall Press, 1990.

Netter, Frank H. *Atlas of Human Anatomy.* West Caldwell, N.J.: CIBA-Geigy Corporation, 1989.

"New Neurobiology Era Parallels Leap in Physics," *Brain-Mind Bulletin* 8, no. 1 (October 14, 1983).

Nicholls, John G., et al. *From Neuron to Brain: A Cellular and Molecular Approach to the Function of the Nervous System.* 3rd ed. Sunderland, Mass.: Sinauer Associates, Inc., 1992.

Nilsson, Lennart. *Behold Man*. Boston: Little, Brown and Co., 1973.

_____. *The Body Victorious*. New York: Delacorte Press, 1985.

Ornstein, Robert. *The Healing Brain*. New York: Simon and Schuster, 1987.

Ostrander, Sheila, and Lynn Schroeder. *Superlearning*. New York: Delta Books, 1980.

Ostrosky, Solís y Ardila A. *Hemisferio Derecho y Conducta. Un enfoque Neuropsicológico*. Mexico: Editorial Trillas, 1986.

Payne, Buryl. *Getting There Without Drugs*. New York: Viking Press, 1973.

Pearce, Joseph Chilton. *The Crack in the Cosmic Egg*. New York: Julian Press, 1971.

_____. *Evolution's End*. San Francisco: HarperSanFrancisco, 1992.

_____. *Magical Child*. New York: Dutton, 1977.

_____. *Magical Child Matures*. New York: Dutton, 1985.

Peat, F. David. *Synchronicity*. New York: Bantam Books, 1987.

Pelletier, Kenneth. "The Hologram and Human Consciousness." *Dromenon* 2, no. 5–6 (1979): 3–10.

_____. *Mind as Healer; Mind as Slayer*. New York: Delta Books, 1977.

_____. *Toward a Science of Consciousness*. New York: Dell Publishing, 1978.

Penfield, Wilder. *The Mystery of the Mind: A Critical Study of Consciousness and the Human Brain*. Princeton, N.J.: Princeton University Press, 1975.

Pietsch, Paul. *Shufflebrain*. Boston: Houghton Mifflin, 1981.

Pinker, Steven. *The Language Instinct*. New York: Harper Perennial, 1995.

Prigogine, Ilya. *From Being to Becoming*. San Francisco: Freeman, 1980.

Prigogine, Ilya, and Isabelle Stengers. *Order Out of Chaos*. New York: Bantam Books, 1984.

Progoff, Ira. *At a Journal Workshop*. New York: Dialogue House, 1975.

_____. *The Symbolic and The Real*. New York: Julian Press, 1963.

Restak, Richard M., M.D. *The Brain*. New York: Bantam Books, 1984.

_____. *The Brain Has a Mind of Its Own: Insights from a Practicing Neurologist*. New York: Harmony Books, 1991.

Richards, Mary C. *Centering in Poetry, Pottery, and the Person*. 2nd ed. Hanover, N.H.: University Press of New England, 1989.

Rilke, Rainer Maria. *Duino Elegies*. New York: W. W. Norton and Co., 1939.

Rose, Steven. *The Conscious Brain*. New York: Random House, 1976.

Russell, Peter. *The Brain Book*. New York: Dutton, 1979.

_____. *The Global Brain.* Los Angeles: J. P. Tarcher, 1983.

Samples, Bob. *The Metaphoric Mind: A Celebration of Creative Consciousness.* Rev. ed. Torrance, Cal.: Jalmar Press, 1993.

Sannella, Lee, M.D. *Kundalini Experience: Psychosis or Transcendence?* Lower Lake, Cal.: Integral Publishing, 1987.

Satir, Virginia. *Conjoint Family Therapy.* 3rd ed. Palo Alto, Cal.: Science and Behavior Books, 1987.

_____. *Making Contact.* Millbrae, Cal.: Celestial Arts, 1976.

_____. *The New Peoplemaking.* Palo Alto, Cal.: Science and Behavior Books, 1988.

Satir, Virginia, and Michelle Baldwin. *Satir Step by Step: A Guide to Creating Change in Families.* Palo Alto, Cal.: Science and Behavior Books, 1983.

Schwenk, Theodor. *Sensitive Chaos.* New York: Schocken Books, 1976.

Sheldrake, Rupert. *A New Science of Life.* Los Angeles: J. P. Tarcher, 1982.

Sky, Michael. *Breathing: Expanding Your Power and Energy.* Santa Fe, N.M.: Bear and Co., 1990.

Springer, Sally P., and G. Deutsch. *Cerebro Izquierdo Cerebro Derecho.* Barcelona, Spain: Editorial Gedisa S.A., 1991.

Sternberg, Robert J. *Intelligence Applied.* San Diego: Harcourt Brace Jovanovich, 1986.

_____. *The Triarchic Mind: A New Theory of Human Intelligence.* New York: Viking Penguin, 1989.

Stevens, Barry. *Don't Push the River.* Berkeley: Celestial Arts, 1985.

Stevens, Peter S. *Patterns in Nature.* Boston: Little Brown & Co., 1974.

Svanborg, P., and M. Asberg. "A New Self-Rating Scale for Depression and Anxiety States Based on the Comprehensive Psychopathological Rating Scale," *Acta Psychiatr. Scand.* 89, no. 1 (Jan. 1994): 21–28.

Teilhard de Chardin, Pierre. *The Phenomenon of Man.* New York: Harper and Row, 1961.

_____. *Toward the Future.* Translated by Rene Hague. New York: Harcourt Brace Jovanovich, 1975.

Theophane the Monk. *Tales of a Magic Monastery.* New York: Crossroads, 1981.

Toben, Bob. *Space, Time and Beyond.* New York: C. P. Dutton & Co., 1974.

Tomatis, Alfred. *The Conscious Ear.* New York: Station Hill Press, 1992.

Venkataraman, I. N. *Bhagavan Sri Ramana.* Madras: Prasad Process, 1981.

Ward, Milton. *The Brilliant Function of Pain.* New York: Optimus Books, 1977.

Wenger, Win. *Beyond O.K.* Gaithersburg, Md.: Psychegenics Press, 1979.

Wilber, Ken. *The Spectrum of Consciousness*, Wheaton, Ill.: Quest Books, 1993.

William, Paul. *Das Energi*, New York: Warner Books, 1973.

Williams, Redford, and V. Williams. *Anger Kills*. New York: Random House, 1993.

Wolheim, Richard. *On Art and The Mind*. Cambridge: Harvard University Press, 1974.

Wurtman, Judith J. *Managing Your Mind and Mood Through Food*. New York: HarperCollins, 1988.

Zukav, Gary. *The Dancing Wu Li Masters: An Overview of the New Physics*. New York: William Morrow, 1979.

Index

For information about
the Mead Institute Lectures and Workshops
please write to:

The Mead Institute
2109 Broadway, Apt. 820
New York, NY 10023

212-866-4229

or send a fax to:

El Instituto Mead de Venezuela
011-58-2-959-1771